THE MYSTERY OF SIN AND FORGIVE-NESS

1

alba house • DIVISION OF THE SOCIETY OF ST. PAUL STATEN ISLAND, N.Y. 10314

THE MYSTERY OF SIN AND FORGIVENESS

Michael J. Taylor, S.J., Editor

Contributors:

Paul Anciaux, O.S.B.
Louis Monden, S.J.
Marie-Bruno Carra De Vaux Saint-Cyr, O.P.
James F. Filella, S.J.
Jerome Murphy-O'Connor, O.P.
Gabriel M. Nissim, O.P.
Robert O'Connell, S.J.
Kevin O'Shea, C.Ss.R.
Piet Schoonenberg, S.J.
Pierre Smulders, S.J.
Paul Tremblay
Bruce Vawter, C.M.
Marcel Van Caster, S.J.
James P. Mackey

244.3
T

Imprimi Potest:
   John J. Kelley, S.J., Prov. Oregon Province

Nihil Obstat:
   Raymond T. Powers, S.T.D.
   Censor Librorum

Imprimatur:
   Joseph P. O'Brien, S.T.D.
   Vicar General, Archdiocese of New York
   November 6, 1970

The nihil obstat and imprimatur are official declarations that a book or pamphlet
is free of doctrinal or moral error. No implication is contained therein that those who
have granted the nihil obstat and imprimatur agree with the contents, opinions or
statements expressed.

Library of Congress Catalog Card Number: 70-140284

SBN: 8189-0198-5

Designed, printed and bound in the U.S.A. by the Pauline Fathers and Brothers of
the Society of St. Paul, 2187 Victory Blvd., Staten Island, N.Y. 10314 as part of their
communications apostolate.

Also by the Editor:

The Protestant Liturgical Renewal: A Catholic Viewpoint. Westminster, Md.: Newman Press, 1963.

Liturgy and Christian Unity. Englewood Cliffs, N.J.: Prentice-Hall, Inc., 1965.

Liturgical Renewal in the Christian Churches. Baltimore, Md.: Helicon Press, Inc., 1967.

The Sacred and the Secular. Englewood Cliffs, N.J.: Prentice-Hall, Inc., 1968.

ACKNOWLEDGMENTS

Acknowledgment is gratefully made to the authors and publishers for permission to quote from the following copyrighted works:

"The Sense of Sin in the Modern World" by Robert O'Connell, S.J. Reprinted from The Way, Vol. 2, No. 1 (January, 1962), pp. 3-18, with the permission of the publisher.

"Missing the Mark" by Bruce Vawter, C. M. Reprinted from The Way, Vol. 2, No. 1 (January, 1962), pp. 19-27, with the permission of the publisher.

"Toward a Biblical Catechesis of the Decalogue" by Paul Tremblay. Reprinted from Lumen Vitae, Vol. XVIII, No. 3 (September, 1963), pp. 507-529, with the permission of the publisher.

"Sin and Community in the New Testament" by Jerome Murphy-O'Connor, O.P. Reprinted from Sin and Repentance, edited by Denis O'Callaghan (New York: Alba House, 1967), pp. 18-50.

"The Reality of Sin: A Theological and Pastoral Critique" by Kevin O'Shea, C.Ss.R. Reprinted from Theological Studies, Vol. 29, No. 2 (June, 1968), pp. 241-259, with the permission of the author and editor.

"The Sacrament of Penance: An Historical Outline" by M.-B. Carra de Vaux Saint-Cyr, O.P. Reprinted from The Sacrament of Penance by Carra de Vaux Saint-Cyr, O.P. and others (Glen Rock, N.J.: Paulist Press, 1966), pp. 3-44, with the permission of the publisher.

"The Ecclesial Dimension of Penance" by Paul Anciaux, O.S.B. Reprinted from **Theology Digest,** Vol. XI, No. 1 (Spring, 1963), pp. 33-38, with the permission of the editor.

"Confession: Psychology Is Not Enough" by Louis Monden, S.J. Reprinted from **Sin, Liberty and Law** by Louis Monden, S.J. (New York: Sheed & Ward, Inc., 1965), pp. 46-62, with the permission of the publisher.

"Confession as a Means of Self-Improvement" by James Filella, S.J. Reprinted from **Catholic Psychological Record,** Vol. 5, No. 2 (Fall, 1967), pp. 141-157, with the permission of the author and editor.

"Communal Penance: A Liturgical Commentary and Catechesis" by Gabriel-M. Nissim, O.P. Reprinted from **Theology Digest,** Vol. XVI, No. 1 (Spring, 1968), pp. 30-34, with the permission of the editor.

"New Thinking on Original Sin" by James P. Mackey. Reprinted from **Herder Correspondence,** Vol. 4, No. 5 (May, 1967), pp. 135-144, with the permission of the editors and the author.

"Evolution and Original Sin" by Pierre Smulders, S.J. Reprinted from **Theology Digest,** Vol. XIII, No. 3 (Autumn, 1965), pp. 172-176, with the permission of the editor.

"Original Sin and Man's Situation" by Piet Schoonenberg, S.J. Reprinted from **Theology Digest,** Vol. XV, No. 3 (Autumn, 1967), pp. 203-208, with the permission of the editor.

"Catechesis on Original Sin" by Marcel Van Caster, S.J. Reprinted from **Lumen Vitae,** Vol. XXII, No. 1 (May, 1967), pp. 147-168, with the permission of the publisher.

CONTENTS

PART THREE:
THE MYSTERY OF ORIGINAL SIN

INTRODUCTION

In a time when belief is undergoing much critical inspection, the mystery of sin and forgiveness, like most doctrines of faith, has come under thorough re-examination. One result is that the subject is being talked about quite differently.

In theological and philosophical literature today sin emerges as more than the doing of evil or the breaking of laws. As some put it, sin is compromising one's personal integrity; it is being untrue to self or dishonest and closed to others. Sin is treating self or the neighbor as a thing, not a person. It is refusing to bring an attitude of love and commitment to the key situations of life. Sin is thus understood in more human, personal terms.

The idea of sin has changed, it would seem, because man's understanding of himself and the world has changed. In former times his destiny was largely in the hands of others. He was a small part of an impersonal world which dictated most of the laws, values, and sanctions of life. He hardly knew who or what he was or what his relationship to others should be or how he could best go about realizing his own humanity. This is still true today, of course, but less so, for the world is somehow smaller and man seems a little better able to discover self and to relate

to others. The process of secularization and technological progress
have left him freer to reflect on who he is and what his responsibilities to self and others are. Psychological reflection has made
him aware of his inner self and how he essentially needs the
other for fulfillment. And modern mass communications have
shown him that the other is not just family and friends — it is
every man.

Christian moralists are very encouraged by this change. A
morality motivated by love, respect, and service seems the only
possible morality that can undo and repair the hateful polariza-
tion that exists between men today. The Christian realizes that
God loves him personally as well as "providentially"; his created
existence is God's way of visibly expressing that personal love.
And ideally man in his thoughts and actions seeks to make grate-
ful response to God for the gift of life. His faith also tells him
that God loves every man with the same personal love. He therefore tries to find in his neighbor the "worth" that God has found.
He tries to see all men as potentially a family, in fact God's own
community on earth. Positive, moral actions are those which contribute to the building up of this community through interpersonal love and service. Negative, sinful actions are those which
selfishly refuse love and service and dissipate community. In this
context sin is what isolates man from his fellows. It is a violation
of community, an irresponsible and immature refusal to grow as
a person by loving and serving others.

With this new emphasis the Christian moralist is not turning
his back on the biblical and traditional teaching on sin. He is
simply putting the traditional doctrine in what he hopes are more
personal and relevant terms. The ancient morality never excluded
love and respect for persons as reasons why we should avoid sin;
it must be said, however, that the stress was often put elsewhere,
usually on individual rewards and punishments. In the new approach sin is not only what deserves punishment. Virtue and sinlessness are not mere ways of winning heaven. Sin is deliberately
choosing to remain selfish and infantile; virtue and restraint simply the necessary steps to manhood. The selfless, serving man is
the true man. Man realizes his humanity not by centering life in

himself, not by using others for his own gratification, but by losing himself in the service of others. This is where his fulfillment lies.

To be sure no one would claim that this kind of "love ethics" is easy morality. Indeed stressing love makes our conduct more demanding, surpassing by far the ethics of reward and punishment. The Christian in his actions is called to do more than the bare minimum. He tries to live according to an ideal, to fulfill a vocation to love and serve, to be with Christ a "man for others."

And yet the Christian often falls short of his ideal and sins. But instinct tells him his infidelity and weakness, though tragic, are not irreversible. Forgiveness is always possible through repentance. And repentance is evident when the sinner sorrowfully admits and confesses that he has refused in a specific way to respond to God's love, that he has abused the gift of life. He is repentant when he confesses that he has somehow misused human freedom and when he resolves to be more respectful of life and freedom in the future. For the Christian this sorrowful awareness and confession of sin is always a moment of sad discovery, but it is also a time of self-realization and an opportunity to begin anew the pursuit of becoming a man. Sin does the salutary work of showing the sinner that he does not yet love enough; it disarms his pride and complacency, the enemies to love and human growth. Since sin closes him to God and creates within him a sense of great loneliness, it reveals to him that his ultimate fulfillment lies in God not self.

Certainly Catholic moralists would not omit the sacrament of Penance from the mystery of forgiveness. They would, however, insist that it must not be used as a "magical," or automatic form of forgiveness. The sacrament must always be a genuine faith-meeting with Christ in the Church. The sacrament for the Christian is the sign that Christ endures among men to forgive, to reconcile, to save. The sinner goes to the sacrament to seek Christ's personal pardon; he sees his visible reconciliation with the Church as his spiritual reunion with the Lord. There he exchanges sin and sorrow for the forgiving, healing love of Christ.

And so sin and forgiveness, even after much re-examination, remains among the "relevancies of life" (at least for the Christian). These essays will, I think, show that sin, even for modern man, is not a pseudo-problem, nor forgiveness an artificial need. All the authors address this point with deep Christian conviction. Their aim is to throw light on the subject, but not necessarily to arrive at identical conclusions or to produce a neat doctrinal synthesis. Their analysis and conclusions are, in fact, sometimes different; but their reflections for the most part complement rather than oppose the insights of others. In every case the contributors have sought to speak in terms modern men can understand. It is hoped that for the reader the sum effect of these essays will be a fresher, deeper, more salutary understanding of the mystery of sin and forgiveness.

Michael J. Taylor, S.J.
Seattle University
Seattle, Washington

THE
MYSTERY
OF SIN
AND
FORGIVE-
NESS

PART ONE: THE MYSTERY OF SIN

Chapter One

THE SENSE OF SIN IN THE MODERN WORLD

ROBERT O'CONNELL, S.J.

The modern world, we are often told (with something like a
note of triumph in the tone of the telling) has lost its sense of
sin. Often enough this becomes a signal for hand-wringing and
head-wagging, in an effort to sound sad about it all. Perhaps
there is even an unspoken prayer of thanks that *we* are not as
modern man? The temptation has to be mentioned, so that we
may be alert to avoid it. We belong no less to the modern world
than do those whom we are tempted to criticize. And that world,
whether we like it or not, exercises a subtle influence on our own
standards and evaluations: an influence that must be faced objectively, and with some degree of sympathy, if we are to be
critically aware of it in our lives.

Perhaps we Christians have not always been entirely lucid in
our preaching – not to mention our practice – of the Christian
morality. It cannot be taken for granted that modern man's sense
of sin is inferior to that of generations that went before him, or,
that he has nothing to tell us Christians of the perennial notion
of sin which our tradition brings down to us.

The Guilt-complex

The modern world's sense of sin is usually identified, by many Christians as well as non-Christians, with what the psychologists describe as the guilt-complex. It is as well known to the confessor as to the psychiatrist. The penitent who glides airily through the first five commandments of the Decalogue and then slams into the sixth commandment like a Mack truck into a stone wall, is not untypical. In the mind of such a person, the entire Decalogue reduces to the sixth and ninth commandments, for all practical purposes. Like the painters of the film advertisements, our penitent thinks that sin and sex are convertible terms; all the rest is secondary. All feeling of guilt, it so often happens, seems to have centered in the area of sexual sins; it has tied the penitent into knots; he (or she) finds confession of these sins an agony, carries around the consciousness of them with a paralyzing sense of shame, inferiority and something very like hatred of self, of his body, of his entire incarnate condition. He is closed in on himself, cramped, stiff in his relations with others, likely to outbursts of impatience or aggressiveness of all sorts. Sanctity is something he longs for: but the sanctity of some disembodied angelic being. If asked why sins of impurity bother his conscience, he replies in such terms as "dirty," "shameful," "soiling," "disgusting." What is their connection with the love of God and of his neighbor? The answer is liable to be far from illuminating.

The results, paradoxically, are often, if not always exactly the opposite of what the penitent would wish. He finds himself so obsessed with the infernal circle of his failings in this regard, that they become even more difficult, if not impossible, to avoid. The sickening round of temptation, fall and temptation again renewed, spirals him downward into discouragement, despondency, and the growing conviction that he can never tear himself out of this morass.

So often the penitent makes life one long purgatory for those about him, conveniently putting out of mind repeated reminders that charity is the fulfillment of the whole law. He frequently takes refuge in scrupulosity, that mask of self-deception, which permits a semblance of delicacy of conscience in one area of activity, while maintaining a hard crust of insensitivity in another area — often the area of charity!

There is nothing more unhealthy than this situation, the psychoanalyst warns; and by dint of a facile equation of such guilt feelings with what the Christian means by the sense of sin, his conclusion is firm: away with it! A recent book written by a French psychoanalyst reads like the moral Magna Carta of our day: *Morale sans Péché*, morality without sin!

But how does such a guilt feeling originate? The psycho-analyst is there with the explanation: it comes from the action of the superego. In layman's language, this amounts to saying that society, represented by the parental authority, teachers, com-panions more generally, imposes certain norms on the conduct of the child, from its earliest moments of awareness. The child is made to feel, since it is incapable of understanding, that the satisfaction of certain of its drives is forbidden, taboo. Dire threats are added to the proclamation of this taboo, and a deep feeling of inferiority, rejection, insecurity, attaches to the action in question, or even to the image, the desire of that action. And yet, since the drive is still there, since the child has not the ghost of a notion *why* it is wrong, no permanent resolution of the desire-situation is achieved. Man's natural reluctance to face un-pleasant truths about himself then forces the memory both of the forbidden act (or desire) and the related feeling of in-security, down into the Unconscious, and the irrational guilt feelings well up from that pit to produce neurosis in later life.

The sociologists, anthropologists, historians and others fill out the background picture. In different societies and at different evolutionary phases, they assure us, different norms of accept-ability apply. And the conclusion is that all norms, whatever their nature, are merely relative to the society in question. The Decalogue of the Bible, for instance, is nothing more than the basic law of Israel at a certain stage of its historical develop-ment, cloaked with the authority of God to make its binding power on the individual Hebrew the more effective!

In accepting these explanations of the "sense of sin," modern man finds a number of moral positions possible to him. Let us sketch out just three of them here, and then ask if there is any fundamental note in his moral consciousness.

Indifferentism

The first of these moral attitudes has to do with sex principally, for this is what first comes to the contemporary mind when the term sin is mentioned. For convenience, we can label the attitude "indifferentism." The act of sexual intercourse, as one author puts it, is as indifferent as drinking a cup of coffee. Sometimes the position is buttressed by a naturalist supposition that the good life for man as for any other animal, consists in the satisfaction of his instinctive drives; sometimes it can be given the anti-Manichaean label, which announces that the body is good and that this drive in particular is not the evil thing such dualisms would make of it. Any taboos in this area, therefore, are to be rejected. If it is pretended that they draw their origin from God, then little time is lost in putting this God out of the picture as well. If nothing is wrong with the instinct, then a God who would forbid such an innocent thing simply does not exist. Here modern man assumes the role of the little boy whistling past the graveyard — "ain't no ghosts here, no sir!"

The irony in all this is that a tendency which started out as anti-Manichaeanism has been sucked into a Manichaeanism of another form. Our culture, which Bergson so aptly labelled "aphrodisiac," with its constant attempt to make sexual satisfaction the center, if not the essence of life, beckons us into a round of pleasures which eventually reduce sexual activity to a sheer, irresponsible enjoyment. Life becomes a series of casual encounters; when any two animals concerned tire of each other, let them seek out another partner. All connection with the ends of life, all moral character is bled from the act; its relation to the power of an enduring human love, "stronger than death," and the corollary of fidelity which follows from that relation, is ignored on grounds that this is just "doing what comes naturally." The soul is for loving, the body for pleasure. The Manichaeans never did better at splitting up the two. And scholars tell us that they drew one of two conclusions from the split: either that sex was dirty and to be despised, or that it was perfectly indifferent, neither good nor bad, just "there": a "fact of life" and nothing more.

The modern world may deride sexual taboos. But their merit lies in the acknowledgment that this act is something special: an encounter in which, mysteriously, the springs of life and of human love coincide. *Terribilis est locus iste,* "a fearful place, this," cried Jacob, in a situation more analogous than modern man is prepared to admit.

Determinism

Often connected with it, determinism is nonetheless a distinct animal from indifferentism. Psychological determinism (the most common form today), informs us that all our actions, despite our illusions of freedom, are in fact dictated by the drives, urges and complexes that lie buried in the dark pit of the Unconscious of each of us. A typical form is the pan-sexual one of popular Freudianism: despite our efforts to explain it away, even to ourselves, even the highest forms of human activity, artistic, religious, heroic, are just sublimations, that is, masks or camouflages, for the achievement of a satisfaction which is, in the final analysis, sexual.

Some sociologist insist that a large measure of determinism issues from the pressures of society. None of us, we are assured, can escape the influence of the "collective consciousness" and its evaluations. It was just such a collective consciousness that was guilty of the Second World War, for example; and the bridge is established to a theory of collective guilt such that an entire group is pronounced guilty *as a group.*

The cult of liberty

The reaction against this determinism finds its term in present-day existentialism with its tenacious proclamation of man's liberty. The authentic individual, we may summarize, is the one who is conscious of liberty as man's typical property. He is the man with the courage to resist the temptation of taking the easy way of conformity to the patterns of his day or society. He becomes a human being in the full sense only when he assumes the terrible responsibility of freely constructing the design of his existence. Right and wrong and good and bad suppose a set of norms received from outside, antecedent to man's action. They suppose a structured human essence which antedates freedom's intervention. But man's essence lies in the future, not in the past; it is the result of his free activity, not some norm that precedes and guides it. What matters, therefore, is not whether man acts in a manner some society or age or church would deem right or wrong. What matters is that he acts freely, independent of any pressures they would put on him. "This above all, to thine own self be true": to the ideal self that lies at the term of every man's freedom.

Here we have Kant's insistence on the personal conscience, become a law to itself, combined with the widespread refusal to accept a morality whose main hinge is a more or less arbitrary connection between certain kinds of action and the corresponding reward or punishment. But the final fruit of this cult of liberty occurs in the so-called "situation-ethics," which stresses that each moral agent and each decision confronting him are both so perfectly individual that no universal laws can possibly be applicable. There is indeed a possibility of right and wrong, good and bad; but there are no rules. Paradoxically: there can be sin, but there are no definable "sins."

Modern morality: the central thrust

"To thine own self be true." In spite of the variety of moral attitudes, the welter of theories that invite modern man's loyalties, here we have a keynote, which brings contemporary moral sentiment (for sentiment it is rather than formulated theory) into a kind of unstable synthesis. Sincerity is the key regarding the *manner* of moral action. As to the *matter,* it can best be summarized in two terms enjoying some vogue at the moment: humanism or, in more determinate form, personalism.

Sincerity

Despite the naturalism that tempts him, despite the appeals of determinisms of all sorts, modern man seems dimly to retain a burning conviction that his freedom makes him fundamentally different from the beasts. Not all his other positions are coherent with this one, and even this consciousness of liberty often remains implicit. But what he sees in liberty, in the first place, is the duty to be sincere. Liberty lays upon him the inescapable responsibility to be true to whatever moral ideal is imposed by personal experience and judgment. He vaguely feels it is all-important that he embrace and sanction **this** ideal personally, rather than let himself be pulled this way and that by the norms which some misty, impersonal "they" seek to thrust upon him. In former times, he feels, it may have been enough for "them" to announce that this or that "simply is not done": and, out of some sheep-like conformity, it was not done. Or at least, not openly. Against what he looks upon as mere exterior conformity to "the rules," modern man puts the primary accent squarely on the interior: the heart must be right, one must do what one is personally convinced is the right thing, and hang the rules. At all costs, don't be (in Salinger's term) a "phoney": even if this means running directly into collision with all the traditional taboos.

Personalism

We can liken sincerity to the limpidity of an eye rinsed clear of the dust of accepted standards, which, in the half-formulated view of the man of our day, merely obstructed the view of the moral landscape. Having swept the slate clean, modern man is left with the terrible possibility of doing wrong, but at first blush with no rules to guide him in avoiding it. If there is any principle regarding the *matter* of moral action which modern man finds himself forced to acknowledge, this will be concerned with what he terms "humanism" or "personalism."

It is not entirely easy to spell out what these terms imply, especially for the ordinary man of our times. Before we begin, however, one objection may be forestalled. If we choose our examples of this concern from the writings of philosophers, playwrights, and from films and other mass media, it is because all these normally take root in that humus of intellectual and artistic activity, the confused and ill-expressed consciousness of the inarticulate mass of mankind. The artist and thinker of any age is always a forerunner, but at the same time a representative of his time: he brings to expression what the men of his age are capable of thinking only in vaguer terms, of being anxious about without being able to locate the seat of their trouble.

Now if there is one phrase that modern man seems to have taken to heart, it is Dostoevski's ringing "we are all responsible for all." Radio, films, television, all seem to have extended the concern of today's man to the further limits of the world he lives in. The Marxist pretension to form the New Man, the concern of socialists, democrats and liberals of every stamp to bring to the masses what were once the privileges of only the few, the tendency of writers, artists, intellectuals to devote their efforts to a constant stream of "causes," the vogue of philosophies containing the terms "humanism" and "personalism" in their labels — all these are symptomatic. Modern man has emerged from what he (somewhat hastily, perhaps) brands as an age of individualism, of isolation. If there is one thing he decries, it is the egotistic posture of unconcern and non-commitment towards the problems that torment the world about him. The value of values is man, and humankind is one great family; each one of us must strain every effort to assure that each member of that family enjoy a life worthy of a man. Despite all his infidelities to it (and which of us is entirely faithful to what we believe in?), this, dimly sensed, would seem the closest thing to an objective ideal envisaged by contemporary man.

But it has only made him more acutely conscious of its unattainability. How do we really get to communicate with others? To understand and be understood? To sympathize and gain real sympathy in return — not some sham of it? Who will consider me as a person, not coldly inform me, in the words of Menotti's consular secretary, "Your name is a number, your story is a case"? We find ourselves all sitting at "Separate Tables," revolted by the distance between us, impotent to get together. It is fascinating to see how Sartre, whose system excludes any meaningful personal relationship, even as a possibility, still beats his wings like a wounded bird against this problem. It is precisely when one sees that all communication, understanding, love is impossible, that one faces the stark realization that *"L'enfer, c'est les autres."* Here, too, is one of the persistent themes of two of the most talented film directors of our day, Ingmar Bergman and Federico Fellini. When the Zampano of *La Strada* crumples up on the seashore crying into the night his final protest, "I don't need anybody, not anybody," even the most ordinary film-goer is aware that the gentleman doth protest too much. The very depersonalization of his world, the bigness of its cold corporate structures, the multiplication of "functionaries" who perform their unfeeling routines with all the icy precision of machines, seem to have set man running frantically about for someone to call him "thou," to call him by his own most intimate name, someone "real" with whom a truly personal relation is possible. And the multiplication of characters, paintings, sculptures in our day, from which eyes stare blank and expressionless out of a self imprisoned in unwilling, unwitting solitude, is testimony not only to a dim awareness that something has gone terribly wrong, but is also an inverted image of a cherished world in which true understanding and love would be possible.

That love, the man of our day is aware, would not imply merely the perfunctory performance of a set of duties one to another, be they sanctioned by Dale Carnegie or the God of Exodus. It could not mean simply giving what one *has* to the other: it must be the self that is given, in a gift that is perfectly reciprocal, with nothing held back. No more explicit recognition of the total exigencies of love could be imagined. It is the very totality of the gift required that makes modern man conscious, perhaps far more than his predecessors, of the sham that all partial loves represent, and at the same time alas, of the quasi-impossibility of genuine love for the poor egotists that we all, Adam's children, are.

But to the products of a change evolution, stray lostlings clinging to a tiny planet, due eventually (perhaps tomorrow) for meaningless extinction, what reason can modern man give to us why anyone should love us? "Unloved, unlovable, in the same kind of a world": this was Clare Boothe Luce's anguished portrait of herself before she found the faith. And this is the source of anguish for the man we have been examining. He feels the need for a relationship that acknowledges an absolute value to the human being and his individual story, but in a world from which all absolutes have been banished. His deep frustration is comparable to the builders of Babel. He is trying to construct a Mystical Body, but without a Christ.

Why Not Christianity?

The reason is that a return to the Christian morality strikes modern man as necessarily a step backwards. Partially because his view of Christian morality is something of a caricature, surely; but neither the practice nor the preaching of Christians has always been exempt of the defects he thinks he has found there. Neither has always been entirely free of a certain taint that tended to devaluate the body and make the sense of sin dangerously analogous to what modern man terms the guilt-complex. A nominalist or purely voluntarist notion of law is not always easy to distinguish from an irrational taboo originating in a perfectly arbitrary will of God, backed up with threats of a hell-fire that seems to have no intrinsic connection with the acts condemned. Doctrinal exaggerations and the imposition of certain practices, all we refer to as "formalism," have not always respected the ineradicable personal element in religion and morality. Nor have the contingent norms of society and class always been kept distinct from the perennial demands of a Christian morality that must find resonance in the deepest heart of man wherever and whenever found.

The historical dimension of the human person, the fact that his liberty and moral responsibility are subject to growth and do not take the same form in childhood as in maturity, the historical axis of Christianity itself, the connection of Law, conscience, and God's Personal Love working out in time; these essential signposts of Christian reflection have sometimes been put in the shade by a timeless scheme of impersonal Law more akin to Stoicism. The paradox of development in dogma, whereby the Scribe in the Kingdom of Heaven is forever drawing out of the same treasure truths which are old and ever again renewed, has not always been accomplished without the danger of misplaced emphasis. And so with Christian morality as well.

To cite but the two main currents of present-day concern, the Christian moralist did not need to wait for modern man to tell him that a personalist morality, emphasizing the values of communion in true charity and underlining a moral teaching based on the Mystical Body, was only caricatured in an individualist morality which emphasizes the apparently egotistic pursuit of one's own "perfection," and the devil take the rest of men. Nor did the Christian moralist need await the philosophies of subjectivity to focus on the paramount importance of sincerity and of personal commitment to what one interiorly believes to be right. The classic distinction of material and formal sin makes this abundantly clear: a man can do what in fact is objectively evil and still get to heaven if he (blamelessly) think it good; another can exteriorly perform what is objectively good and still be damned because, in the modern term, the heart is not right.[1]

---

1. Cf. Karl Adams, **The Spirit of Catholicism** (London, 1934), pp. 225-9.

Modern Sense of Sin: A Christian Appraisal

We may begin by pointing out that the guilt complex, far from being the equivalent of the Christian sense of sin, is rather a masquerade of it. In certain conditions, in fact, it can be a virulent foe of the true Christian sense of sin. This latter must have as its point of reference God and not the self; especially if that self pretends to be ideally some disembodied angelic being better than the union of body and soul God made and saw to be very good. A Christian sense of sin, moreover, would bear fruits of "charity, joy, peace, patience"— all fruits of the Holy Spirit; the guilt complex produces almost the exact opposite. Instead of being a springboard to progress, it is a disease that paralyzes all progress, particularly on that central point which is the whole of the law, charity.

From Taboo to Law to Conscience

And yet, in his moral life, that historical creature called man must begin as a child under a law which he cannot understand, a law that is imposed from without, often couched in the form of a prohibition where the connection of the act and the threatened punishment must strike his infant understanding as perfectly arbitrary. The abuse of such parental authority can, granted, be extremely harmful, can tie the child into neurotic knots in later life. But the mistake would come in thinking either that all impositions from parental authority are to be dispensed with, or that the child is meant to stay forever at this infantile stage. Parental authority, like most teaching, has the function of putting itself eventually out of a job, precisely by producing an individual who is reasonable and responsible enough at last to stand on his own feet. Only at this stage can the value of actions be scrutinized in the light of a mature vision of reality: only then can the child see that not all "taboos" of society are on the same footing, nor all, from table manners to incest prohibitions, on a moral footing. Only then can he be expected to compare

the code he has *received* with the code his personal conscience
has not merely the privilege but the *duty to construct* and ratify
interiorly.[2] The process does not mean rejection *en bloc* of all
imposed morality, but the lucid discernment of where taboo
and a mature vision of reality coincide, and where they differ.

A continuous reading of the Old and New Testaments, in
fact, leads one to speculate whether the infancy of our race did
not have to pass through the same pedagogy as the individual
moral agent. From an original accent on an almost material
notion of sin, akin to ritual impurity, without discernible relation to interior dispositions, backed by the often inscrutable
punishments of a "jealous" Yahweh, the moral consciousness of
Israel advances to a notion of law as God's wise ordering of
things for our own good. The God of the Decalogue is more
frequently underlined as the God who, even prior to Exodus, is
the God who promised our fulfillment to Abraham. The Law
never becomes that merely impersonal Logos, the "immanent
reason of things" of Stoic philosophy. The Torah remains always
God's personal word addressed to a people that is the object of
his entirely unaccountable love: "I have called thee by thy
name!"

Then sin becomes plain as a rebellion of the first-born to his
Father, the adultery of the bride to her Spouse. Then God's
jealousy becomes plain as the other face of his inexplicable love
for men, all the more inexplicable in that he has no need of man.
And sin is seen as the *hamartia*, the missing of the mark that is
none other than our happiness: *gloria Dei vivens homo!*

The evolutionists, then, are not entirely wrong: there is an
evolution of moral consciousness, not only humanity more generally, but even in the pedagogical process of God's long revelation.

And yet, is the evolutionist prepared to show that all notion
of a perennial structure of human nature is to be discarded? Or
that man, wherever and whenever found, is incapable of per-

---

2. It is taken for granted, of course, that this process takes place in the
context of faith.

ceiving a certain basic set of ethical principles? The Decalogue, for instance?

In considering the thirst for sincerity which we find in contemporary man, we are reminded of Thomas Wolf's determination to cast methodic doubt on all accepted literary judgments. He embarks on years of voracious reading in the effort to form his own personal opinions, only to confess at the end, perhaps with some disappointment, but with a candor that does him credit, that he has wound up in substantial agreement with the evaluations of the great tradition. The quest for a personal set of values can drive us into a tenacious refusal to agree with an opinion we finally see to be true, for the simple reason that someone else has managed to utter it before we did. This is the satanic temptation lying in the path of modern man: a sham sincerity more monstrous even than the sheep-like conformity he sees infecting the morality of former ages.

Can the personalism of contemporary morality sanction, sincerely sanction, unbridled robbery? or random murder? Or are these, as the great tradition insists, unchangeable features of the moral landscape which the limpid eye of personalism must acknowledge? Agreement here may be a first step down to Graham Greene's *Potting Shed*, the test of whether sincerity is sincere enough to admit the vision that waits there. Men have proposed literally hundreds of theories on where and how man is to find happiness. For us, our nature trails off into mystery — man, the unknown, Carrel calls him — and reason may not always be able with its flickering lamp to light up *all* its dark passageways. To the Israelite, the Decalogue becomes increasingly clear as the map of human life his Father has given him in loving care for him. Sincerity will lead to a love that finds it normal to believe, trust, confide itself to One who is Father as well as Law-giver; it will lead to that Personal Word, his Son, then to that Church which continues his Incarnation down to our own day; it will lead us to find life, and find it more abundantly.

The Church and modern man, are, in fact drilling the same tunnel starting from opposite ends. The one begins from the exigency of interior sincerity; its initial probings are in the direction of objective standards. The former, starting out with the objective standards which her God has drawn out of the man he fashioned, must forever remind her children of their need to interiorize those standards in a faith unfeigned, a trust that is never confounded and a charity that bears all things. Let modern man read the Sermon on the Mount once again — let all of us do so, in fact. There, beside the most eloquent demand for inwardness ever uttered, we shall find the Law, not abolished but fulfilled. We are asked now to furnish, not works of a purely exterior observance, but the unreserving gift of ourselves. How, and why? The answer lies in the piece of the puzzle that man of our day seems hardly to know is lacking to him.

That piece is a God who is Personal; who loves us and out of love gives us his Law; and — incredible — can be *personally* offended by our rejection of his gift. The entire atmosphere of the Sermon on the Mount is bathed in a childlike trust in the Father; the key to the love it demands of us lies in the fact that His Son affirms "you do it unto Me." Of each of us he wishes to say nothing less than "This is My Body."

Here is the missing foundation for the modern world's obscure sense of being responsible all for all, for the unlimited extension of its concern, for its mute detestation of all egotistic unconcern. And here alone can it find the love, the communication, the oneness it seeks so sorely: "One, Father, as You and I are One." To the exigency of this sincere love, "Love one another as I have loved you," modern man is honest enough to reply that such love is impossible to us. And Christ said nothing different: "Abide in My love." "For without Me you can do nothing." That love must be given, that gift is the Spirit of Jesus, soul of his Mystical Body: at one and the same time the bond of all the members one to another, and the voice that cries from within each of them, *Abba, Father!*

This Gift, this love, and not, as in the guilt complex, some ideal image of himself, is the focus for the Christian's apprehension of the tragic seriousness of sin. Our constant temptation is to think that God loves us because we are somehow lovable in ourselves. But the exact reverse is true: sin is our own strictly personal property, all the rest is God's gift. God loved us first, while we were still sinners, and in loving us, makes us lovable. The foundation for man's dignity and worth which contemporary man seeks in vain, is nowhere else than in that love which God pours out in his unflagging creation of man, a creation which always has in view the adoption of man into the Sonship of Christ.

This is why the Cross will always remain the final embodiment of a single truth with two faces, each implying and reinforcing the other. It shows us what sin is, but precisely and only because it shows sin's antithesis, God's inexhaustible love. Only then was it plain that the secret, dimly avowed aim of sin must always be deicide, the destruction of God. To a love which would draw us out of our egotism, pride and selfish adoration of our own independence, man's answer is "Crucify him." But not until Calvary did sin amazedly rub its eyes at finding its Victim at last within reach, not until then could it unleash all its lurking fury. The miracle is that this moment was not the last in human history.

And yet, when man has vented his utmost, when he sees the dead figure on the gibbet as wordless testimony to his hatefulness, just as he is tempted to descend that hill to final despair, the lance thrusts home and there rushes forth blood and water. All the hate we could fling against Him, God had endured, absorbed, outlasted. At the end, our sinful strength is spent, yet His Love still lives. Lives and creates in us a new heart, one that can love with a love that is poured out of his own heart.

Once sin is seen, in the only way a Christian can look at it, against the backdrop of that Crucified Love, a peculiar inversion occurs. The very recognition of our sins brings with it the simultaneous revelation of that same Love. And the Christian sense of sin becomes suffused with a trust, a liberating joy and a response of love that reminds us of St. Paul's word that we live no longer for ourselves but for Him who loved and died for us. Progressively the Christian is conscious of being, as it were, only secondarily concerned with *his own* perfection, *his own* getting to Heaven, *himself* generally. The final bolt of egotism has been slipped. It is the immense outpouring of God's love that becomes central for him, it is this which must not go to waste. The Blood that was poured out for our Atonement, to "unite the scattered children of God," must not have been poured in vain.

But the vision of that Love shows at the same time why sin's punishment is not arbitrarily but intrinsically connected with the nature of sin itself. All sin ultimately comes down to the proud refusal of God's love that would bring us out of our egotism into communion with him and all his scattered children. Sin is sin exactly in the measure embodied in that refusal: whether it take the slack form of a sensuality too soft to face the challenge of that commitment, or the terrifying form that avarice, or even lust, can assume, ruthlessly reducing everyone in its entourage to mere objects of its own exploitation. Hell is our isolated selves having finally obtained the wish expressed by our lives; self-entombed, eternally frozen in the attitude of refusal that becomes at death the résumé of our entire life. Love cannot be forced, even by Infinite Love. And once faced with a life that culminates in final rejection, even the omnipotent God is helpless. "How oft would I have gathered thee together . . . and thou wouldst not!"[3]

Only the Christian view of man can attribute such substance, such meaning to human life: this temporal, bodily creature can freely choose heaven or hell. For as Christians we believe in the whole man, embodied spirit, a creature made by God to be wholly native to space and time, body and soul indivisibly the object of God's creative as well as his redemptive action. We believe in a body whose positive value is such that without its handmaid the soul is gaping incompletion; a body whose union with the soul is essential, not accidental, not to say somehow monstrous.

Much is said of the Unconscious dictating our conscious acts; but the fact of psychoanalytic cure indicates that even in psychic sickness liberty can impose a new organization in the depths of

---

3. Mt 23, 37.

our soul. Hence our drives and quasi-determinisms can be checked, tamed and eventually, in limits known only to God, personalized in this life through the patient action of an incarnate liberty in constant growth; till eventually we stand forth, in the image of the risen Christ, our bodies become the perfect embodiment of our accomplished personality. Nothing man does is entirely "indifferent" or completely refractory to this process, whether we "eat or drink or whatever else we do"—including sex. Our contemporaries see in the Unconscious nothing but demons, pulling down everything to the level of mere biology. The Christian may prefer to look on Christ's descent into the "lower regions" as a liberating invasion of that realm as well; now the seed planted in our depths at creation is once more free to bring forth the fruit of its hidden yearning and can at last become the incorporation of a personal, life-producing love. Even instinct has a "desire" to be transformed by the charity of Christ; even the lower creation "groans and travails," "awaits with eager longing" and eventually "will be delivered from its slavery to corruption into the freedom of the glory of the sons of God."[4]

But this "assumption" of instinct into liberty, a term we prefer in hope of avoiding the connotations of "escape" and "camouflage" that beset the term "sublimation," must then be seen as a long, continuous, life-time project. In this long pedagogy, even our sins can assume a positive function, if brought to the One who knew what was in man, and who has given sinful men like ourselves the power of changing wounds into glorified scars. In this patient pruning of time, all the various ages of man, each building on the work that went before it, each bringing its typical challenges, trials, temptations, purifications, each with its characteristic joys and its proper moral perfection; all of them have an irreplaceable contribution to make to us. Not only the "big decisions" that set the course of our lives for years to come, but the long series of grey days where there is neither storm nor sunlight: all have an indispensable brushstroke to add to the canvas that is our finished portrait.

---

4. **Rom** 8, 18-22.

For the actions of our lives are not an unrelated, discontinuous series. Sins do not make us just "someone who sinned yesterday" but "someone who today is a sinner." Each one alters, however slightly, the helm of our basic life-course, forcing the fundamental direction of our being either towards or away from the communion God would give us, till at the end we take form like some living tableau, set in an attitude expressive either of acceptance or refusal.

In St. Matthew's account of the judgment, the damned ask indignantly: "Lord, when did we see Thee hungry . . . thirsty . . . naked?" Christ's answer suggests that despite the opaque tissue of our temporal existence, he insists on our duty to see the strands of God's love working through our lives and the lives of those he expects us to love. We are asked to recognize Christ in Magdalene's gardener, in the quite ordinary traveller to Emmaus, or in the dim figure on the shore which John detects as "the Lord." Our eyes must be sharpened by long fidelity, to the penetration of a faith that is already clairvoyant with the light of knowledge, understanding and wisdom.

Perhaps his persistence in assigning a kind of absolute value to the person and personal love puts contemporary man "not far from the Kingdom of God" after all, closer than we imagine to the implication that "you do it unto Me." If the shadow of any momentary sparrow (to borrow an image from Chesterton) can be a message from the Sun, perhaps the smile of any love can tell us Love exists and loves us. Perhaps his sincerity will lead our groping brother to "be watchful," his good intentions to burgeon into a continued effort of attention, till one day he detect, however faintly the music of God's love which all the raucous cries of Calvary could not drown.

Chapter Two

MISSING THE MARK

BRUCE VAWTER, C.M.

Etymologies are handy things. They frequently tell us what our fathers, who first coined the words that we nowadays use so casually, really meant by what they said, which is sometimes a little different from what we mean. On the other hand, etymologies can just as often be misleading, since it is use that really determines a word's meaning for those who use it, and use may have parted company with etymology even from the very beginning. Ordinarily we will find that it is at least instructive to examine etymologies, even though in the end we may not have to treat them too seriously. This classic Scholastic approach to a new term has always been through *quoad nomen* and *quoad rem,* the etymological definition first, then the real meaning.

At the outset, then, it is interesting to observe that none of the words used in the Bible for "sin" has of itself that exclusively moral association to which hundreds of years of Christian use have accustomed us. It is interesting, because this fact throws some light on certain aspects of the biblical idea of sin and especially on some attitudes adopted by later Judaism. It cannot, however, give us any adequate appreciation of the biblical theology of sin.

In the Hebrew Old Testament the word most commonly used for sin, the word that we customarily translate "sin" in our Bibles, is *hattah*, which literally means "to miss the mark." The mark that is missed need not be a moral mark, nor need it be missed immorally. The author of Pr 19, 2 uses "missing the mark" of the hasty traveller who loses his way through inadvertence to road signs.

The Hebrew word used most commonly after *hattah* in the biblical vocabulary of sin, *pesha*, is entirely of the same order. It means "overstep" or "rebel." In 2 K 8, 20, when the author states that Edom successfully rebelled against the rule of Judah, he is passing no moral judgment on the revolt but simply recording a political fact. Other Hebrew words that are used on occasion to signify a moral lapse — such as "err," "wander," and the like — also have of themselves no necessary moral application.

The same must be said of the Greek word *hamartano*, used in the Greek Old Testament to translate *hattah*, and in the New Testament in its own right as the word for "sin."

Hamartano is the exact equivalent of *hattah*. It, too, means "miss the mark," and in profane Greek it often refers to a man's losing his way on the road. For that matter, the Latin *peccare, peccatum*, with which our own liturgy has made us so familiar and which have as their root meaning "stumble," originally did not necessarily connote anything moral. When the Italian says *che peccato!* he is not saying "what a great sin!" but rather, "what a pity!" Thus it is that terminology alone cannot tell us a great deal about the biblical theology of sin. We must see, rather, how the terminology is used. The terminology doubtless assisted what was a tendency of the later Judaism, to make of the notion of sin something purely formal and legalistic. Wellhausen was able to assert that what the Law of Moses demanded was not rightdoing, but rather the avoidance of wrongdoing. With respect to the later legalism, Wellhausen's charge was well founded. He was certainly wrong, however, in extending this indictment to the Law itself and to the way it was understood in the biblical period. This much we can easily see, I believe, by examining a few of the passages that go to make up the biblical theology of sin.

See, for example, how the word *pesha* is used by the prophet Amos, one of the earliest of our biblical authors. If we read his first oracles we find that "transgressions" of which he repeatedly speaks embrace inhumanity, cruelty, social injustice, violation of contract, acceptance of bribes, violation of the public trust, greed, lust, and hypocrisy, on the part of Gentiles as well as of Israelites.[1] There is obviously no question here of sin as the merely formal, mechanically computed, violation of a law. Rather, it is clear that for Amos *pesha* is a transgression of the moral law, a rebellion against God's moral will, a will that had been made known to the Gentiles as the norm of rightdoing. Amos does not, it is true, elaborate any doctrine of natural law, to explain how Israelite and Gentile alike were under the same moral obligations; no such doctrine is anywhere elaborated in the Hebrew Old Testament, which addressed itself always and exclusively to the people of God who were recipients of his revelation. Yet in 6, 12 Amos does state that the rejection of the justice and rightdoing which God required of Israel — here in specific reference to the corruption that had taken place in Israelite courts of law — was as absurd and unnatural as tracking horses over rocks and ploughing the sea with oxen. Sin for the Israelite, certainly, was the violated will and law of the Lord. But it was will and law that found a response in man's mind and heart; it was never arbitrary whim or caprice.

This conception of *pesha* that we first encounter in *Amos* is common to the rest of the prophets. It is not incorrect to do as we are doing, to find the spirit of the Law expressed in the prophets. The criticism of the past century tried to oppose the two, as though the spiritual, prophetic religion and the priestly religion of the Law had been separate, mutually antagonistic developments in Israelite history and tradition. Criticism now recognizes

---

1. Am 1, 3-2, 8.

that in this attempt it, too, had taken the wrong track and missed the mark. Prophecy and Law were, of course, two different emphases of Israelitic religion, which correspondingly spoke two different languages. But they were emphases of the same religion and were directed towards broadly the same ends. If we do not expect to find the moral and devotional teaching of Catholicism in the Code of Canon Law or the Roman Ritual, neither do we oppose what we do find there to the *Summa* of St. Thomas or the *Introduction to the Devout Life*. In much the same fashion, it is now agreed that we rightly interpret prophetic teaching as supporting in its way a doctrine that the Law upheld in its own.

In the Law the favored word for sin is *hattah*. The "mark" or norm that was "missed," in the mind of the Israelite authors, was that of the Covenant of Sinai, of which Israel's Law was the spelling out of the people's obligations with respect to its covenant God.

Here, too, if we would understand rightly in what this covenant duty consisted, we must have a clear idea of what covenant meant, first and foremost, in the ancient Near East. The closest analogy to covenant in our own society is the bilateral contract; but while the analogy is valid as far as it goes, we have sometimes tended to overlook the fact that analogy is not identity. In other words, covenant was *like* a contract in some ways, but covenant was not precisely a contract. Specifically, whereas the binding force of a contract consists in legal justice, the covenant obligation was not conceived primarily as one of justice but as one of love.

The word customarily used in the Old Testament to convey the notion of the covenant bond is *hesed*, translated variously as "mercy," "loyalty," "devotion," "lovingkindness," or simply "love." It was in *hesed* that God had chosen Israel and bound it to himself; *hesed*, correspondingly, was the duty of every Israelite in return, towards God and towards the other members of the covenant community. The covenant idea, therefore, was modeled after a family rather than a legal relationship. When an Israelite committed *hattah*, sinned, his offence was not terminated by the letter of the law which he had violated, but by the familial piety which he had ruptured, the *hesed* of which the Law was a formulated norm and expression.

Sin and evil to the Semite were not the negation, the "deprivation of good" that they have achieved in our thinking under the influence of other thought-forms. Sin was a positive thing that had been done, that therefore continued to exist until done away with. What we think of as "guilt," the condition of the sinner as the result of sin, and the punishment that we conceive of as a kind of act of reciprocity on the part of God or offended authority taking vengeance on the sin, were to the biblical authors hardly distinguishable from the sin itself. In *Nb* 32, 23 "sin" and "the consequences of sin," as we would have to render the thought in English, translate the same Hebrew word, and this is typical of the biblical viewpoint. It is from this viewpoint that we must understand the Old Testament conception of sins committed in ignorance, for which expiatory rites and sacrifice were provided by the Law. From this viewpoint, too, we can see how a whole community could share in the guilt of one of its members, or generations yet unborn in the guilt of their progenitor. It was not that they were being "held" guilty of another's wrongdoing, but that they were caught up in the consequences of an act that were actually the continued existence of the act itself. The Deuteronomic law of personal responsibility[2] that was laid down as a necessary rule in the human administration of justice, and its application by Jeremiah[3] and Ezekiel[4] to the divine dispensation under the new covenant, were restrictions placed by God on the "natural" extension of guilt.

Similarly, punishment was not so much as retribution "visioned" upon the sin (though this idea of retribution is also, at times, the biblical conception) as it was the inexorable running of sin's course. God, it is true, could forestall this consequence — there is nothing in the Bible akin to the fatalism of Greek trag-

---

2. Dt 24, 16.
3. Jr 31, 29f.
4. Ezk ch. 18.

edy. For sins of ignorance he did so by accepting the expiatory sacrifices of the Law. For other sins there was the recourse of prayer, coupled with the contrition and the confession of the sinner, of which we have so many examples in Psalms. But God's forgiveness of sin did not automatically entail his remission of punishment, as can be seen from the famous judgment passed on David's sin with Bathsheba.[5] The Catholic teaching on the temporal punishment of sin is a true echo of this biblical doctrine.

Finally, we can see from this "objective" nature of sin as it was understood by the Old Testament why that which is sinful was broader in its extent than that which is immoral. Legal purity, by which was meant the external holiness of a people consecrated to God, a reminder, in turn, of the need of interior holiness,[6] could obviously be violated without the performance of any immoral act. A woman had to make a "guilt offering" after the "uncleanness" of childbirth because legal purity had been offended; but no question whatever of morality was involved in the matter.

Here we may pause to note the difference between the world of the Old Testament and that of the New. While most of what has been said above applies equally well to the thinking of the Old and the New Testaments, there is in the New Testament, for reasons that we shall explain more fully later on, no trace of the conception of purely legal holiness. The old formulas are used, but they are used within the new dimension of a salvation and a regeneration of which the former figures were but a type and a foreshadowing. The "holy ones" to whom St. Paul writes are not those merely consecrated to God, but those of whom personal holiness is expected as a consequence of the indwelling Spirit. With the entire apparatus of formal sanctity superseded in a new and spiritual covenant, sin and immorality are fully identified. The law of Christians is the code of conduct that

---

5. 2 S 12, 10-14.
6. Cf. Lv 11, 44ff.

befits those removed in principle from this world and joined to
the Source of all that is holy and to Holiness itself. Charity is
the *hesed* of the new covenant.

The nature of sin in the Bible can aptly be perceived in the
effects that are attributed to it. These are described in various
ways and under various figures, but the idea that emerges is
much the same. In the Law, sin is represented as an *obex,* an
obstacle that stands between God and people — once again we
see the relevance of the "objective" conception of sin. The rites of
expiation are not directed to God in the thought that he is to be
placated or changed from an unfavorable to a favorable disposition; God is never the object of the verb that we translate "ex-
piate." Expiation, rather, has sin for its object. Sin must be removed, this obstacle in the path of man's approach to the Holy.
Man, not God, must change. When sin has been wilful, committed "with a high hand," a sin of mind and heart, then the
mind and heart of man must be changed. This is contrition or
repentance.

In the famous sixth chapter of *Isaiah* we find this same notion
of sin as it was experienced by the prophet at the time of his call
to prophesy. If this chapter is read attentively, it is apparent that,
despite the awesome and grandiose terms in which God is
described in theophany, it is in the moral order rather than in
the order of being that man is seen to be most separated from
God. Sin, in other words, the sin that Isaiah confesses of himself
and of his people, is what lies behind his recognition that he is
"lost" in the presence of the Holy. Much the same idea must be
in the background of the English word "sin" (cf. the German,
Sünde) that has been formed by Christian thinking, namely that
it *sunders* one from the other.

One of the most fruitful sources of the biblical theology of sin
are the penitential psalms of the Old Testament. The New Testament would certainly open up a wider vision of the riches of
God's salvation and his grace, but not even the New Testament
can tell us more about the sense of sin and of the lostness and
meaninglessness which are its inevitable concomitant. Among

the penitential psalms none is richer in its content than *Ps* 50 (51), the well-known *Miserere.*

This psalm begins with a plea to God, the covenant Father, to honor his *hesed* in responding to the sinner's appeal. Three words are used for sin throughout the psalm: the two of which we have already spoken above, together with *awon,* "guilt," the state of a sinner who has transgressed the will of God and who now stands in a condition of disharmony with that will. Sin, in other words, appears as a rebellion, an offence against the covenant bond, and therefore a state of aversion from the God of the covenant. Correspondingly, three different words are used to express the sinner's conviction of what God alone can and must do with regard to his sinful state.

It is important to see precisely what these words mean, since all of them involve vaguely the same figure, and it would be easy to conclude mistakenly that they are more or less arbitrary synonyms. "Blot out," "wash," and "cleanse" are their usual English equivalents. The "blotting out" in question is a ritual obliteration or washing away: in this sense the same verb appears in *Nb* 5, 23. The "washing" that the psalmist has in mind does mean this, certainly, but we need to recall the type of washing with which he was familiar. The washing of clothes,[7] not of the hands or feet, is what the verb denotes. More literally still, it could be rendered "tread out"— the Oriental flung his soiled clothing in a stream and stamped on it enthusiastically. The "cleansing," finally, to which the psalmist refers is a ritual or declaratory cleansing of the kind provided for in *Lv* 13, 6.

The psalmist petitions of God, therefore, what a later theology would distinguish into a forensic and a real justification. Justification is forensic: God must simply forgive, declare the sinner to be a sinner no more. There is a simple truth preserved in this conception, for the committed sin, of course, is a reality that is never annulled or annihilated. The historical fact that is a past human act cannot be done away with as though it had

---

7. Cf. *Ex* 19, 10.

never occurred. But justification is also real: the guilt that has remained in the sinner and that prevents his access to the God of holiness must be stamped out and obliterated.

The nature of this real justification is brought out beautifully and profoundly towards the middle of the psalm. The psalmist calls upon the Lord to *create* in him a clean heart, and to *renew* within him an upright spirit. The same word (*bara*) is used that we translate "create" in the creation narrative of *Gn* 1, 1. It is a word reserved in the Old Testament exclusively for the wonderful, unique action of God alone. For the Israelite, "heart" was much more than a metaphor for the emotions or, as we sometimes use it, for a kind of better self or good will. The heart was conceived as the seat of *all* emotion, will, and thought; for the Semite, we must always remember, thought or "said" things in his heart, not in his head. The heart was the Self. The "spirit," or breath, was the power residing within man, a power that could come from God only, by which he was able to think and will in his heart. It, too, therefore, might be called the Self. The psalmist clearly knew, as a consequence, that the justification of the sinner entailed a divine work of re-creation, the renewal of a personality that had been distorted and turned aside from its true purposes by the act of sin. Create, he says, a new *me*. Such an idea is boundless in its commentary on what he believed the effect of sin to be in the sinner, an effect which obviously far transcends any notion of purely formal or legal rectitude. Sin was, in his eyes, an involvement from which man could not emerge without an alteration in his inmost being.

Because of the similarity of this passage to the language of Jeremiah[8] and Ezekiel[9] some authors have concluded that the psalmist must have been dependent on the teaching of these great prophets. In their preaching about the new covenant, however, Jeremiah and Ezekiel seem merely to have articulated an ancient Hebrew conception. Similarly, the psalmist's conviction (expressed in v. 6) that every sin is a sin against God, contains

8. Jr 24, 7; 31, 33; 32, 39.
9. Ezk 36, 25ff.

nothing that was new in Israel, as can be seen from the ancient Joseph story[10] and David's confession at the finding out of his sin with Bathsheba.[11]

One other value *Ps* 50 has in setting forth for us the biblical theology of sin. In v. 7 the psalmist declares, "Behold, I was brought forth in guilt, and in sin did my mother conceive me." He makes this utterance as a motivation to God to be merciful, as a reminder that man's proclivities are sinful — *Gn* 8, 21 has God himself acknowledge this and accept it in his announced plan or his economy of dealing with man. The biblical authors were well aware that the introduction of sin into the world and its continuation were the achievement of human malice against the will of God. They testified that man's disposition to sin was not of God's designing, but was part of consistent history in which the will of a saving God had from the first been resisted and thwarted.[12] It was this belief that St. Paul would further develop[13] and which we understand more comprehensively as the doctrine of original sin. The Bible does not profess this belief, of course, to excuse man's continued sinfulness; it merely seeks to explain it.

As we have mentioned above, most of the Old Testament theology of sin is discernible in the thinking of the New Testament authors, who had been formed completely in the tradition of their biblical fathers. There is, however, a decisive difference that results from the new and definitive revelation of Christianity. For while sin was taken for granted and elaborately provided for in the life of the Old Covenant, the New Testament Church saw in itself the fulfillment of the prophets' prediction of a new covenant,[14] which was to be an everlasting covenant in which sin should have no part.

The New Testament writers were well aware, of course, that

---

10. **Gn** 39, 9.
11. 2 S 12, 13.
12. Cf. **Gn** 3ff. and similar passages.
13. Rm 5, 12ff.
14. Cf. **Jr** 31, 31-34; 32, 37-41.

Christians could and did commit sin — the apostolic epistles and the letters to the churches in the first chapters of the *Apocalypse* testify to a refreshing and total lack of naïveté in this respect. Sin, however, together with the Law, and the "flesh," and death, and everything imperfect, belonged to this sinful world in which the Christian by rights no longer had any share. It was only by returning to this sinful world or to any of its works — and hence St. Paul's polemic against the attempt of the "Judaizers" to impose the Mosaic Law on Christians — that the Christian could become guilty of sin. Sin was, therefore, always a kind of apostasy. The salvation achieved by Christ, the New Covenant ratified in his blood, had freed mankind in principle, through grace, from the reign of sin and this world. Because what was done now in principle would be accomplished definitively only at the end of all, in the final fulfillment of the divine economy;[15] because, therefore, the Christian though freed of this world continued to live in it and could always relapse into its ways, sin was an ever present possibility. Yet he could sin only by abandoning the total commitment involved in Christian faith, which he could regain only through the new heart and spirit that must once more be bestowed on him by divine grace.

The sense of horror and of enormity in the presence of sin[16] never deserts the New Testament, even though it is under no illusion as to the weakness of Christians and to their consequent recurring need of the forgiveness of Christ and the ministration of his Church. If we today can summon a somewhat more casual attitude to the function of the confessional in the sacramental life of the Church, undoubtedly this is partly due to the fact that modern man, even Christian man, has to a greater or less extent forgotten what sin really is.

Probably man can never really lose his sense of sin, though today he seems to have great difficulty in defining for himself what he means by it. When we look about us at a world in which

---

15. 1 Cor 15, 53-56.
16. Cf. 1 Cor 6, 13-20.

men give witness, by action far more eloquently than by word, to a feeling of rootlessness and purposeless existence, to a life bereft of meaningful experience in which event follows event in witless sequence and where men can achieve no community together, we perceive, in a groping sort of way, what biblical man understood as sin.

Chapter Three

TOWARDS A BIBLICAL CATECHESIS
OF THE DECALOGUE

PAUL TREMBLAY

Since the fourth century the Decalogue has played an important part in the catechetical instruction of the Church. Earlier
centuries had usually employed the plan of the two paths — path
of life, path of death — in moral instruction, but St. Augustine
was the first to give the Decalogue a predominant place in his
catechesis. His example was followed and passed down the ages,
without excluding the earlier plan nor the appearance of others,
notably that of the virtues, followed by St. Thomas.[1] The Decalogue is still taken as the basis of very recent text-books and
catechisms, as for example, the book on morality, *The Law of
Christ* by Häring, and the new German catechism.

Here we wish to examine the *root position in the Bible* of the
Decalogue. The exigencies of modern moral teaching often make
the Decalogue seem too negative, too individualist, too authoritative, unscientific, either too strict or too vague, often too exacting.

---

1. For the history of the Decalogue and its place in catechesis see the
article "Decalogue" in D.T.C., col. 171-173.

In a word, the Decalogue is certainly the best-known passage in the Bible, it is also perhaps the least well understood.

In face of this incomprehension, we wish to try and reach the exact meaning of the Decalogue, by simply returning to the Sacred Books. From this biblical reading of the Decalogue, it may be possible to draw certain orientations for use in teaching it.

I. DECALOGUE: PASCHAL LAW

The Decalogue is inseparable from Israel's Pasch. To understand this we need only remember the literary and historical context of the "ten Words," in chapter 20, right in the middle of the most important book of the Old Testament. The Decalogue belongs to the astounding series of facts of the Exodus.

Exodus, as we know, develops two subjects: the deliverance from Egypt (chs 1-15), and the alliance (chs 19-40). The story opens with a reminder of the oppression of the Hebrews by the Pharaohs. But God "remembered" them. He called Moses in Sinai, and gave him the mission of seeking the people in their servitude, and to lead them to the same spot. "I will be with thee. And this thou shalt have for a sign that I have sent thee: When thou shalt have brought my people out of Egypt, thou shalt offer sacrifice to God upon this mountain" (*Ex* 3, 12). God certainly did not fix this trysting-place, so that the people should settle in this rocky desert; on the contrary, he promised to lead them "into a good and spacious land, into a land that flows with milk and honey" (*Ex* 3, 8). Sinai was a stage, planned by God between Egypt and the Promised Land, for the celebration of a great mystery. Before considering this mystery of the Alliance, whence proceeds the Decalogue, we must mark carefully the poles, historical and geographical, which confine it, Egypt and the Promised Land.

The Decalogue, with the Alliance, fits in with the passing of the Hebrew people from the condition of slavery to that of free men, thanks to the strong hand of God. We must never forget that it is meant for men free already, impressed by the power shown by God in their deliverance, still on the way to the Promised Land. In other words, the Decalogue is given to men engaged in a Paschal life. It is not by chance that it begins with an historical reminder: "I am Yahweh, thy God, who brought thee out of the land of Egypt and out of the house of bondage" (*Ex* 20, 1).

As the Decalogue is inseparable from the history of the first Exodus, the new commandment which Christ gave us to perfect the old law, has its roots in his Pasch. Not only was it promulgated at the last meal with his disciples, that is, at the anticipated ritual celebration of the Death — Resurrection of Christ; but the very measure of the charity it indicates refers us to the fact of his Paschal Death. "A new commandment I give unto you: That you love one another, as I have loved you, that you also love one another" (*Jn* 13, 34). This measure of love, "as I have loved you," refers to the infinite love of Christ on the cross. St. John describes the life of Christ culminating in his "Hour," in the background of the Exodus.[2]

Besides, in the context surrounding the new commandment of Christ, there is question of his mysterious departure. In the verse preceding the precept of love, our Lord declares: "Little children, yet a little while I am with you. You shall seek me . . . whither I go you cannot come" (*Jn* 13, 33). We know Christ's journey: he "passes from this world to his father . . ." by death. Only through death can his disciples follow him. Immediately afterwards he speaks to Peter of the day of his martyrdom: "Whither I go, thou canst not follow me now; but thou shalt follow hereafter" (*Jn* 13, 36). Christ, therefore, gave his new commandment once engaged upon the "Hour" of his exodus, and entrusted it to his disciples in the perspective of their own "pasch." Passing on this same commandment to the faithful, John the Apostle will use words and perspective of the Exodus: "A new commandment I write unto you . . . because the darkness is passed and the true light now shines" (1 *Jn* 2, 8).

---

2. See Durrwell, F.X., **La Résurrection de Jésus, mystère de saint**. Paris, Mappus, 1954, pp. 31-38.

The whole history of salvation rests on two chief facts: the Pasch and the Alliance. We have just seen the Decalogue in the frame of the Exodus, we must now place it in the religious setting of the Alliance. There is so close a connection between the two that the Decalogue of Exodus 34, 10-26 presents the "ten Words" as *"words of the Alliance."*

Let us first examine the biblical text. The Decalogue is in chapter 20. Although exegetes have difficulty in discriminating sources from chapters 19-24, it is clear that the literary context of the Decalogue is not the primitive one. The list of commandments appears rather *ex abrupto* after chapter 19, and is not directly connected with what follows: 20, 18. This does not mean that the Decalogue is misplaced, and we must not ignore the intention of the last inspired compiler who settled the final arrangement of chapters.

Modern exegetes mostly agree on attributing the Decalogue to Moses. It is believed that an earlier text, going back to the days of the great prophet, must have contained the substance of the Decalogue as we know it, though probably composed of sentences as short and simple as the fifth, sixth and seventh commandments still are. With the passage of time and traditions, this original Mosaic Decalogue received several revisions and additions until it was definitely fixed about the fifth century. The place then settled for it by the sacred compiler reveals a profound theological intention. He inserted it between the proclamation of the Alliance (ch. 19), and its ritual celebration (ch. 24), thus making the Decalogue an integral part of the Alliance. This weaving the commandments in with the Alliance shows clearly the source and motivation of morality. This finds its root in God, in Yahweh who shows himself in the fearful storm on Sinai. The laws of the Decalogue may materially resemble the moral codes of neighboring peoples, like the Hammurabi, there will always be an essential difference: the biblical Decalogue is part of the Alliance with the one God, it can only be read properly in the light of the gleaming halo of the manifestation of Yahweh surrounding it.

The Alliance is often defined as a contract between God and the people, a bi-lateral pact, calling for precise promises on both sides. This over juridical notion has two tiresome consequences: it presents the Alliance as a past fact, and makes the morality derive juridically from it. "The Alliance is not a treaty, but an engagement, a way of living together, relationship between people, which must be maintained in the varying circumstances of life, and according to the deep solicitations of the spirit of communion." The Alliance is a beginning, it inaugurates a new way of life. It is not an idea, a treaty on parchment or on stone, it is the "life-together" of God and the people. The promise of life in communion, the Alliance foresees certain roles and responsibilities. God undertakes to protect his people; in return, the people promise to live in the service of God.

The engagement of God is faithful, irrevocable. One word suffices: "I will be your God." The people's engagement is precarious, needing to be repeated daily, to be expressed in various ways. The ten commandments enumerate clearly some of the ways of remaining faithful to the Alliance. For the weak human will, they spell out concretely the people's reply: "I will be thy people." They are the multiform expressions of a movement of love, corresponding to the first love of God ready to make alliance.

The relationship between the Alliance and the Decalogue can be compared with the marriage-contract and conjugal life of every day. The Alliance is love promised and lasting. The Decalogue is the small coin of this love's fidelity. Sacred writers, especially the prophets, have always interpreted the people's history in this double aspect: love-unfaithfulness, marriage-adultery.

The Decalogue, then, is inseparable from the Alliance. God ordered Moses to place the tables of the Law inside the ark of the Covenant (*Ex* 40, 20). In the course of Israel's history, public proclamation of the Law will serve as ceremony of renewing the Alliance (2 *K* 23, 1-3). This was but normal; faith in the Alliance without works was dead faith.

The history of Israel teaches us also not to confuse Alliance with Decalogue. The Decalogue is not the whole Alliance, and of the two, Alliance comes first. The Alliance obviously fades away if unaccompanied by observance of the commandments. But fidelity to these, without the spirit of the Alliance, leads to moral catastrophe. The Decalogue is no substitute for the Alliance. This was the mistake of the Pharisees and Doctors of the Law, separating fidelity from love. They forgot the Alliance, and kept the Law only. Or rather, of the Alliance they only kept a juridical aspect, the bi-lateral notion called Pharisaism: When I observe the exact letter of the Law, God is bound in justice to reward me. All the prophets labored against this *do ut des,* and preached the interior reality of the Alliance.

Christ himself will do the same. He asks for servants "in spirit and in truth" (*Jn* 4, 24), and corrects the Pharisees' aberrations over the commandments (parents, bigamy, etc. *Mt* 5, 17-48). Christ, however, was more than the prophet of the interior religion; the New Alliance was realized in him personally. It was just when he was about to seal this New Alliance in his blood, that our Lord announced his new commandment. This took place at the Cenacle, where fifty days later the Holy Spirit would come to invigorate this new law in the hearts of the disciples. This new commandment is love, as love also prompted the first inauguration of the Alliance on Sinai.

Since then, it is with a "heart of flesh," with the Spirit of God, that we have been able to read and to practice the Decalogue. Now, the Spirit makes us understand what the "finger of God" wrote on Sinai. He makes us understand love's plan and will behind the words of the first Alliance, and which endure in their fulfillment in us.

III. THE DECALOGUE: WORD OF GOD

We have seen that in the perspective of the Alliance, the Decalogue contains concrete expressions of man's answer to God's initiative love. We must take care all the same not to form too juridical an idea of the Alliance, as a treaty or pact, leading us to place the Decalogue entirely on man's side; "What man must do to be faithful!" It must not be forgotten that, before being man's practical answer, the Decalogue is first of all God's Word *"a tenfold word of God."* This is all-important when presenting the moral code of the commandments. It is a moral code of God's Word.

Let us read the very pages of the Bible. The first verse of *Exodus* 20 tells us: "the Lord spoke all these words." The Decalogue contains the "ten Words" which God uttered before the assembly at Sinai. "The Lord said to Moses: Lo, now will I come to thee in the darkness of a cloud, that the people may hear me speaking to thee . . ." (*Ex* 19, 9). Not only was it "written by the finger of God" (*Ex* 31, 18; *Dt* 9, 10), in Deuteronomy Moses goes so far as to say: "Yahweh spoke to us face to face" (*Dt* 5, 4), and he speaks of the tables of the Law as "containing all the words that he spoke to you in the mount from the midst of the fire" (*Dt* 9, 10). It is stated that the people heard "the voice of his words" (*Dt* 4, 12). The Decalogue is the result of God speaking to his people. It comes from God, and like all God's Works, it nourishes. "Not in bread alone does man live, but in every word that proceeds from the mouth of God" (*Dt* 8, 3). God who can create all things by his Word, makes his people live, not only on manna, but also from the commandments issuing from his lips.

This is the text Christ will repeat to Satan, at the moment of his temptation, thus alluding to his vocation which was to give "the words of the Father" (*Jn* 17, 8). In his opening discourse, when announcing the completion of the old Law, our Lord marks his declarations with the words: "It has been said . . . but I say to you . . ." (*Mt* 5, 17-48). At the end of his life, he sums up his whole work and all he expects from his disciples in these "words." "The words which thou gavest me I have given to them . . . (*Jn* 17, 8) . . . If anyone love me, he will keep my word . . . He that loves me not, keeps not my words. My word is not mine, but the Father's who sent me" (*Jn* 15, 23-25). His enemies are they who "cannot hear his words" (*Jn* 8, 43), and they seek to kill him because his word "has no place in them" (*Jn* 8, 37). The Christian's duty is none other than that of the Jew under the Old Law; it consists "in keeping the Word" (*Dt* 4, 1; *Jn* 8, 31-32).

The Decalogue inaugurates a morality entirely centered on the Word of God. This assertion has immense import. It obliges us to place the Decalogue in the mystery of the Divine Word, and all morality with it.

What does that mean? That God's Word is creative, efficacious; pronounced by the prophets, or without them as intermediaries, it makes history, revealing and accomplishing God's plan. This Word, uttered in the Decalogue and the Law, fixes the moral ideal of the Alliance as well as realizing it already in men's hearts. The grace of the ancient Alliance was of course not the grace of the New, but the Old Law must have had a certain efficacity, rather difficult to define. The Law was, in fact, the "pedagogue in Christ" (*Gal* 3, 24), and Christ came himself as the apex of the people, poor (*anawim*) and righteous, trained under the Law. Christ is the personal "Word" of the Father (*Jn* 1, 1), Creator of the world, Legislator of the New Law, and at the same time its most perfect realization ("servant" obeying the Father). The Old Law, "perfected" in the Law of Christ, belongs to the mystery of the Word, issue of the Father, descending to earth with power and efficacity. In these perspectives the Decalogue finds quite a different origin than is allotted to it often by natural moralists.

Every Word of God is both noetic and dynamic, both revelation and fulfillment. The Decalogue is no exception. Because it comes from God, it must contain some dogmatic truth about God himself, as well as instructing us on what God does for us or expects from us. It is very important to see these two facets of the Decalogue, because the revelation it contains of God enlightens and motivates man's subsequent conduct.

It must be realized that the Law is a channel through which God communicates his wisdom to man. The whole poem from the book of Baruch (3, 9-4, 4) could be quoted here. "He found out all the way of knowledge and gave it to Jacob his servant" (3, 37).

Each commandment is first an indication of some important

good to be protected; life, marriage, personal possessions, etc. Our gaze must first concentrate on this specified value. On this head, the negative form of most of the commandments must not limit our ideas to the evil acts forbidden only. "It should even be noticed that a negative command is often more positive than it appears, and is often more universal than an affirmative one. If you say to someone: You must take this path, all other paths are ruled out, but if you say: Do not take that path, all other paths remain open to him. The negative form can be more precise; the precept, Be honest, is vague, but not: Do not tell lies, do not steal."

In the last analysis, all the commandments have a still higher finality. Beyond the protection they intend to assure for certain basic values, all ten are an affirmation of God's absolute power over all creation. They reveal one only God, who will not be annexed in any way by man (graven images, use of his name), who is master of time (the Sabbath), of life (Thou shalt not kill) and its propagation down the generations (honoring parents, respect in sexual matters), who is Lord of the earth and its goods, whose care and fruits are entrusted to man, the intimate Ruler of man's heart (no covetousness). Thus is the Decalogue a Word revealing the nature of God.

Life of communion supposes a certain degree of communion in being. The meeting between God and the people on Sinai demands that the people should rise a little towards the holiness of their God. The Decalogue intends to create in the people a reflection, a glimmer of God's holiness which is needed for the life in alliance. In its precepts the Decalogue seeks to convert, to turn, man towards God. It is entirely theologic and theocentric. In the codes found in Deuteronomy and Leviticus, the prescriptions are often stressed by the words: "I am the Lord thy God" (*Lv* 19, 1-37; *Dt* 7, 6), or they bear as head-line: "Be holy, because I am holy" (*Lv* 11, 44; 19, 2; 20, 7, 26; *Dt* 14, 21).

This shows that the Decalogue of the Bible is much more than the cultivated flower of a natural, anthropocentric morality. It is a revelation of God, God's Word, revealing and converting. "Dearly beloved, I write not a new commandment to you, but an old commandment which you had from the beginning. The old commandment is the Word which you have heard" (1 *Jn* 2, 7). "This commandment which I command thee this day, is not above thee, nor far off from thee . . . But the word is very nigh unto thee, in thy mouth and in thy heart, that thou mayst do it" (*Dt* 30, 11, 14).

IV. THE DECALOGUE: LAW OF THE ASSEMBLY

The Decalogue is God's Word addressed to God's people. It is eminently a *community law*. This stands out clearly from the Old Testament text, and in giving the New Law, Christ chose to adopt the same community perspective.

The Alliance first bound the Israelites together as a people. "You shall be my peculiar possession above all people" (*Ex* 19, 5), and each individual of that people. The Decalogue is addressed to the people first. Even more, just as the people of Israel came into being on Sinai, created by the words of the Alliance, it can be said that the Decalogue fashions them as a people.

In fact, Yahweh convoked the whole people to Sinai, all were to prepare for the theophany (*Ex* 18, 12). On the day fixed, the "day of the assembly" (*Dt* 10, 4; 18, 16), Moses leads the whole people "to meet the Lord" (*Ex* 19, 17). When the prophet came down from the mountain, and "told the people all the words of the Lord and the judgments," the people answered with one voice: "We will do all the words of the Lord which he has spoken" (*Ex* 24, 3). Then, at the celebration-rite of the Alliance, Moses read the book of the Alliance to the people, he poured the two halves of the blood upon the altar and upon the people (*Ex* 24, 7-8). The responsive value to the Alliance and the Decalogue is the people. "That thou mayst pass in the covenant of the Lord thy God, and in the oath which this day the Lord thy God makes with thee, that he may raise thee up a people to himself, and he may be thy God" (*Dt* 29, 12-13). Notice in passing, the actuality of the Alliance and the Law: "thee," "today." These imperatives bind actually the whole people, all its generations (*Dt* 29, 13) and obviously each member of this people, as the form of address constantly used by God suggests: thou . . . you . . . A tone of dialogue binding the people and each person.

This statement gives the Decalogue a new color. All the commandments are laws for God's people, they concern this people's God, and the different circumstances of this people, time, generations, possessions, relations. It would destroy their meaning to consider them as "personal" laws, or only as those of an upright human society. They are the laws, the Charter of God's people, a people chosen from among all others. It would also falsify the spirit of the Decalogue to approach it with the mentality of strict commutative justice. For the Decalogue is the law of a people entirely bound over to God. "God's special treasure," accepting to live according to this first principle: God is absolute ruler, he has given Jacob the use of his domain. At the same time, the Decalogue is the law of a people who have freely accepted to be at God's service. God willed to deliver Israel before proposing the Alliance to them. "The Decalogue asks nothing from slaves; the human condition of freedom is indispensable to answer the Ten Words."

The New Law also was given to a new people come to birth, freed from the slavery of Satan. Christ's Hour is both the Hour of the Alliance, Hour of the New Law, Hour of the New Assembly. Christ willed to shed his blood "for many," and tradition sees the birth of the Church in the piercing of his Side upon the cross. The New Law, accomplished by the coming of the Holy Spirit into the body of the Risen Christ, has grown among the faithful since the day of Pentecost. But the Holy Spirit will not force man's liberty. As God said to the people in the beginning, "If, therefore, you will hear my voice, and keep my covenant . . ." (*Ex* 19, 5), as our Lord said, leaving his listeners free: "If thou wilt . . . if any one loves me . . . if . . . ," so today, the Holy Spirit invites with equal gentleness and tact. Each one is called to understand that the Alliance is for all and for each. "He delivered himself up for me" (*Eph* 5, 25). "If thou wilt possess eternal life, keep my commandments."

Finally, notice that behind the "Thou" of the precepts of the

Decalogue, there was already the mystery of God's people. Since
Christ came, this collective "Thou" has become much more personal. Grafted on Christ, the new people is so welded together,
that it is no longer possible to find a completely other personality
in its members. Paul learned this on the way to Damascus: "Why
persecutest thou me?" We can discover the same reality behind
the "Thou" of the Decalogue.

V. THE DECALOGUE: LAW OF TESTIMONY

The Alliance, misunderstood, "could turn, for Israel, into satisfaction at being chosen, self-congratulation over an exceptional
and exclusive vocation." The Decalogue was then in danger of
becoming a means for self-justification, a matter for egoist boast-
ing before other nations and even before God. The Pharisee's
temptation exists in every age: "O Lord, I thank thee that I am
not like the rest of men, extortioners, unjust, adulterers . . ." (*Lk*
18, 11). But this danger is avoided if we pay attention to the
duty of testimony which falls on the servant of the Law.

Let us first look at the biblical texts themselves. The tables of
the Law are called "tables of the testimony" (*Ex* 32, 15, 18), that
is, they are the memorial, the witness of God's coming to Sinai.[3]
The word testimony becomes a synonym for the Law; Psalm 118
uses it for precept, commandment, words (20 times). Psalms 78
does the same: "they tempted and provoked the Most High God;
and they kept not his testimonies" (v. 56), "God set up a testimony in Jacob; and made a law in Israel" (v. 5).

This testimony was given to Jacob so that he might give testimony in his turn to God before other nations. The privileged
choice of Israel and the gift of the Law was made in the perspective of all nations. This perspective is already indicated in the
promise of the Alliance: "You shall be my peculiar possession

---

3. The tabernacle where the Ark of the Covenant lay, containing the
tables of the Law, is called "tabernacle of the testimony" (**Ac** 7, 44), i.e.,
sacrament of a certain presence of God among his people.

above all people; for all the earth is mine. And you shall be to me a priestly kingdom . . ." (*Ex* 19, 5-6).

Israel is the people of God among all peoples. The Alliance that God makes with Israel is the "Covenant of the Lord of all the earth" (*Jos* 3, 11). The people of God is not unique because they have a God whom others have not, who will belong to them alone. The privilege of God's people is "to know" the God of all, to know, to be able, to be obliged to do on this account, what others do not know, or are unable to do. Israel's quite exceptional privilege is not being brought out of Egypt, God having done the same for some detested pagans (*Am* 9, 7); it is not the grace of salvation reserved for them alone. Israel is the one to whom God, still unknown to others, has shown himself and has spoken. Is it for themselves alone? For the moment the accent is on the specialness of the chosen people, on its separateness, put apart, its consecration to Yahweh. Nevertheless, even if the text does not yet declare it, already it implies something like a responsibility for Israel towards other nations, a mission resulting from the gift of revelation.

The missionary perspective of the Law accords with the universalist vocation of the people. It is included in the oracle with a universal horizon uttered by Isaiah: "Let us go up to the house of the God of Jacob; and he will teach us his ways . . . For the Law shall come forth from Sion" (*Is* 2, 3). Deuteronomy also stresses testimony: "You shall observe, and fulfill them (the commandments) in practice. For this is your wisdom, and understanding in the sight of nations, that hearing all these precepts, they may say: Behold a wise and understanding people, a great nation" (*Dt* 4, 6, cf. *Dt* 31, 12). In a great poem on the Exodus, the book of Wisdom sums up Israel's role among the nations; through them "the pure Light of the Law was to be given to the world" (*Ws* 18, 4).

We know that this mission would concentrate one day upon the "Servant of Yahweh," who would be "the light of nations." Christ came to accomplish the New Alliance, open to all men without exception. His law has the same universal dimensions, and its fulfillment by the disciples is a testimony before all men.

At the beginning of the discourse on the new justice, St. Matthew places these words of our Lord: "Let your light shine before men that they may see your good works and glorify your Father who is in heaven" (*Mt* 5, 16). This very concrete "visibleness" is also intimated in Christ's new commandment: "Love one another as I have loved you" (*Jn* 15, 12). The signs of Christ's love have been public, and the love he asks from his followers is a love that bears witness to the very love that he had. The unity of brethren in this love will be a "sign" to the world: "That they all may be one . . . that the world may believe" (*Jn* 17, 21). The coming of the Paraclete enkindles the dynamism of this love in the hearts of the disciples, and clearly shows the universal diffusion of the New Law (*Ac* 2, 1-17).

For Israel of old, the law was first consent to the Alliance, showing itself by rejection of everything contrary to it. This behavior of the people was bound to raise the problem of the truth of the God of Israel for the neighboring peoples. For the new Israel also, there is the concrete question of not behaving like those who have not received the revelation of Jesus Christ: "I, therefore, a prisoner in the Lord, beseech you that you walk worthy of the vocation in which you are called . . ." (*Eph* 4, 1; cf. 1 *P* 4, 1-4), so as to win others to Christ: "Be without offense to the Jews and to the Gentiles and to the church of God; as I also in all things please all men, not seeking that which is profitable to myself but to many; that they may be saved. Be followers of me, as I also am of Christ" (1 *Cor* 10, 32-11, 1; cf. 9, 19-23; *Col* 3, 17, etc.).

The gift of the Law must be thus understood: it is a light revealed by God, which cannot be put under a bushel, without failing in what God expects from all peoples. The Decalogue is not only precept, it calls for testimony. "You are a holy nation, a purchased people; that you may declare his virtues who has called you out of darkness . . . Having your conversation good among the Gentiles; that whereas they speak against you as evil-doers, they may by the good works which they shall behold in you, glorify God in the day of visitation" (1 *P* 2, 9-12).

VI. THE DECALOGUE: LAW OF WORSHIP

The prophetical function of Israel towards other nations is an aspect of the priestly vocation of the people who must stay nearer the living God as mediator for other nations. For Israel was made a *priestly people* on Sinai, priest-people among other peoples. They exercise their priesthood first in their worship of God. The assembly in Horeb ended with a liturgy. The Decalogue was received in a ritual and liturgical context. Its precepts ensure, so to say, the continuation of worship throughout life. We see already how dogma, morality and liturgy are very closely united in the Bible.

The Decalogue was given to a nation of priests: "You shall be to me a priestly kingdom and a holy nation" (*Ex* 19, 6). The whole nation, therefore, will be consecrated to the worship of God. The essential character of priests, is that they are vowed to the divine service, to fulfill the sacred functions of the liturgy. That Israel is to become a priestly kingdom means that they are called to be entirely consecrated to God's service, carrying out the functions of this service. Such was already a key-theme in *Exodus, chs.* 7-11: "Let my people go that they may serve me." The Decalogue can be seen as the detailed explanation of this cultural function. Israel's morality is one of worship.

All the commandments, in fact, are directed towards worship. The first two obviously are, since they concern the worship of the one only God. The Sabbath precept is also plainly ritualistic; it demands a deduction from man's time to be consecrated to God: "The sabbath is the tithe of time, the offering of working days, the sacrifice of ordinary occupations by their momentary cessation." The other precepts also aim at the consecration of the world to God. Respect for parents, as God's instruments in the transmission of life: to kill is forbidden because man is "in the image of God" (*Gn* 9, 6), and blood belongs to God (*Lv* 19, 11-14); respect for all that concerns life, for sexual matters which belong to the order of mysteries, since their source is in God; responsible use of earthly goods, for the whole earth is the

Lord's; no interior greed, since everything is consecrated to God, even the desires of the heart. Leviticus sums up all these commandments and adds the reason: "You shall not steal. You shall not lie; neither shall any man deceive his neighbor. Thou shalt not swear falsely by my name, nor profane the name of thy God. I am the Lord" (19, 11-12). Everything is worship of the Name, all Israel's activity must be service of God. We have already seen formulae of the Decalogue centered on the holiness of God and of the people, the spirit of religion (*Lv* 19; *Ps* 15).

In the New Testament, we notice how Christ proclaimed his new commandment at the Hour of his sacrifice, at the hour when he ordained his disciples priests of the New Alliance. In his "sacerdotal" prayer he says: "I sanctify myself, that they also may be sanctified" (*Jn* 17, 19). After the coming of the Holy Spirit at Pentecost, Peter quotes the words of Exodus to the multitude of newly-baptized: "You are a chosen race, a kingly priesthood, a holy nation, a purchased people, that you may declare his virtues who has called you out of darkness into his marvellous light" (1 *P* 2, 9). The Decalogue is again the law of the people whom God has acquired "unto the praise of his glory" (*Eph* 1, 14).

VII. THE DECALOGUE: WORDS OF LIFE

This is how the deacon Stephen speaks of the tables of the Law, when summarizing the whole history of salvation, before his persecutors; "This is he (Moses) who received the *words of life* to give unto us" (*Ac* 7, 38). Here we find another major characteristic of the biblical presentation of the Decalogue, which we cannot pass over in silence when we transmit it in our turn.

The text of the Decalogue itself only speaks of life once: "Honor thy father and thy mother, that thou mayst be long-lived upon the land which the Lord thy God will give thee" (*Ex* 20, 12). But we know that it is included in the context of the Alliance, that the Alliance also does not go without promises (the Greek word διαΘηκη can mean alliance, covenant, testament, promise). The Alliance itself was a relation of life with the Master of life, that is why blood was the sacrament of it. It was to be made visible in a happy and peaceful life in a land "flowing with milk and honey." The Decalogue was first received as a guide to a country of joy and happiness.

In spite of deceptions and vicissitudes in Israel's history, the prophets and sacred writers never ceased to represent the Decalogue in a light of joy and life. When a siege of Jerusalem was imminent, Ezekiel preaches "the commandments of life" (33, 15). He then refers to the Deuteronomic reform a little earlier, which has insisted so much upon the "double path," one of observance of the Law leading to life, the other of infidelity, leading to death. "Consider that I have set before thee this day life and good, and on the other hand death and evil. That thou mayst love the Lord thy God, and walk in his ways and keep his commandment . . . and thou mayst live, and he may multiply thee. . . . But if thy heart be turned away . . . I foretell thee this day that thou shalt perish" (*Dt* 30, 15-20; cf. 4, 1; 5, 29; 6, 24; 8, 1; 9, 1). Five centuries later, Baruch shows the same devotion to the Law because it gives life: "This is the book of the commandments of God, and the Law which is for ever. All they that keep it shall come to life; but they that have forsaken it to death" (4, 1).

Notice that Christ will use phrases to speak of his New Law. Before passing to that, note the enthusiasm with which Old Testament writers extol the Law. Psalm 118 is the most renowned and best known praise of it. The psalmist cannot desist from praising this law that gives life (vv. 17, 25, 37, 40, 50, 88, 93, 107, 116, 144, 149, 154, 156, 159), that makes him happy and delights him (vv. 14, 16, 24, 35, 39, 47, 74, 77, 92, 111, 143, 162, 174). It is not a restricting law, it is wide, its horizons are vast: "I have run the way of thy commandments, when thou didst enlarge my heart" (v. 32; cf. 45, 96; *Ps* 18; *Ps* 3, 36-4, 4).

Christ came to fulfill these "precepts of life" (*Ba* 3, 9). He was himself the "Word of Life" (1 *Jn* 1, 1), the "Living Word" (*Heb* 4, 12). On this head he fulfilled the Old Law, in revealing the new content to be put into the word "life." Henceforth, there is no question of long vitality, security, fertility of the soil. Christ has "the words of eternal life" (*Jn* 6, 38). This new life is participation in the very life of the Son of God, "Eternal Life" in person (1 *Jn* 5, 20); it is new birth, in and through the Son; Christians are "born again from a seed not mortal but immortal: the Word of God who lives and remains for ever" (1 *P* 1, 22-25). The Decalogue remains a condition of entrance into this higher life. "If thou wouldst enter into life, keep the commandments" (*Mt* 19, 16-18). Especially must we observe his new commandment (*Jn* 13, 34-35).

Christ also insisted on the spirit in which we must observe the Law. It is significant that Matthew placed the beatitudes as preface to the discourse on the new Law. "Blessed are they who. . . . Blessed are . . ." Christ did not come to confirm the too heavy, legalist, interpretation of the Pharisees. Quite the contrary, he liberated the Law from the mountain of narrow, human additions, to restore its spirit and life. "The words which I have spoken to you are spirit and life" (*Jn* 6, 63). Christ did not come to stifle life. Quite the contrary, that men might have life in abundance, he laid down his own in order to rise again as "Author of Life" (*Ac* 3, 15). He gave his new commandment not to extinguish the joy of his disciples, but to make it greater: "These things I have spoken to you that my joy may be in you, and your joy may be filled. This is my commandment, that you love . . ." (*Jn* 15, 11-12).

What we have just said shows sufficiently that the commandments direct us towards life, towards a life understood and lived in Christ's Paschal Mystery. For in Christ's "Hour" were accomplished perfect obedience, perfect Life, perfect joy.

We have to carry on the work of the Apostles who received the mission to go and speak boldly "in the temple to the people of this life" (*Ac* 5, 20).

CONCLUSION

What has been the aim of these pages? We have examined

the scriptural roots of the Decalogue, embedded in the faith of the people and their alliance with God, how it was understood when it was given on Mount Sinai, how it was lived afterwards, and how Christ confirmed it in his New Law. If we now had to define the Decalogue, we would say this: the Decalogue is, during the Exodus and within the Alliance, a Word uttered by God before the chosen people, a Word accepted by the people in a worship, lived by them in testimony to their God, and efficacious in life and happiness. None of the elements of this definition should be underestimated in catechesis on the Decalogue desirous of fidelity to the revealed content.

Read thus, in the perspectives we have adopted, it seems to us that "in spite of its negative form, in spite of casuist commentaries, which have burdened it with a too high co-efficient of negativity, this age-old Decalogue can be freshened and can carry real weight of personalism."[4] We can see too, in the light of Christ's words, and with the discernment given us by the Holy Spirit, that the Decalogue becomes simply the moral side of our faith. It is the answer of a people saved and in alliance with God, it is the other side of Israel's faith. It can never be anything else for the Church and for every Christian.

---

4. A. Danet, **La morale chrétienne, morale des mystères du Christ.** Lille, 1962, p. 38.

Chapter Four

SIN AND COMMUNITY IN THE NEW TESTAMENT

JEROME MURPHY-O'CONNOR, O.P.

The explanation we find in *Matthew* of our Lord's proper name is a perfect summary of a key aspect of the primitive preaching: "you shall call his name Jesus, because he will save his people from their sins" (1, 21). It was a fundamental assertion of the kerygma that Jesus came into the world to save sinners and that he in fact did so by his death.[1]

The awareness of the intimate relationship between sin and the mission of Christ was born during the earthly ministry of Jesus. Many passages of the Gospels attest the tenderness and compassion with which he received those considered by the authorities as unpleasing to God (*Lk* 15, 2). He was even taunted with being "a friend of tax collectors and sinners" (*Mt* 11, 19; *Lk* 7, 34). Jesus in reply defends his association with sinners on the grounds that "those who are well have no need of a physician; I came to call not the righteous but sinners" (*Mk* 2, 17; cf. *Mt* 9, 12-13; *Lk* 5, 32).[2] There is, moreover, a

---

1. Cf. 1 **Cor** 15:3; 1 **P** 2:24; 3:18; **Heb** 9:26; **Apoc** 1:5.
2. This text may be contrasted with the statement of the Teacher of

further series of texts in which Jesus is mentioned not merely in connection with the reception of sinners, but as mediating the forgiveness of sins.[3]

The culminating point of this aspect of our Lord's mission is found in the sublime words with which he is represented as setting the seal of his ministry: "This is my blood of the covenant which is poured out for many *for the forgiveness of sins*" (*Mt* 26, 28). The italicized phrase is missing in the parallel accounts of the Words of Institution, and in particular in that of *Mark*, on which *Matthew* depends. The liturgical character of these texts makes it very probable that these words represent the primitive Church's understanding of the eucharistic sacrifice as the summit and summing-up of the total ministry of Jesus.

The early Church was also conscious that her function in the world was to be a continuation or prolongation of the ministry of Christ. The relationship of the risen Christ to the community he founded is beautifully expressed by J. A. Moeller when he defines the Church as "the Son of Man manifesting himself ceaselessly among men in his human form, eternally renewing and refreshing himself."[4] Many other authors could be cited in the same sense, for example Karl Adam: "The true Ego of the Church is Christ Jesus."[5] Such clarity is the result of two thousand years meditation on the mystery of the Church, and it may be doubted that the penetration of the primitive Church was as profound. This is not to say, however, that it was not present in an embryonic form. The Church was always aware that Christ had arranged for the continuation of his work through the double mission of his Spirit and of his apostles,[6] and the succes-

---

Righteousness, who described himself as 'a snare for evildoers and a physician for all who have turned from sin' (1 **QH**. 2, 8). In other words his ministry was only to those who were already pure.

3. Cf. **Mk** 2:5 and par.; **Lk** 7, 48; 19, 9; 23, 43; **Jn** 5 ,14; 8, 11.

4. **Symbolik**, n. 23.

5. **Das Wesen des Katholicizmus**, Düsseldorf 1928, 24.

6. Cf. Y. Congar, "Le Saint- Esprit et le Corps Apostolique réalisateurs de l'oeuvre du Christ," **RSPT** 36 (1952) 613-625; 37 (1953) 24-48; id. **The Mystery of the Church**, New York 1960, 147-180.

sive epistles of Paul reveal the evolution of his mind as he penetrated ever more deeply into his concept of the Church as the Body of Christ, the starting point of all future development.

The object of this study is to examine one precise aspect of the Church in her relationship to Christ: her power to forgive sins. We shall study first the power of the Church with regard to sins committed before baptism, and then her authority with regard to sins committed by members of the community. The second part obviously presents many more problems than the first, and while there seems to be a definite evolution in the Church's self-understanding in this respect, it is not possible to establish the various stages with certitude. Hence we shall examine in turn the practice of the Church with regard to post-baptismal sin, the factors that forced her to take cognizance of the problem, and finally the relationship she discerned between her power and that of Christ.

PRE-BAPTISMAL SIN

The most explicit account of the primitive Church is given us by Luke in the *Acts of the Apostles,* and a number of passages refer to her practice and doctrine relating to baptism. The dates attributed to this work range from the sixties to the eighties of the first century, and on the supposition that some of the features of earlier days must inevitably have become blurred in memory, a number of authors hold that Luke modified the teaching of his sources on baptism so as to conform it to the ecclesiastical practice in force at the time of writing. Weiss[7] and Jackson-Lake[8] consider Luke anachronistic in introducing baptism as early as the first Pentecost.

The principal argument against this opinion, which in fact has won little or no support, is that the administration of baptism in the earliest days of the Church is taken for granted by

---

7. The History of Primitive Christianity, London 1937, 50ff.
8. The Beginnings of Christianity, I, London 1942, 383ff.

Paul. His own conversion, which took place not long after the death of Jesus, was marked by the reception of baptism, and it is hard to see how he could have bracketed himself with other Christians in his use of the first person plural in *Rm* 6, 1 if baptism had not been for him, as for others, the critical turning point in his life, marking his deliverance from sin and his experience of the new life of the Spirit.[9] We are asked to assume an intolerable position if we are asked to believe that baptism could have brought that experience to Paul several years after his conversion. Hence we can assume that Luke's allusions to baptism are substantially accurate. In fact, we shall see that the doctrine on baptism found in *Acts* is definitely more primitive than that found in the Pauline Epistles.

From the very beginning we find baptism associated with the remission of sins. In his Pentecost speech Peter is represented as saying: "Repent and be baptized every one of you in the name of Jesus for the forgiveness of your sins" (*Ac* 2, 38). This is echoed in the command given to Paul by Ananias: "Rise and be baptized and wash away your sins, calling on his name" (*Ac* 22, 16; cf. 9, 18). We need not delay on the problems that the phrase "in the name of Jesus" has given rise to.[10] It is certain that we have to do with a rite that draws its whole meaning from the person of Christ and the relationship established with him. This is suggested by the formulation of another passage of *Acts*: "The God of our Fathers raised Jesus whom you killed by hanging him on a tree. God exalted him at his right hand as Leader and Savior to give repentance to Israel and forgiveness of sins" (*Ac* 5, 30-31).

Inevitably the question arises at this point: what is the precise relationship between the two events (the death of Christ and baptism) to which the forgiveness of sins is attributed?

---

9. Cf. G. P. Beasley-Murray, **Baptism in the New Testament,** London 1962, 95.

10. Cf. W. Heitmüller, **Im Namen Jesu. Eine sprach- und religions-geschichtliche Untersuchung zum Neuen Testament, speziell zur alchristliche Taufe,** Göttingen 1903.

Beyond the affirmation that they are in some way linked by faith *Acts* tells us nothing ("Everyone who believes in him has forgiveness of sins through his name"— 10,43). Nor are most of the other New Testament writings more helpful. Either they content themselves with variations on the fundamental assertion of the kerygma that Jesus came into the world to save sinners,[11] or merely juxtapose the two events.[12]

It is only in the later epistles of Paul that we find baptism and the death of Christ synthesized and held within a single perspective. Baptism is an inclusion in what happened to Christ. Today we can no longer establish with certainty whether Paul came to this interpretation of his own accord, or whether he was able to appeal even at this early date to the outlook of the Church. What little information we have strongly suggests that the synthesis was effected by Paul himself.[13] In the *locus classicus* for his theology of baptism (*Rm* 6, 1-11) he starts from the current affirmation of the kerygma ("Do you not know . . ." v. 3) that baptism sets the believer in a new relationship to Jesus and his death without specifying what the connection between the two is. Then by combining his notion of Christ as a corporate personality[14] with the fruit of his contemplation of the symbolism of the essential rite of baptism[15] he is able to say: "We were buried with him by baptism unto death" (v. 4), and two verses later: "Our old man was crucified with him so that

---

11. **Apoc** 1, 5; 1 **P** 2, 24; **Heb** 9, 26.

12. 1 **P** 3, 18-21; **Tit** 3, 5-6.

13. Cf. R. Schnackenburg, **Baptism in the Thought of Saint Paul**, New York 1964, 33, 136; G.P. Beasley-Murray, op. cit., 128.

14. This idea is found explicitly in the theme of the Two Adams (**Rm** 5, 12-21; 1 **Cor** 14,45-49; 15, 21-22), and underlies the concept of the Church as the Body of Christ.

15. This is indicated by the fact that while Paul's key idea in **Rm** 6 is that in baptism we **die** with Christ (v. 5-8) what he says in v. 4 is that we were **buried** with him. This was obviously suggested by the rite of immersion, which in view of the loose link already established between baptism and the death of Christ was conceived as a symbolic descent into the tomb.

body of sin might be destroyed, and we might no longer be enslaved to sin." The positive facet of this doctrine finds expression
in *Colossians*: "And you who were dead in trespasses . . . God
made alive together with him having forgiven us all our trespasses" (2, 13; cf. 2 *Cor.* 5, 19).

Thus, while there was a definite evolution in the understanding of baptism in the primitive Church, the awareness of its
efficacy to forgive sins was present right from the beginning.[16]
In the oldest explicit baptismal creed known we find the candi-
date professing his faith thus: "I believe in the Father Omnipotent, in Jesus Christ our Savior, in the Holy Spirit the Paraclete,
and in the remission of sins."[17] But, as *Acts* makes clear, in addition to faith repentance (*metanoia*) is an essential prerequisite.
There is no suggestion that the sacrament is performed for the
automatic fulfillment of a predestined purpose. It is an encounter between a penitent sinner and a merciful Redeemer.

In addition to forgiving sins baptism also has another effect
which it is important to keep in mind. It effected the entry of
the believer into the new messianic community. After the appeal
of Peter, "Repent and be baptized" (*Ac* 2, 38), a final summary
of his message is added: "Save yourselves from this crooked
generation" (2, 40). Whereupon, "those that received his message were baptized, and on that day about three thousand souls
were added (to the Church)" (2, 41). That baptism is a rite of
initiation is also suggested by Paul's terminology when he terms
it "the circumcision of Christ" (*Col* 2, 11), but this aspect is
not emphasized in the context. Finally, it is Paul's realistic view
of the intimate union of the Christian with Christ effected in baptism that forms the basis of his view of the Church as the Body

---

16. The position of M. Barth (**Die Taufe ein Sakrament?**, Zollikon-
Zürich 1951, 140) that baptism was received merely in hope of forgiveness
fails to do justice to the explicit statements of **Acts**.

17. This formula is found in a Christian gnostic work, written in Coptic,
and dated in the middle of the second century. It is quoted in P. Galtier,
Aux origines du sacrement de Pénitence, Paris 1951, 40, note 10.

of Christ.[18] The implications of this are manifold, but two are particularly relevant for our purpose.

(a) *The Church is de jure sinless.* This inference, which is but an extension of the consciousness that baptism remitted sins, finds confirmation in a passage from *Ephesians* where the Church and not an individual appears as the subject of baptism: "Christ loved the Church and gave himself up for her that he might sanctify her, having cleansed her by the washing of water with the word, that he might present the Church to himself in splendor, without spot or wrinkle or any such thing, that she might be holy and without blemish" (5, 25-26). The same idea underlies certain sections in the Pauline Epistles, notably the apostle's conception of the Church as a Temple in which the Spirit dwells (1 *Cor* 3, 16-17; 2 *Cor* 6, 16), and his collective designation of the members of the Church as "saints" (1 *Cor* 1, 2 etc.). It is discernible also in the statement of *Hebrews*: "For by a single offering he has perfected for all time those who are sanctified" (10, 14).

It will be noted at once that the affirmation of the sinlessness of the Church in *Ephesians* is much more formal and explicit than in the other writings attributed to Paul. This is hardly surprising in the light of recent investigations into the relationship between this epistle and the Qumran literature. F. Mussner has established that in the central section of *Ephesians* constituted by chapter 2 we have a thematic association of ideas which is also in evidence in the Scrolls,[19] and K. G. Kuhn has brought to light the many points of contact between Qumran and the first part of chapter 5.[20]

Now, in the Essene writings the sanctity and sinlessness of the community is repeatedly affirmed. It is "the holy community"

---

18. Cf. **Gal** 3, 26-29; 1 **Cor** 12, 27; B. Ahern, "The Christian's Union with the Body of Christ in Corinthians, Galatians and Romans," **CBQ** 23 (1961) 199-208.

19. "Beiträge aus Qumran zum Verständnis des Epheserbriefs," **Neutestamentliche Aufsätze** (Festschrift J. Schmidt), Regensburg 1963, 86-99.

20. "Der Epheserbrief im Lichte der Qumrantexte," **NTS** 7 (1960-61) 338-341.

(1 QS. 9, 2), "the council of holiness" (1 QS. 8, 21), "the assembly of the holy fabric" (1 *QH*. 10, 8), "the company of infinite holiness" (1 *QS*. 1, 5). While the radical sanctity of the community is thus asserted it is clear that a more profound purification was awaited at the time of visitation: "Then God will cleanse by his truth all the works of every man . . . and he will cause the spirit of truth to gush forth on him like lustral water" (1 *QS*. 4, 20-21).

The eschatological character of this final text (the last phrase of which presents a certain analogy with *Eph* 5, 25) is very much in evidence. But the others also carry eschatological overtones, because behind the affirmation of the sanctity of the community in the Qumran literature lies the conviction that it represented the first fruits of the messianic age. There was a continuous tradition in Judaism, found in the prophetic,[21] sapiential,[22] and apocalyptic writings,[23] that the messianic community would be sinless, due to the presence of the spirit in the souls of the elect. It was in the light of such ideas that the early Christians and the Essenes viewed themselves. This eschatological perspective, seen at its most striking on the individual level in 1 *Jn* 3, 9,[24] was also not without influence on the primitive Church's comprehension of the mystery of the forgiveness of post-baptismal sin.

(b) *Sin has a corporate dimension.* The reference here is naturally to the sins of the "new man." In virtue of his baptism he has been admitted to the community of the saved, and thenceforward he can never be considered on the religious plane as an isolated individual. "None of us lives to himself and none of us dies to himself" (*Rm* 14, 7), because all are members of the Body of Christ. It is through the Church that he is sanctified,

---

21. **Is** 60, 21; **Ezra** 36, 27-28.

22. **Pr** 9, 6; **Sir** 24, 22.

23. **Test. Lv** 18, 9; **Jubilees** 5, 12; **Henoch** 6, 8.

24. Cf. I. de la Potterie, "L'impeccabilité du chrétien d'après 1 **Jn** 3, 6-9," in **L'Évangile de Jean** (Rech. Bibl. III), Bruges-Paris 1958, 161-177 (reprinted with corrections in I. de la Potterie and S. Lyonnet, **La vie selon l'Esprit, condition du chrétien**, Paris 1965, 197-216).

and should he sin, he not only offends God but injures the Church. The primitive Church knew this, if not theoretically, certainly existentially. A number of explicit statements of Paul tend in this sense,[25] but the clearest evidence is to be discerned in the practice of the Church. This took two forms, which we may term preventative and curative.

(i) Preventative: The community felt a keen obligation to ensure its freedom from sin. This obligation fell principally on its leaders,[26] but was not limited to them. All the members were expected to play their part in aiding the new man to overcome the old: through avoidance of the creation of occasions of sin (1 *Cor* 8, 11-12; *Heb* 3, 12), through advice and exhortation (1 *Thess* 5, 11, 14; *Jude* 22; *Heb* 3, 13-14; 10, 25), and through mutual prayer (*Jm* 5, 16; 1 *Jn* 5, 16-17). The immediate source of this mutual solicitude was charity. "May the Lord make you increase and abound in love to one another and to all men as we do to you, so that he may establish your hearts unblameable in holiness" (1 *Thess* 3, 12-13). The surest bulwark against the infiltration of sin was the intense fraternal charity that should animate the community, and whose source was Christ himself.

(ii) Curative: The community also felt itself obliged to expel the pertinacious sinner from its midst. The profound reason for such exclusion is to be found in the awareness of the holiness of the Church outlined above. The Christian is not saved as an individual but in the spotless Body of Christ, and this belonging gives him a constant and effective title to the inpouring of the life of the Spirit. To rebel against this influx of grace by sin contradicts his membership in the Church. Instead of being a sign of his possession of the Spirit his membership is a lie. It

---

25. "Do you not know that a little leaven [= malice and iniquity] leavens the whole lump?" (1 **Cor** 5, 6). 'If anyone has caused pain [by sinning] he has caused it not to me, but in some measure — not to put it too severely — to you all' (2 **Cor** 2, 5). This explicit stress on the corporate dimensions of sin, which is found only in **Corinthians,** is no doubt a ᴄ⁻ quence of the emphasis of the corporate character of our redempti˙ ᴎ necessitated by the divided state of the Church in Corinth.

26. Cf. 2 **Cor** 11, 28, and the Pastoral epistles passim.

would be contrary to her very nature for a sinless Church to tolerate this state of affairs. Hence the first thing she must do, and precisely to save the sinner, is to restore truth to its rightful place by expelling him.[27]

POST-BAPTISMAL SINS

The Practice of the Church

The first point to be noted is that the judgment of sin is reserved to the community (*Mt* 18, 17). This is thrown into relief by the absolute prohibition of private judgment in this matter (*Rm* 14, 4, 10; *Jm* 2, 4; 4, 12). In the case of evident sin the community, in the person of its leader(s) has the right and duty to judge and act. "As for those who persist in sin, rebuke them in the presence of all" (1 *Tm* 5, 20). If the sinner refuses to amend, there are two possibilities, obviously dependent on the gravity of the sin. In the case of the Thessalonian who disobeyed the apostle's injunction not to be idle, Paul simply recommends that the others do not associate with him (2 *Thess* 3, 6, 14). This, apparently, is not an excommunication, because he is still considered as a brother (3, 15).[28] The ultimate object of such action is "that he may be ashamed" (3, 14). Exclusion from the community is inflicted for more serious sins, which we may

---

27. Cf. K. Rahner, "Forgotten Truths Concerning the Sacrament of Penance," in **Theological Investigations,** II, London 1963, 136-142; M. Schmaus, "Reich Gottes und Bussakrament," **Münch. Theol. Zeit.** 1 (1950) 20-36.

28. Cf. **Didache** 15, 3: 'If anyone has injured his brother let no one speak to him and let him not receive any word from you until he repents.' As Audet points out this indicates a situation in which the Church was still governed by the law of small numbers, for only in a restricted group with strong interior cohesion could the temporary interruption of social relations be expected to exert effective pressure on the wayward (**La Didachè,** Paris 1958, 467-68).

presume to be those sins which exclude from the kingdom of
God (1 *Cor* 6, 9-10; *Gal* 5, 19-21; *Eph* 5, 5). "As for a man who
is factious, after admonishing him once or twice have nothing
more to do with him, knowing that such a person is perverted
and sinful; he is self-condemned" (*Tt* 3, 10). The tone here is
much more severe than in 2 *Thessalonians* and suggests that it is
a question of a true excommunication, even though the ritual
formula "to hand over to Satan" is lacking.

This formula appears in two passages. "By rejecting conscience certain persons have made shipwreck of their faith,
among them Hymenaeus and Alexander, whom I delievered to
Satan, that they may learn not to blaspheme" (1 *Tm* 1, 19-20).
According to 2 *Tm* 2, 17-18 the error of Hymenaeus was to deny
the resurrection of the body by holding the only resurrection to
be that effected spiritually in baptism. In the second text the
handing over of the guilty individual to Satan is again the personal responsibility of Paul. This, together with the specialized
formula certainly attests the gravity of the case, but perhaps also
the exceptional character of such judgments. "Though absent in
body I am present in spirit and as if present I have already
pronounced judgment in the name of the Lord Jesus on the man
who has done such a thing. When you are assembled and my
spirit is present with the power of the Lord Jesus you are to
deliver this man to Satan for the destruction of the flesh that his
spirit might be saved in the day of the Lord Jesus" (1 *Cor* 5, 3-5).

The quotation from *Dt* 13, 6 in v. 13 (Drive out the wicked
person from among you") makes it indisputable that "deliverance
to Satan" is an excommunication. The difficulty arises in the
purpose clause "for the destruction of the flesh." There is no
reason for saying, as Cornely does,[29] that there is question here
of a special power proper to Paul to decree a corporal punishment of which Satan would be executant, and still less to understand it as a sentence of death as many of the older Protestants
did (Godet, Lietzmann, J. Weiss, etc.). "Flesh" and "spirit" here,
as elsewhere in the epistles, are modes of being of the whole

---

29. **Prior Epistola ad Corinthios,** Paris 1909, in loc.

man. Paul's idea would seem to be that once the protection of
the Church was withdrawn the sinner would find himself exposed without defence to the attacks of Satan, the author of all
the calamities that have afflicted humanity since the sin of
Adam.[30] In Jewish thought of the first century, sickness, which
might be expected to have a salutary effect, was attributed to
demonic possession; for example, *Lk* 13, 16: "And ought not this
woman, a daughter of Abraham, whom Satan bound for eighteen
years be loosed from this bond?" In view of the idea of binding
and loosing which has such importance in the Gospels the notion
of binding in this text is very significant. It is also encountered
in the Pastorals where those in Satan's power are considered
to be bound by him (1 *Tm* 3, 7; 2 *Tm* 2, 26; cf. 1 *Tm* 6:9;
2 *P* 2, 20). The underlying idea is of an Aeon divided between
two powers. He who is not free by union with Christ, is enslaved
to Satan (cf. *Rm* 6, 16-23).

If we add *Mt* 18, 17, these are the principal passages of the
New Testament in which mention is made of exclusion from the
community because of sin. With one possible exception, nowhere
do we find an allusion to the reconciliation of a sinner, but the
stress on the medicinal value of the penalty that is so clear in the
Pauline letters suggests that restoration to full communion was
accorded on evidence of true repentance.

Other New Testament writers manifest a rather more pessi-
mistic attitude to the possibility of such repentance. John, for
example, prescinds from the whole question completely: "If anyone sees his brother committing a sin which is not unto death
he will ask and he [God] will give him life for those whose sin is
not mortal. There is sin which is unto death: I do not say that
one is to pray for that. All wrongdoing is sin, but there is sin
which is not unto death" (1 *Jn* 5, 16-17). What is new in this
text is to find intercessory prayer limited to a particular class of
sins, i.e. those which do not merit eternal death. An exhortation
to fraternal intercession for sin is also found in *Jm* 5, 16, but without any such limitation: "Confess your sins to one another and

---

30. So Allo, Dibelius, Robertson-Plummer.

pray for one another that you may be healed."[31] To understand the "to one another" of this text as necessarily implying a liturgical act is to force their sense. The way in which the exhortation is introduced in no way suggests that it was an established practice, and in the perspective of James the sole purpose of the "confession" is to motivate the intercession of the brethren. This would seem to imply that the sins in question were not public, and, in consequence, not subject to the judgment of the community. In 1 *Jn,* on the other hand, both types of sin are public, but beyond that the definitions given are rather obscure. The "sin which is not unto death" would appear to be a sin, which while not in itself very grave, is such as to indicate a dangerous state of spiritual tepidity.[32] The "sin which is unto death" is a sin of extreme gravity. It is futile to speculate as to which sins could be so qualified, but it seems very probable that they were such as to merit expulsion from the community (cf. 2, 19; 4, 4-5; 5, 12).

It should be noted that John does *not* say that such sins are unforgivable.[33] All the text implies is that he is abstracting from

31. While this verse is closely related to the remission of sins connected with the anointing of the sick (v. 14-15), both by the particle οὖν and the allusion to "healing," it is nonetheless concerned with a distinct, but analogous, situation: if the intercession of the presbyters is effective for the sick, then so are our prayers for one another. Cf. F. Mussner, **Der Jakobusbrief,** Freiburg 1964, 233.

32. Cf. R. Schnackenburg, **Die Johannesbriefe,** Freiburg, 1963, 277.

33. The distinction between sins that could be forgiven and those that could not is not found before Tertullian (cf. B. Poschmann, **Busse und Letzt Olung,** Freiburg 1951, 24). The "Unforgivable Sin" logion in **Mk** 3:28-29 and par. deals with a different case altogether. In the more primitive perspective of Mark the saying stems from a situation in which Jesus rebuked those who refused to recognize the Spirit working through him in his victory over the demons. The form of the logion in **Mt** 12, 32 and Lk 12, 10 indicated a complicated literary evolution. These two authors draw a distinction between blasphemy against the Son of Man and against the holy Spirit, thereby suggesting a distinction between the earthly ministry of Jesus and that of the risen Christ in his Spirit-guided Church. Rejection of the revelation witnessed to by the latter is now the unforgivable sin. Cf. G. Bornkamm, in G. Bornkamm — G. Barth — H. J. Held, **Überlieferung und Auslegung im Matthäus-Evangelium,** Neükirchen 1960, 31.

them completely. The motive for this attitude is not made explicit. From the context we can only infer that the author was not sure if the petition for their forgiveness was according to God's will (v. 14). This scruple is indirect witness to the power of prayer emanating from a fraternal charity whose measure is the love of Christ (4, 10-11). So confident is John of God's desire to save that, given a minimum of good will on the part of the sinner, he makes forgiveness an almost automatic consequence of fraternal intercession. His judgment as to the presence or absence of this minimal disposition is formed on the basis of the type of sin committed. In the case of less serious sin he assumes that the sinner will respond to the divine love as manifested in the charity of the community. His uncertainty with regard to grave sins is perhaps conditioned by a view prevalent in the primitive Church that certain sins imply an attitude that could never, under normal circumstances, be transformed into repentance.

Evidence of this view is found in the *Epistle to the Hebrews*: "It is impossible for those, who having been once enlightened, and having tasted the heavenly gift, and having become partakers of the holy Spirit, and having tasted the word of God, (and) the powers of the age to come, and who have fallen, to renew again to repentance, (that is) those who are crucifying the Son of God on their own account and are holding him up to public contempt" (6, 4-6; cf. 10, 26, 29; 12, 16-17).[34] This passage is only concerned with the subjective dispositions of the sinner; there is nothing to suggest that the sin of apostasy as such is unforgivable. The severity of tone must be understood in function of the religious psychology of the first Christians for whom the experience of salvation was so vivid as to make deliberate sin seem an impossibility. This aspect is underlined by the fourfold manifestation of the divine generosity. This mercy the apostate repays by a double crime. The total rejection that apostasy im-

---

34. On these passages cf. C. Spicq, **L'Épitre aux Hebreux,** II, Paris 1953, 167-178; M. Goguel, **La doctrine de l'impossibilité de la seconde conversion dans l'épitre aux Hebreux et sa place dans l'évolution du Christianisme,** Milan 1931.

plies is nowhere more evident than in the statement that apostates "crucify the Son of God on their own account," because in baptism they were "crucified *with* Christ" (*Gal* 2, 19; 4, 19). It is impossible to reach by any human means one whose rejection of the light is so total. The sinner's refusal is so absolute that he has made himself impervious to the ordinary solicitations of grace. Of what has he to repent, since he no longer believes in Christ, or in God, or in grace, or in sin, or in judgment? Thus on the human level the impossibility of repentance is absolute, but if we include God within our horizon the impossibility is only relative. A new divine initiative, as gratuitous and as unmerited as the first, could change his disposition, could infuse a light in which the decision of faith would again appear as truth.

We must now turn to the one possible exception to the statement that nowhere in the New Testament do we find an allusion to the reconciliation of a sinner with the community. In the third century the imposition of hands formed part of the rite of reconciliation. St. Cyprian writes: *Hos enim oportet cum redeunt acta paenitentia per manus impositionem solam recipi* (*Ep* 74, 12; cf. also 15, 1; 17, 2; 18, 1). Similar formulae are to be found in Eusebius (*Hist Eccl* 7, 2) and in *Const Apost* (2, 18). This fact has led a number of scholars [35] to interpret 1 *Tm* 5, 22 as a rite of reconciliation, rather than to see in it an allusion to ordination, which is the common opinion. The passage reads: "Rebuke those who (persist in) sin in the presence of all so that the rest may stand in fear. In the presence of God and of Christ Jesus and the elect angels I charge you to keep these rules without favor, doing nothing from partiality. Do not be hasty in the laying on of hands, nor participate in the sins of another μηδὲ κοινώνει ἁμαρτίαις ἀλλοτρίαις)."

In the view of the majority, Paul has in mind only the presbyters, and the point of the passage is a warning against hasty ordination of candidates who may be unworthy. Were Timothy

---

35. Notably P. Galtier, "La reconciliation des pécheurs dans S. Paul," **RSR** 3 (1912) 448-460; id. art. "Imposition des mains," **DTC**, VII 1306-1314; but also Lock and Dibelius in their commentaries on the Pastorals.

to act imprudently in this respect he would be responsible for
their sins. While we readily admit with Spicq that the quality of
the clergy is a prime concern of Paul in the Pastorals, it would
seem that he had adequately expressed himself on this point in
3, 1-10. It is true that the apostle speaks again of the presbyters
in v. 17 but is it as clear as the majority opinion would have it
that he has them in mind up to v. 22? Is it not equally possible
that "those who persist in sin" (v. 20) should have a wider extension than the presbyters of v. 19? Given the structure of chapter 5 it is not impossible that Paul begins a new section in v. 20.
Hitherto he has been concerned with Timothy's attitude towards
various sections of the community: different age groups (v. 1-2),
widows (v. 3-16), presbyters (v. 17-19), and it may be plaus-
ibly suggested that in v. 20-22 he is concerned with his attitude
towards sinners in general, being led into this through mention
of an elder's sin in v. 19.

It must be admitted, however, that an equally good case can
be made for the homogeneity of v. 17-22. Hence we must look
for other arguments that may weigh the balance to one side or
the other. In *Ac* 6:6, 1 *Tm* 4:14, and 2 *Tm* 1:6 the imposition of
hands forms part of an ordination rite, but it is also clear that
this gesture was capable of other symbolic values in the primitive
Church. It was, for example, closely associated with baptism
and the gift of the Spirit (*Ac* 8, 17; *Heb* 6, 2). The usage of the
formula in 1 *Tm* 4, 14 and 2 *Tm* 1, 6 cannot, then, be absolutely
determinative with regard to the meaning of 1 *Tm* 5, 22.

A more fruitful approach is by way of the phrase "to participate in another man's sins." The closest of the parallels that might
serve to elucidate its meaning is 2 *Jn* 11.[36] Here it is question of
the reception of a heretic into one's home. The apostle forbids
the Christian even to greet him, "because he who greets him
participates in his evil work (κοινωνεῖ τοῖς ἔργοις αὐτοῦ τοῖς
πονηροῖς)." In this case the "communion" is established by the
greeting, which was normally a blessing (cf. *Mt* 10, 13). Given
the corporate dimension of sin, it follows inevitably that the

---

36. Cf. also **Apoc** 18, 4; **Eph** 5, 11.

Christian is involved if he establishes solidarity with the sinner. This case would appear to be exactly parallel to 1 *Tm* 5, 22, because the imposition of hands is a perfect symbol of solidarity. By admitting an impenitent sinner to communion Timothy would become solidary with him in his sin.

This parallel, however, is not absolutely conclusive, because if the imposition of hands establishes communion with regard to present sin, then it also does so with regard to future sin, which is the position of those who favor ordination, rather than reconciliation, as the meaning of the passage. In the light of the available evidence, therefore, it does not seem possible to come to any firm conclusion with regard to the meaning of 1 *Tm* 5, 22. It is possible, but not by any means certain, that in it we have an allusion to a rite of reconciliation.

The Self-Understanding of the Church

In the New Testament we find not one but many theologies of the Church, in the sense that each author gives us his faith-inspired vision of the community of salvation. Most often these are partial insights into the mystery rather than a systematic development, but one trait is common to all. All were conscious that the Church is the eschatological community of salvation. This awareness was based on the conviction that the promised Messiah had come in the person of Jesus of Nazareth, that he had been raised from the dead, and that he had sent the holy Spirit to the community he had founded. This is not to say that the future held nothing new. The Second Coming of Christ was awaited with a fervor and intensity that varied according to time and place. This eschatological longing was shared by other sectors of Judaism, notably by the community of Qumran, but with this important difference. At Qumran, as in the rest of Judaism, this hope was based on the divine promise and a profound faith in the fidelity of God,[37] but in the Christian com-

---

37. It is extremely doubtful that the Essenes ever attributed a messianic

munity its basis was the conviction that this promise had already
been realized. One effect of this awareness was a tremendous
sense of the privilege of belonging to the messianic community.
"Though you do not now see him you believe in him and rejoice
with unutterable and exalted joy" (1 P 1, 8). It is understandable
that this exaltation, very intense at the beginning (on the individual as on the community level) should have become somewhat
attenuated with the progress of time. While it existed it opposed
an effective barrier to sin, but as it diminished the Church was
forced to reflect on the problem posed by the presence of sin in
her midst. Two factors that polarized this reflection were participation in the liturgy, and the scandal given to weaker members of the community.

The Liturgy

Of the two forms of the *Pater Noster* found in the Gospels
Luke's is considerably shorter than Matthew's, and there is also
a difference in the wording of the petitions. Recent scholarship
has come fairly close to a consensus in its attempt to explain
these facts. It is generally agreed that the Lucan number of petitions is more original, but that the formulation of Matthew ap-
proximates more closely to the original Aramaic of our Lord.[38]
The fifth petition in *Matthew* reads: "And forgive us our debts
as we have forgiven our debtors" (6, 12). The eschatological
tenor of the prayer in *Matthew* has been firmly established by
Brown in the article referred to. This quality is in evidence in
this petition not only by virtue of the initial "and," which links
it with the preceding, but by virtue of the two aorists ἄφες

---

role to the Teacher of Righteousness (cf. A. van der Woude, **Die mes-
sianische Vorstellungen der Gemende von Qumran**, Assen 1957), and no
text permits us to suppose that they expected his return (cf. J. Carmignac,
"Le retour du Docteur de Justice à la fin des jours?" **Revue de Qumran**
1 [1958] 235-248).

37. Cf. R. E. Brown, "The Pater Noster as an Eschatological Prayer,"
Theol. Studies 22 (1961) 178.

and ἀφήκαμεν which emphasize not the temporal quality of the acts but their *Einmaligkeit*. In the last days the followers of Christ will receive the fullness of sonship. Their forgiveness of one another, and their forgiveness by the Father are but two facets of this great gift.[39] The Matthean "as" simply implies that human forgiveness is the counterpart of the divine. In this petition, then, the Christians, who in the first part of the prayer have begged for the advent of the last days (which include the definitive judgment), deal with the consequences of that request.

This eschatological tone is not maintained in the parallel petition in *Luke* where instead of the second aorist we have an indicative: "And forgive us our sins, for, indeed, we ourselves forgive our every debtor" (11, 4). The stress here lies on the mutual forgiveness being practiced in the community here and now. This is presented as though the condition for divine forgiveness has already been realized.

The ethical tone is even more marked in the commentary that Matthew attaches to his version of the Lord's Prayer: "If you forgive men their trespasses, your heavenly Father will forgive you also, but if you do not forgive men, your heavenly Father will not forgive you" (6, 14-15). It is certain that this logion was not originally associated with the Lord's Prayer, and it may be asked if it does not come from the pen of the evangelist himself. It reflects a dominant preoccupation of Matthew, and is closely paralleled in content by the conclusion with which he modifies the original import of the Parable of the Pitiless Debtor: "And so my heavenly Father will do to every one of you if you do not forgive your brother from the heart" (18, 35). The modification consists in the fact that, in order to heighten the effect of the parable on the members of the Church, Matthew restricts its original entirely general application to the Christian brother.[40] But the parable in its original sense completely legitimizes his commentary on the *Pater Noster*. It combines exhortation with

---

39. Cf. Brown, art. cit., 203; P. Bonnard, **L'Évangile selon S. Matthieu**, Neuchâtel-Paris 1963, 86-87.

40. Cf. J. Jeremias, **The Parables of Jesus**, London 1963, 109.

warning: God has extended forgiveness to you in the Gospel, but God will revoke that forgiveness if you do not wholeheartedly share the forgiveness you have experienced.[41]

A more fundamental question must be raised at this point. Why did Matthew feel it necessary to add such a commentary to the Lord's Prayer? The approach to a solution is suggested by *Mk* 11, 25: "And whenever you stand praying, forgive, if you have anything against anyone, so that your Father also who is in heaven may forgive you your trespasses."[42] In *Mark* this logion is immediately consequent on a saying concerning the power of prayer ("Whatever you ask for in prayer, believe you will receive it and you will"). The effect of this juxtaposition is to suggest that the efficacy of prayer is conditioned by faith, but also by the Christian's readiness to forgive. In pointing out that in this verse we have the sole instance of Mark's use of the term "Father in heaven" Stendahl makes a remark that merits attention. To him it suggests "a liturgical language known to Mark but not quite natural for his own style."[43] The significance of this emerges if we remember that the *Pater Noster* is essentially a community prayer, as is evident from the consistent use of the first person plural, and from an early stage it must have been in use by the community in its liturgical assemblies.[44] At this point we must recollect what was said above of the Church's conviction of the essential sinlessness of the messianic community. In this perspective we see that Matthew's commentary is grounded in the very nature of the eschatological community. In essence it is an assertion that the right to utter this prayer belonged only to a mutually reconciled, and therefore sinless, community.[45] The *Sitz im Leben* of

41. Cf. J. Jeremias, op. cit., 213.

42. K. Stendahl, "Prayer and Forgiveness," **Svensk Exegetisk Arsbok** 22-23 (1957-58), 76-77, argues convincingly against the view that this verse is a gloss influenced by **Mt** 6, 14.

43. Art. cit., 76, note 8.

44. For the history of the liturgical use of the Lord's Prayer cf. T. W. Manson, "The Lord's Prayer," **Bulletin of the John Rylands Library** 38 (1956), 99-113, 436-448.

45. Cf. K. Stendahl, art. cit., 83.

the logion is, then, liturgical, and it supposes a community some distance removed from its first fervor.

At its origin lies a saying of Jesus, whose authenticity can only with difficulty be questioned:[46] "If you are offering your gift at the altar and there remember that your brother has something against you, leave your gift there before the altar and go; first be reconciled to your brother and then come and offer your gift" (*Mt* 5, 23-24). This injunction, whose intention is not to minimize sacrifice but to ensure its being taken seriously and not as a magical rite, finds an obvious setting in the life of Jesus, whose disciples certainly frequented the Temple (cf. *Jn* 7, 8).[47] It was inevitable that this rule should have been adapted to new circumstances when the first Christians began to hold their own liturgical assemblies. It is even likely that *Mk* 11, 25 is a more specifically Christian form of this directive.[48]

In all these texts concerning mutual reconciliation the sinner's demand for pardon addressed to the brethren he has offended is considered to render him acceptable to God. They suggest a stage in the Church's development when the presence of sin in her midst had become a problem, and, further, that this problem made itself felt in terms of who could participate in the liturgical assembly. We know, for example, that at Corinth the question of unworthy participants in the Eucharist posed a very actual problem (1 *Cor* 11, 17-29). This must have given rise to reflection on the communities' power with regard to sin among its members. Did a sinner automatically exclude himself permanently from participation?

---

46. Cf. A Descamps, "Essai d'interpretation de Mt 5:17-41: 'Formgeschichte' ou 'Redaktionsgeschichte?' " in **Studia Evangelica**, Berlin 1959, 170.

47. προσφέρειν indicates actual offering as opposed to merely bringing a gift to the altar. The idea of a lay person offering sacrifice is unheard of in Judaism, but the Greek can be explained on the basis of a misunderstanding of the original Aramaic, which witnesses to the antiquity of the logion. Cf. J. Jeremias, "Lass allda deine Gabe (Mt 5:23f)" ZNW 36 (1937), 151.

48. Cf. R. Bultmann, **Die Geschichte der synoptischen Tradition**, Göttingen 1931, 140.

The "Little Ones"

The Church, while in no sense condoning sin,[49] never conceived of herself as a community of the *perfect*. Perfection was an ideal towards which one was expected to strive, but which was not required as a condition of entry. Jesus repeatedly warned that the company of the disciples was not a purified community, and that at the end their ranks must undergo a process of purification (cf. *Mt* 7, 21-27; 22, 11-14, 10-12). In the Pauline Epistle it is evident that some members of the community were weaker and less stable than the others, and Paul's concern lest they should be led into sin is very marked (cf. *Rm* 14; 1 f; 1 *Cor* 2, 6-3, 4; 8, 7-13). The same situation is perceptible in the first part of *Mt* 18 (v. 1-14, paralleled by *Mk* 9:33-50), which contains three logia of Jesus which perhaps underlie the teaching of Paul in *Rm* 14.[50]

In this section (*Mt* 18, 1-14) we find a number of sayings concerning "children" (παισία) or "little ones" (μίϰροι). For Bultmann[51] and H. Braun[52] all such texts originally referred to real children, and only later were used in a transferred sense of the disciples. This is perhaps an over-simplification, for Michel has shown that the concept was known and used in this sense in Palestine at the time of Christ.[53] In any case Matthew certainly uses these terms to designate the disciples. In view of the recommendation addressed to them in v. 3-4 to become as "children" the expression "one *such* child" (v. 5) can hardly be understood otherwise. This is confirmed by v. 6 which speaks of "little ones

---

49. Note the rather obscure case of Ananias and Sapphira (**Ac** 5, 1-11) where none of Qumran's gracious casuistry applies to "one who has lied in matter of wealth" (1 **QS** 6:25). Cf. K. Stendahl, **The Scrolls and the New Testament,** New York 1957, 8.

50. Cf. C. H. Dodd, **Morale de l'Évangile,** Paris 1958, 69.

51. Op. cit., 152.

52. **Spätjüdischer-häretischer und fruhchristlicher Radikalismus,** II, Tübingen 1957, 86 note 3.

53. **TWNT,** IV, 650-661. In rabbinic circles the term most frequently carried a pejorative connotation: those of low intelligence.

who believe in me." The question arises here: by these terms does Matthew mean all the disciples or part of the community? That the latter alternative is correct is suggested by the fact that in the context of chapter 18 the formal point of the image is neither simplicity nor sinlessness but weakness or helplessness.[54] The "little ones," then, are a definite religio-sociological section of the community: the weak and lowly.[55] Matthew explicitly warns the stronger element that these are not to be despised (v. 10; cf. 10:41); and adapts the parable of the Lost Sheep (v. 12-14) to demonstrate in a positive fashion how they are in fact to be treated. In its original setting (cf. *Lk* 15, 3-7) this parable is a defence of the Gospel against the Pharisees, and the conclusion is an implicit condemnation of its critics. Matthew makes the audience the disciples, and, by means of a new conclusion, modifies the point of the parable so that the stress falls on the assiduity of the shepherd's search for those who have gone astray.

That the danger of the weak being led into sin is not a mere theoretical possibility is made very clear in the logia found in v. 7-9: "Woe to the world for temptations to sin. For it is necessary that temptations come, but woe to the man by whom temptation comes. And if your hand or your foot causes you to sin cut it off and throw it from you; it is better for you to enter life maimed or lame than with two hands or two feet to be thrown into eternal fire. And if your eye causes you to sin pluck it out and throw it from you; it is better for you to enter life with one eye than with two eyes to be thrown into eternal fire." These admonitions are generally understood on the individual level; for example, Lagrange: "In the preceding passage Jesus insisted on the need to avoid giving scandal. He did not say what was necessary to avoid being influenced by scandal. This is the lesson presented here."[56] In this perspective the fact that Matthew has

---

54. Cf. G. Barth, in Bornkamm-Barth-Held, **Überlieferung** . . . , 114-115.

55. Cf. W. Pesch, 'Die sogennante Gemeindeordnung Mt 18,' **BZ** 7 (1963), 226.

56. **L'Évangile selon S. Matthieu**, Paris 1927, 350. Similarly Bonnard, op. cit., 270.

already included these logia in the Sermon on the Mount (5, 29-30) would be explained as a desire to accentuate their message.[57] Such simple repetition is very strange, and creates an assumption that Matthew has a different object in view here. The whole context of the chapter in fact suggests that the metaphor should be understood on the community level.[58] The warnings are directed against all those who by word or example cause the "little ones" to sin (cf. v. 6). The Pauline Epistles provide adequate evidence that such were not wanting in the primitive Church. Here their expulsion from the community is insisted upon.

As Pesch points out, *Mt* 18, 1-14 suggests that the state of the community is anything but happy.[59] The original enthusiasm has waned, and the charity it inspired has cooled. The danger this entailed for weaker members was very probably a second factor that forced the community to face the problem of sin in its midst. Given the Church's deepening consciousness of the nature of her mission, expulsion of sinners could never be considered a final solution.

Christ in His Church

An early tentative to provide an adequate solution is to be found in Mark's treatment of the Cure of the Paralytic (2, 1-12). The classic interpretation of this episode in Catholic exegesis accepts all its details as objective historical record. The central issue was Jesus' personal power to forgive sin which he vindicated by a miracle. Protestant opinion is unanimous in denying the unity of Mark's account—it is a fusion of two distinct events, a miracle and a controversy with the Pharisees—but divided on the question of their historical value. Bultmann considers both unhistorical.[60] Dibelius admits the historicity of the cure, but denies

---

57. Cf. W. Trilling, **Das Wahre Israel**, Leipzig 1959, 90.

58. Cf. A Humbert, "Essai d'une théologie du scandale dans les Synoptiques," **Biblica** 35 (1954) 8; W. Pesch, art. cit., 223-224.

59. Art. cit., 226.

60. Op. cit., 12-14.

historical value to Jesus' claim to personal power over sin.[61] The historicity of both elements is maintained by Taylor.[62] It is impossible here to go into all the reasons that motivate the literary judgments involved in these opinions,[63] and to test their validity. A recent study, however, has clarified the problem greatly by highlighting v. 10 ("But that you may know that the Son of Man has authority on earth to forgive sins—he said to the paralytic") as the fundamental cause of the disharmony evident in the narrative.[64]

In fact, when read in conjunction with v. 5 and v. 12, v. 10 certainly appears in a curious light. A greater claim is made in v. 10 than that first implied in v. 5. V. 5 ("Your sins are forgiven") centers on the forgiveness of sins *by God,* for Jesus proclaims forgiveness in a fashion very reminiscent of the Old Testament prophets. Compare, for example, 2 S 2, 23: "David said to Nathan, 'I have sinned against the Lord.' And Nathan said to David, 'The Lord has pardoned your sin' (transposed into the passive = your sin is forgiven)." Nothing in the verse suggests Jesus' *personal* power over sin. Yet just this is the key-point of v. 10, which is concerned precisely with Jesus as the forgiver of sins. If we move now to v. 12 we at once notice that it falls far short of v. 10. It does not fail to attribute to the audience the recognition of the fact that Jesus has established the reality of the forgiveness of the paralytic's sins, but it does not claim for them a recognition of Jesus' personal power to forgive sins.

If v. 10 is removed, the narrative becomes greatly simplified and focuses on a question of fact: are the words of forgiveness uttered by Jesus effectively true? The fact of forgiveness is stated in v. 5, verified by the miracle in v. 11, and recognized by the crowd in v. 12. The homogeneous development firmly establishes the literary unity of the pericope, and throws into clear relief the

---

61. **Die Formgeschichte des Evangeliums,** Tübingen 1959, 63-66.

62. **The Gospel according to Saint Mark,** London 1955, 191-192.

63. A convenient summary is to be found in R. T. Mead, 'The Healing of the Paralytic — a Unit?,' **JBL** 80 (1961) 349.

64. C. P. Ceroke, 'Is Mk 2:10 a Saying of Jesus?' **CBQ** 22 (1960), 369-390. We are much indebted to his study in this paragraph.

adventitious character of v. 10. We must agree, then, with Ceroke, that v. 10 is not a saying of Jesus but an editorial addition.

The construction of v. 10 presents its own problems. To the majority of exegetes the initial ἵνα followed by the subjunctive suggests a final clause. Hence the translation "But in order that you may know." The difficulty here is that the expected principal clause is lacking. There is evidence, however, that in Hellenistic and Byzantine Greek ἵνα plus the subjunctive was used to introduce an independent proposition expressing a decision, or more frequently, a mild command, a prayer, a wish.[65] In this perspective we should translate "Know that. . . ." This latter alternative concords better with the redactional character of the verse, and makes more obvious the function of the phrase "he said to the paralytic" with which v. 10 concludes. It indicates the end of the comment, and a return to the episode being narrated.

What is the purpose of the comment? It can hardly simply be a declaration of Jesus' personal power to forgive sin. To a Christian who believed in Christ's divinity this would have been sufficiently clear from v. 5-7. Ceroke finds the clue to a deeper meaning, and I think rightly, in the title "Son of Man." He discerns evidence of a tradition that applied this title to the risen Christ precisely as conceived to be exercising a divine function as head of the messianic community.[66] *Mark* 2, 10 fits perfectly into this tradition, especially if we adopt a translation that differs slightly from that commonly found in the vernacular versions, but which is equally possible grammatically: "The Son of Man has power to forgive sins on earth." A heavenly power is attributed to Jesus as the risen Christ, but this power is exercised on earth.

The implications of this for the life of the Church only become evident if we take into account the allusion to the oracle of *Dn* 7 that is implicit in the title "Son of Man." There it is question of the coming of "one like a son of man," who is endowed with power. In the New Testament this power is understood as

65. Cf. J. Duplacy, "Marc 2:10 — Note de syntaxe," **Mélanges bibliques redigées en l'honneur de A. Robert**, Paris 1957, 424-426.

66. Art. cit., 383-387.

a power of judgment.[67] What is important for our purpose is that this oracle also suggests an extension of the power attributed to the Son of Man.[68] After speaking of this power in v. 14 the author continues: "The Ancient of Days came and judgment was given to the saints of the Most High, and the time came when the saints received the Kingdom" (v. 22).[69] Implicit, then, in Mark's comment is a claim that the community participates in the power of its Lord, and in the context this can be nothing other than the authority to forgive sins, which, moreover, is intimately related to the power of judgment. If the hour of judgment is advanced it is not in order to punish sin but to pardon. It is less a question here of vindicating a right to forgive sins, as Bultmann thought,[70] than that of a consciousness of having experienced the messianic forgiveness of sins through the ministry of Jesus and of an awareness that that forgiveness is being extended to men.[71] The function of the forgiveness of sins is exercised by Jesus present in the community, physically during his earthly ministry, through his Spirit in his exalted state.

The relatively primitive state of the tradition from which *Mk* 2, 1-12 stems is attested to by the lack of any allusion to post-baptismal sins. We have here an initial stage of the Church's awareness of her participation in the power of her Lord. A much more profound comprehension of the mystery is evident in Matthew's treatment of the same episode, particularly when viewed in the context of his whole Gospel.

Matthew introduces nothing new into the narrative, but by reducing the miracle story to the minimum he gives added emphasis to the central point of Mark: the forgiveness of sins. His specific contribution is to be found in the conclusion: "When the crowds saw it they were afraid and glorified God who had given

---

67. Cf. **Mt** 16, 27; 25, 31f.

68. This is well brought out by A. Feuillet, "L'exousia du Fils de l'Homme," **RSR** 42 (1954), 179-181.

69. For a defence of this translation, cf. J. Dupont, "Le paralytique pardonne," **NRT** 82 (1960), 957 note 66.

70. Op. cit., 13.

71. Cf. Ceroke, art. cit., 390.

4

such power to men." Obviously the crucial words are the final
two. What does Matthew mean by "to men"? Various solutions
have been proposed,[72] but the only satisfactory one is that which
takes into account the fact that Matthew is writing in the context
of the Church for Christian readers. His description of the crowd's
reaction is an invitation to the Christian community to give thanks
to God for the power which, after Christ's departure, remains
with the men to whom he communicated it. It does not seem
possible to give any other adequate explanation as to why he
should have modified Mark's conclusion in precisely the way he
did, particularly since Held has demonstrated that Matthew's
treatment of the Gospel material shows an evident preoccupation
with the problem of the participation of the community in the
power of its Lord.[73]

This preoccupation shows up very clearly in *Mt* 18, which also
helps us to define more accurately the repositories of the power
spoken of in 9, 8. The discourse enshrined in this chapter is
formed from a number of sayings of Jesus, whose original historical setting it is very often impossible to determine. It is quite
clear, however, that a number of them were originally addressed
to the community in general. Does it follow, then, that the discourse in its actual state must be considered as addressed to *all*
the disciples? This opinion has been upheld most recently by W.
Pesch,[74] but he has failed to take into account the study of E. R.
Martinez, which, on the basis of a careful study of Matthew's
use of the term "disciple," adduces strong evidence that the evangelist has in mind not the disciples in general but the Twelve.[75]
The same conclusion emerges from an investigation of the literary history of the discourse. In a study devoted to *Mk* 9, 33-50 R.
Schnackenburg comes to the conclusion that this text served as

---

72. These are classified and discussed by J. Dupont, art. cit., 950-953.
73. Bornkamm-Barth-Held, **Überlieferung** . . . , 258-262.
74. "Die sogennante Gemeindeordnung **Mt** 18," **BZ** 7 (1963), 234.
75. "The Interpretation of 'oi Mathetai in Mt 18," **CBQ** 23 (1961), 281-
292.

Matthew's source for the first part of the discourse,[76] and it is clear that *Mk* 9, 33 (= *Mt* 18, 1) has the apostles in view. To L. Vaganay the problem is a little more complex, and he postulates as the source of *Mt* 18, 1-14 an Aramaic document made up of seven sections joined by link-words, but once again the first section which sets the tone for what follows is concerned solely with the Twelve.[77] In the course of the discourse there is no evidence of a change of address. Furthermore, it can hardly be denied that certain logia have much greater force if they are considered as addressed to the leaders of the community. The parable of the Lost Sheep is a case in point. It is on them that the burden of ensuring the protection and development of the "little ones" weighs most heavily, and the responsibility of expelling from the community those who are a source of scandal (v. 7-9; 15-17) is primarily theirs — as we know from the procedures in force in the Pauline communities.

The key passage of the discourse for our purpose is found in v. 18: "Truly I say to you, whatever you bind on earth shall be bound in heaven, and whatever you loose on earth shall be loosed in heaven." Because of its place in the promise of the primacy to Peter (*Mt* 16, 19) the formula "to bind — to loose" has been the object of continued discussion throughout the history of the Church. The most widespread interpretation today among both Protestants and Catholics, based on the rabbinic use of these terms brought to light by Paul Billerbeck,[78] holds that "to bind — to loose" means "to declare a thing forbidden and to declare a thing permitted," or, more strictly, "to excommunicate and to lift an excommunication." The power to lift an excommunication might justly be considered to include the authority to remit sins,

---

76. "Mk 9:33-50," in **Synoptische Studien** (Festschrift A. Wikenhauser), München 1953, 184-206.

77. "Le schematisme du Discours Communautaire à la lumière de la critique des sources," **RB** 60 (1953), 203-244.

78. (H. Strack) — P. Billerbeck, **Kommentar zum Neuen Testament aus Talmud und Midrasch**, I, München 1922, 738-747.

but in this interpretation, the relation between the two remains rather obscure.

Recently, a forgotten patristic interpretation (Ignatius, Justin, Clement of Alexandria, Ephraem), which has the great advantage of clarifying the relation between sin and the power to bind and loose, has been revitalized by H. Vorgrimler.[79] For these authors the phrase has a demonological value. This connotation is far more widely attested than the rabbinic usage, and it certainly antedates the formation of the Gospels. It is found in the Jewish apocalyptic writings, and traces are evident also in both Old[80] and New Testaments.[81] In this perspective "to bind — to loose" connotes "the power with which the kingdom of God takes possession of the Aeon hitherto dominated by the Evil One."[82] For the authors of the New Testament there were only two possibilities of being open to man: submission to the Evil One in sin, or submission to Christ as a member of his Church. No neutral middle state was possible (cf. *Mt* 12, 30; *Mk* 9, 40; *Lk* 9, 50; 11, 23), and man found himself in one state of being or the other as the result of a free personal decision. While ostensibly a member of the Church the sinner had, in fact, changed his allegiance from Christ to Satan. Hence "to bind" means to intensify the claim the Evil One has on a sinner by withdrawing from him the protection of the Church. It is thus in practice equivalent to excommunication. This view preserves the essential of the "rabbinic" interpretation, because an action that merited excommunication was certainly forbidden. In a similar way "to loose" means to break the bonds with which Satan restrains a man from his true destiny.[83] In itself this power could be exercised

---

79. "Mt 16:18 s. et le sacrement de pénitence," in **L'homme devant Dieu** (Mélanges H. de Lubac), I, Paris 1963, 51-61.

80. **Ps** 58, 6; **Dt** 18, 11; **Job** 36, 13; 40, 13; **Is** 47, 9, 12; **Tob** 8, 13.

81. **Mt** 12, 22-29; **Mk** 7, 35; **Lk** 13, 12-16; **Ac** 2, 24; 1 **Jn** 3, 8; **Apoc** 9, 14; 20, 1, 3, 7.

82. H. Vorgrimler, art. cit., 59.

83. A rather close parallel is found at Qumran. Of the Overseer of the camp it is said: "He shall carry them in all their despondency as a shepherd his flock. He shall loose all the bonds that bind them that there may no

in baptism, but it can also imply the lifting of an excommunication, and in view of the juxtaposition of this verse with v. 17 this would seem to be the meaning intended by Matthew here.

It should be obvious how closely this interpretation harmonizes with what we have seen of the practice of the Pauline churches. Moreover, it has the added advantage of enabling us to draw a clear distinction between the power accorded to Peter alone (the power of the keys, implying supreme dominion) and that accorded to the apostles (the power to bind and loose).

Is it possible to discern when *Mt* 18, 18 was spoken by Jesus?[84] In *Mt* 18 the logion is divorced from its historical context, but a parallel transmission of power is narrated in *Jn* 20, 22-23: "Receive the Holy Spirit. If you forgive the sins of any they are forgiven; if you retain the sins of any they are retained." It has been commonly held (e.g., Wescott, Meinertz) that John here adapts the Matthean text for Gentile readers on whom the implications of the expression "to bind-to loose" would have been lost. C. H. Dodd, however, has shown that it is impossible to derive *Jn* 20, 23 from *Mt* 18, 18.[85] He has likewise pointed out the presence of two Johannine *hapaxlegomena* (to forgive sins, to retain) makes it highly improbable that the passage is a free creation of John. Hence, he concludes, we must postulate "an alternative form of the tradition regarding the authority committed to the apostles by the Lord, akin to, though not identical with, the tradition followed by Matthew."[86] It is possible, then,

---

more be any oppressed or broken among his congregation" (**CD** 13, 9-10). This seems to be a reference to spiritual bonds, i.e., sin (cf. **Is** 58, 6). Cf. J. Schmid, "Contribution à l'étude de la discipline pénitentielle dans l'Église primitive à la lumière des textes de Qumran," in **Les Manuscripts de la Mer Morte** (Colloquium de Strasbourg 1955), Paris 1957, 89.

84. The authenticity of the logion is well defended by A. Vögtle, "Messiasbekenntnis und Petrusverheissung," **BZ** 1 (1957), 252-272; 2 (1958), 85-103.

85. **Historical Tradition and the Fourth Gospel**, Cambridge 1963, 349.

86. Ibid. Though his reconstruction is perhaps too perfect to win wide acceptance and is marred by several errors of interpretation v. 21-23 is included in John's source by G. Hartmann in his study "Die Vorlage der Osterberichte in **Jn** 20," **ZNW** 55 (1964), 197-220.

that in locating this logion in a post-paschal context John has preserved its original historical setting.[87]

Over and above witnessing to the transmission of power to the apostles, these texts establish a relationship between reconciliation with the community and divine forgiveness. What is formally stated in Matthew's "what you shall loose on earth shall be loosed in heaven" is implicit in John's use of the passive "they are forgiven."

The certitude of divine ratification of the communities' decision with regard to sin is already hinted at in *Mt* 5, 22bc: "Who ever says 'Raca' to his brother shall be liable to the council (τῷ συνεδρίῳ), and whoever says 'You fool shall be liable to the Gehenna of fire." The casuistic style of this incision sharply distinguishes it from the apodictic style of the antithesis immediately preceding (5, 21-22a), and it is very likely that it was composed by Matthew himself, who elsewhere displays a tendency to add casuistic commentaries.[88] Συνέδριον is understood by many exegetes to designate the Sanhedrin, the supreme court of the Jews in Jerusalem, and the "judgment" mentioned in v. 22a is taken to mean the local tribunal. This distinction demands that a gradation be seen between the faults of anger and two forms of insult.[89]

This interpretation rests on very fragile ground. "Judgment" in v. 22a stands in antithesis to that referred to in v. 21, and

---

87. Christ's washing of the feet of the apostles and his order to them to do likewise (Jn 13, 2-17) was reinterpreted in the Johannine tradition and applied to the penitential practices then in force. The opposition between the complete bath (most naturally understood of baptism) and the washing of the feet alone suggests the necessity and possibility of a purification subsequent to baptism. In view of what we have seen above, relative to the problem of participation in the liturgy, it is probably not pure chance that this episode is situated in the framework of Christ's last meal, i.e. in an implicitly eucharistic context. Cf. P. Grelot, "L'interprétation pénitentielle du Lavement des pieds. Examen critique," in **L'homme devant Dieu** (Mèlanges H. de Lubac), I, Paris 1963, 75-91.

88. Cf. A. Descamps, art. cit., 164; R. Bultmann, op. cit., 142.

89. A recent example of this interpretation is to be found in P. Bonnard, op. cit., 64.

obviously designates the eschatological judgment in opposition
to human punishment. Furthermore, it is highly unlikely that
Matthew would mention the Sanhedrin in connection with
Christian sin. And finally, it is impossible to establish any
gradation between the two insults, particularly since the meaning of "Raca" is anything but clear.

It is preferable to understand the two insults as parallel
examples chosen more or less at random, and intended to make
more explicit the teaching of Jesus on fraternal anger. If v. 22b
and c are in fact parallel then there must be some correlation
between the συνέδριον and the "Gehenna of fire." What can this
be if not that the decision of the συνέδριον has eschatological
implications? It is this precise aspect that provides the link with
the preceding antithesis. Fraternal anger is subject to the decision of the συνέδριον which has an eternal dimension. Who, then,
are the constituent members of the συνέδριον? Ignatius uses the
term to designate the college of the Twelve,[90] and it is hard to
escape the conclusion that this is the meaning intended by
Matthew here. If our interpretation is correct we have here a
good parallel to the first part of *Mt* 18, 18, but this aspect is not
without an echo in Judaism.[91] The most original part of the
logion is that which concerns the reconciliation of sinners.

The formulation of *Mt* 18, 18 implies the certitude of divine
ratification of the communities' decision. Whence this certitude?
Undoubtedly from the promise of Jesus, but Matthew affords us
a very welcome clarification by juxtaposing to this verse the

---

90. **Mg** 6, 1; **Philad** 8, 1; **Trall** 3, 1.

91. M. Weise ("**Mt** 5:21 f-ein Zeugnis sakraler Rechtsprechung in der
Urgemeinde," **ZNW** 49, 1958, 116-123) has brought to light an interesting
parallel from Qumran by juxtaposing 1 **QS** 8, 5-7 ("The Council of the
Community . . . [is appointed] to bring down punishment on the wicked")
with the Levitical curse uttered on 'the men of the lot of Belial' in 1 **QS** 2,
6-7 ("May God make of thee an object of dread by the hand of all the
Avengers of vengeance . . . Be thou damned in the night of eternal fire").
The parallel is deficient to the extent that "the wicked" = "the men of
Belial" were never members of the community, but valid in that it sees
the decision of the Council as endowed with an eschatological value.

logion recorded in v. 19, 20: ". . . where two or three are gathered together in my name there am I in the midst of them." It is quite clear that in its original setting this logion had nothing to do with the forgiveness of sin, but to deny it any relevance to the preceding saying in its present context is to completely misunderstand the evangelist's technique. It is the presence of the saving Christ in his Church that guarantees the validity of her decisions with regard to sin.[92] We find precisely the same doctrine in the parallel passage in *John,* but transposed into his own theological framework, for the promise of power is immediately preceded by the gift of the Spirit. It is also very close to the teaching of *Mk* 2, 10, though the formulation there is rather more subtle.

The most striking impression that remains as a result of this survey of the teaching of the New Testament on sin in its relation to the Christian community is that sin is always viewed in a perspective of charity. This is obviously true of the forgiveness of sin operated in baptism, for Christ's death, into which the believer is incorporated by this sacrament, is the supreme expression of God's love. In this act Christ took upon himself the sins of his brethren (*Heb* 2, 11-14). From this flows the obligation of fraternal charity which is the bond of the Christian community. But, just as Christ's, this love has a special relevance to sin. It motivates the brethren in their concern for the purity of the community, and while it may demand the exclusion of a member in order that the messianic community might not be a living lie, it is always with a view to his restoration. Brotherly love inspires the continual mutual edification which is the surest defence against the rejection of the love of God; to be lacking in love is to create an occasion of sin. More important, however, is the role that fraternal charity plays in the forgiveness of sins.[93]

---

92. Compare 1 *Cor* 5, 3-4 "I have pronounced judgment in the name of the Lord Jesus on the man who has done such a thing. When you are assembled and my spirit with the power of the Lord Jesus is present you are to deliver this man to Satan."

93. Cf. B. Langemeyer, "Sündvergebung und Brüderlichkeit," **Catholica** 18 (1964), 290-295.

The charity of the community towards sinners, which manifests itself in prayer (*Jm* 5, 20; *Jn* 5, 16) patience 1 *Thess* 5, 14), gentleness (*Gal* 6, 1; 2 *Tm* 2, 25) and mercy (*Jude* 22), is the incarnation of the salvific love of God in Christ. To respond to this love by true repentance for the offence that has insulted God and injured the community is to be reconciled not only with the community, but with God who is present in it. As G. Barth has well pointed out, the "Rule of the Community" (*Mk* 18) is but a commentary on, or better an application of, the Great Commandment of Charity.[94]

---

94. Bornkamm-Barth-Held, Überlieferung . . . , 79.

Chapter Five

THE REALITY OF SIN: A THEOLOGICAL AND PASTORAL CRITIQUE

KEVIN F. O'SHEA, C.SS.R.

Modern catechetical writing usually presents sin as a refusal of love for God. Sin, we are told, means "saying no to God" in the voluntary heedlessness of a human action; it is a failing, freely and responsibly, in the duty of personal love for God. Sin is in the heart of a man and disrupts the personal communion he must live with God in every action.

This essay will offer a critical assessment of this point of view. Theologically, it will argue that it is insufficiently realistic, insufficiently historical, and insufficiently communitarian to convey the insights of the biblical revelation on sin. Pastorally, it will argue that it is useful, and even necessary, to describe what happens when most ordinary people say that they "sin," since in these things the full biblical malice of sin is not normally achieved. In this we shall show that the modern catechetical point of view is insufficiently alert to the biblical sources of revelation on the reality of sin, and that it is insufficiently alert to modern pastoral psychology on the reality of sin. At the same time we shall show that it has instinctively stressed authentic values and can retain its usefulness.

This is but a tentative. It desires to underscore the importance of the problem of developing a theology of sin in real accord with biblical revelation and with the experience of contemporary man.

THEOLOGICAL CRITIQUE

Insufficiently Realistic

Biblical thought about sin is dominated by the horizon of covenant.[1] Sin is, at root, a violation and a rupture of covenant with the living God. Modern thought about sin is dominated by the horizon of "the human act" (usually taken to mean "each particular human act"). Sin is a refusal of love in and through a detailed human action. This is why modern thought is insufficiently realistic to convey the biblical realism of sin.

In covenant, God enters freely into a bonded relationship with his people; He becomes literally "their" God and they become literally "His" people. We have in our modern attitudes, an a priori idea of God as sufficient to himself, and then gratuitously entering into relations with others. The biblical writers would not have thought much of such a "God." For them, this was not to be understood as though God had to create a people; for them, it would not have been worth God's while being "God" if he were not the "God *of*" Israel. Israel is not just a people (already fully constituted) which then, further, accidentally happens to be the people of God; Israel is only a people to the extent that is the "people *of*" God. This is the value of covenant: it makes God God; and it makes Israel the people of God.

Sin is the violation of this covenant. Its result is that Israel is no longer the people of God; Israel, in effect, is wiped out in its real meaning. Its result is that God is no longer God, since he is no longer the God of Israel; God, in effect, is wiped out in his real meaning. The mystery of sin stands at the opposite pole

---

1. Cf. R. Koch, **Grâce et liberté humaine: Réflexion théologique sur Génèse I-XI** (Paris, 1967); S. Lyonnet, "Péché: Dans le judaïsme, Dans le Nouveau Testament, Péché originel," **Dictionnaire de la Bible, Supplément** 7 (Paris, 1966) 480-567; L. Hartmann, "Sin," **Encyclopedic Dictionary of the Bible** (New York, 1963) cols. 2218-32; P. Schoonenberg, **Man and Sin** (London, 1965).

from the mystery of covenant, which it destroys. The direct opposite to the concept of sin in Scripture is the concept of God. The malice of sin includes a terrible realism not usually read into the simple formula "saying no to God."

The New Testament is the eschatologically final covenant between God and the redeemed world in the crucified and risen Jesus, in the mystery of the Church, the new people of God. It is the absolutely indefectible outpouring of God's love in covenant. God's covenant bond with the Church cannot be broken. It can, however, be broken by particular persons, in so far as they refuse to allow it to hold sway in their own lives; for it is in them that the Church seeks its own fullness. When a person, in the New Testament era, commits sin, he excludes the new covenant bond from his personal life, and in his whole personality and bearing he ruptures the new covenant in so far as it pertains to him. He ceases to exist as a "man in Christ" and he makes the "God of our Lord Jesus Christ" cease to exist for him; it is as though neither of them, the partners of this final bond of love, ever existed. He indeed says "no" to God, but in a much more realistic sense than is usually read into the formula.

In the parable of *Lk* 15 (wrongly titled "The Prodigal Son," more correctly called "The Mistaken Elder Brother") we see a Pharisean concept of sin contrasted with this authentic covenant concept. The mistaken elder brother tells his father: "Look, all these years I have slaved for you and never once disobeyed your orders, yet you never offered me so much as a kid to celebrate with my friends." For him, avoiding sin means observing public order, not being wanted by the police, keeping regular observance. It is an external matter. The repenting prodigal tells his father: "Father, I have sinned against heaven and against you. I no longer deserve to be called your son." For him, sin does not mean the squandering of his inheritance, the evil life he has led with women, the days of his shame in the land of his wandering; for him, sin means the violation of the bond that unites him to his father, as son the violation of the covenant of sonship, of his personal relations to his father and the family. The other matters are merely the effects and the symptoms of this fundamental malaise. When the father receives the prodigal in forgiveness, he rejoices that he has returned to sonship — not that he has come home safe and well, as the servants mistakenly tell the mistaken elder brother. The language of the newly-risen son is full of tender respect for his father, in the restored bond of covenant, and contrasts with the disrespect of the language of the elder brother, who lives and works on the family property in the spirit of a mercenary. Indeed, at the end of the story the father truly has only one son: the forgiven prodigal, restored to covenant life. The lesson, on the meaning of sin in the New Testament, is obvious, and it is a much more realistic lesson than that usually given by the formula "saying no to God."

In 1 *John* we learn two contrasting principles: "He who is born of God cannot sin," and "He who commits sin is of the Evil One." As long as we are actually being engendered in God's love as his son in Christ, as long as we are actually living in that filial bond of covenant with our Father, then we cannot sin at all. Covenant and violation of covenant do not stand together. The practical secret of living without sin is a perpetual awareness of this living covenant in our hearts. Yet, if we do sin, this covenant is broken, and a new one is set up with our new "god," the personified power of the Evil One. The significance of our sin is not simply that of an evil act, in which we have said "no" to God; it is the establishment of a total personality-involving relationship with our new god, with the Evil One.

Paul told the Galatians: "I live, now not I, but it is the Christ that lives in me" (2, 20). Yet he told the Romans: "If I sin, it is not so much I that sin, as the power of sin that dwells in me" (7, 20). Here, graphically, is covenant, and broken covenant; covenant, and its substitution by covenant with evil. This is the realism of Scripture concerning sin. Is it sufficiently conveyed in the current formulas of catechetics?

Insufficiently Historical

Biblical thought about sin is dominated by the theme of the

Sin of world.[2] We should write it with a capital: the Sin, the Sinfulness, of the world. Modern thought about sin is dominated by the idea of the "human act" in which "sin" happens. St. Paul would have called that a "transgression," he would not have called it "Sin." Sin is a deeper thing, a powerful virus of evil which has a history of its own, on the cosmic plane.

The Sin of the world is a virus of evil which entered the world as a personified force through original sin and dynamically unfolds itself and tightens its grip on humanity and on the world in an escalating fashion down the ages of history. It is the hidden power which multiplies transgressions in the history of mankind. They are merely its symptoms; it is greater and deeper than all of them. It forms human history into what we might call "perdition history" (to coin the opposite of "salvation history").

This is the viewpoint of the Yahwist in Genesis, the viewpoint of Paul to the Romans. It is the viewpoint of biblical wisdom. It treats a subject too much neglected in modern moral theology of "transgressions."

In the coming of Christ, and in his rejection and crucifixion, this virus of evil in perdition history reached its climax once and for all. The Pasch of Christ is not simply the high point of salvation history, as we have been taught so well in recent times. On the first Good Friday Pilate the Gentile joined the clamoring Jews before him in rejecting Christ; it was truly the second fall, when the cosmos, prompted and ruled by the sin within it, broke its covenant with Love. It was the cosmic rupture of the covenant God held out to the cosmos in his given Son. At this point the virus of evil became absolutely visible: it played out its strength in public for all to see. And in the same moment it was forever vanquished in the mystery of Christ's resurrection. "Mors et vita duello conflixere mirando," as the paschal sequence tells us.

The present time, after the resurrection, as we await the *parousia*, is indeed the end-time of both salvation and perdition

---

2. Cf. Schoonenberg, **op. cit.**; A. Dubarle, **The Biblical Doctrine of Original Sin** (New York, 1965).

history. The Lamb of God has blotted out the Sin of the world in principle, but his victory is still being realized, still being achieved in struggle, as the history of this end-time unfolds. In this present history two mighty forces are in conflict, and their power is now fully at work: the force of the Sin of the world, and the force of the risen Lord of the world. It is Christ who remains the victor, but we still live in a time of historical struggle when he is still achieving his victory in us. We need to fear sin's power in our world now, as we need to revere more deeply Christ's power to conquer it now.

St. Paul called those who live justly in Christ at present "those who are being saved" in a continuous present tense. He equally called those who allow the virus of sin to have its play in their lives "those who are being damned"— again in a continuous present tense: they are being brought now, historically, into final perdition.

In Scripture, then, our present history is a drama where Christ's dawning Easter victory must ascend to the full light of day in our lives. And for some it is a tragedy, in that in them this light is overpowered by their darkness.

The Sin that is in the world now is not primarily the small matter of "saying no to God" in a bad act, but the great matter of the historical power that has already struggled to crucify Christ and that struggles now, as a beaten but still violent force, to claim men for the Evil One. It is legitimate to suggest that the historical realism of this meaning of Sin is not sufficiently brought out in current formulas.

INSUFFICIENTLY COMMUNITARIAN

Biblical thought considers the situation in which we live our lives in the human community to be tainted by the Sin of the world.[3] Here it finds the concrete power of Sin. Modern thought

---

3. Cf. Schoonenberg, op. cit.; K. Rahner, *Spiritual Exercises* (New York, 1965); L. Monden, *Sin, Liberty, and Law* (New York, 1965).

looks rather to the individual, and seeks the fruits and the sources of sin in him, in isolation.

Because of the active presence of sin, the human person is not able, in the present world, to enter into the dialogue of love-relationships with other human persons, and so is unable through them to enter into the dialogue of love-relationship with God. It is said — in a clumsy phrase which brings out the point — that our present situation is one in which horizontal and vertical dialogue are impossible: we cannot relate as we ought and as we would with others and with God. The world — the atmosphere, the spiritual climate, the milieu, the human situation — in which we live our own personal history is truly infected by the Sin "of the world."[4] This means that true community life is impossible unless sin is overcome and blotted out. The gift of God in Christ, redemption itself, consists in the new openness to community that men have together in God's "people," where they are "together" and God is "with" them.

When transgressions, or sinful acts, occur, much of the root cause to which they ought to be imputed lies in the tainted situation of men, in the milieu in which personal relationships in community are obstructed. The power of sin is *around* us, as a circumscribing influence, as well as in our hearts.

Once again the present approaches, portraying sin as a refusal of love for God, look to be too individual to suggest such community values, and so fall short of the full reality of sin.

PASTORAL CRITIQUE

A New Problem

We have shown that the current description of sin ("saying

---

4. Cf. Vatican II, **Gaudium et spes** (Pastoral Constitution on the Church in the Modern World) nos. 1-22.

no to God") does not contain the full biblical reality of Sin. In doing so, we have actually suggested more: we have suggested that what ordinary people do when they say they "commit sin" does not contain the full biblical reality of Sin. We are faced, then, with a dual problem: that of identifying the ways in which the biblical reality of Sin can be found in the lives of ordinary people, and that of identifying what happens when ordinary people say they "commit sin."

In our modern attitudes we look directly to the human act — literally to "the" human act. We take it for granted that in each and every human act the full reality of sin is possible. Human life is the sum total of all our human acts, some of them good, some of them sinful. But it seems, at least prima facie, impossible to find the biblical reality of Sin in any ordinary human act.

It would seem, again prima facie, that the biblical reality of Sin could be found in its fullness not in any particular act but in the whole mystery of a human *life*. This new kind of Sin is not something that can be done in half a minute or half an hour. It takes a whole lifetime, including death, to commit this kind of Sin. Only then could there be, in an absolute sense, a final covenant rupture with the God of New Testament grace; only then could there be a definitive expression of the historical virus of evil in the personal life of a particular man.

It is our intention to examine "human life" as the proper subject of the biblical reality of Sin. There are difficulties in doing so. We are too used to considering human life as a series of roughly univalent human acts. We are not used to considering the value of human life itself as one unit of meaning, and then going back and situating each "human act" into its horizon.

A Point of View

Our point of view can be expressed as follows: (1) Sin means the absolute and permanent violation of covenant relationship with God. It is a total and final position of man, in his freedom, before God. (2) This can only happen at the very deep level in which man is present to himself wholly as a person, fully master of his freedom, fully face to face with the God of covenant. (3) This cannot happen in an ordinary, isolated act, but only in the projected course of a human lifetime, climaxing in the personal position taken in death. It is not a matter of "falling into sin" haphazardly, but of being in one's life and inner personality, a "sinner," a man who is "unto-sin-death," and who thus enters death.[5]

In any realistic assessment of man's life in relation to biblical values, it can only be *at death* that the mystery of iniquity called Sin in Scripture is truly and fully present. In practice, this means that much of the inherited Catholic horror of "mortal sin" really finds its object in the sin of final impenitence. In this first principle, what are we to make of so called "sins," called "mortal" and "venial" in accepted language, that happen during life?

An Analysis

Beyond the consummating death-experience, there will be situations during *life* when, relatively, a person will be aware of himself as a person, and will be master of his freedom, and will encounter the presence of the God of covenant inviting him to communion, and will take a position. These are times when the center of personality is exposed fully, as it is at that moment of its development and maturity in personal history. Given that particular stage of his particular vocational pathway to death, the person is opened up and presented to his own consciousness com-

---

5. Some dependence is therefore acknowledged in this study on the theories of the "horizon of the human spirit" (K. Rahner and others) and of the "final option" in the experience of dying (L. Boros and others). This dependence is not absolute; it is rather practical and pastoral. We believe that even for those who may not follow in these paths theologically, many helps are there to see more deeply into their own system of thought and to reduce it to useful pastoral conclusions. For an excellent blend of both viewpoints and presentation of the meaning of sin (to which we owe much), see J. Fuchs, "Sin and Conversion," **Theology Digest** 14 (1966) 292-301.

pletely, so that he has to act with all his personal resources and
commit himself as a person. He is really unveiled in his inner
selfhood at that stage of his growth, and called upon to take
a position that shows what he then is in a complete way. The
situation must in some way be a foretaste of death, and the
awareness of the person must anticipate in some way the complete awareness he will have in dying.

In such a situation it is possible to have a genuine self-realization of the person against the God of covenant he then knows.
It is possible to have a violation of covenant proportioned to the
stage of maturity and of personal awareness he has then reached.
If that happens, it is Sin — not in the total sense which can only
take place in death, but in a true relative sense; for the person,
as he exists and lives in the hands of his own counsel there and
then, violates the covenant as it stands before him there and
then. This, of course, cannot happen every day, and it will not happen
in the same way and the same degree in different persons, but situations do occur when in a relative, progressing personal awareness the covenant bond with God can be violated. In such a
situation what really happens?

Sometimes the sin-act then performed will entrain, dynamically and infallibly (prescinding from the redeeming grace of
Christ), a further course of personal life in a sin-state which
leads to death-in-sin and the final Sin. This sinner, through his
option, has become truly a "sinner" in his personality and will
continue to act as such, even in the final option of death. It seems
to me most natural to use the word "mortal" to describe such a
sin, because its whole virus is to entrain the person of the sinner unto sin-death. This, of course, is to use the word "mortal" in
a much stricter sense than is current.[6]

---

6. In "mortal" sin in this sense, there is an actual bringing on of the
consequent life-drive to death-in-sin, an actual coloring of the personality,
so that the man will, by force of the "mortal" sin, continue in this state
henceforth, prescinding from the grace of Christ. In such a state it is not
intended necessarily that the induced death-in-sin actually does occur; the
saving grace of Christ may intervene.

In the same situation we have described, another sin-attitude is possible. There can be a true selfish realization of the person against God, a true rupture of covenant with Him, *without* it entraining this consequent sin-dynamism and *without* it affecting the whole personality as sinful henceforth unto death. In this case the climate, the atmosphere, the ambient, the spiritual "air" in which the person is immersed, the overshadowing presence of Christ and of Love inhibit the inner character of the position that has been taken from assuming its true proportions in that person and in his future life. It is indeed question of a very radical self-position against God, and indeed question of violation of covenant with God, but without the involvement of a life drive as a result, so that covenant life is envisaged and even expected for the future.

We do not intend here the case of a so called "immediate" conversion after a full-blooded act of "mortal" sin, such as we described in the preceding case. The restrictive influence of the Christian ambient, to which the person clings despite his present act, is psychologically experienced by the person, is known to him in the act of his sin, and in that act he is somehow favorable to it. He wants to take a very radical position against God right now, and he does, but at the same time he does not want to be that kind of person for good and all. He stands back from involving himself as a person in the drive to sin-death which such an act really does lead to by its own intrinsic implication.[7]

No ordinary person, in the critical moment of decision to sin or not, would express his attitudes in such language; yet we think that such language does express his real mentality at that moment. We believe that many theologians, following our argument, would instinctively apply to this case the usual term "mortal sin." We prefer to call it "serious," not "mortal," sin. It is not mortal in the sense in which we used the word previously: it is

---

7. In "serious" sin, the induction of a life-curve unto death-in-sin does not happen, even at the actual time the sin is committed. It does not happen precisely because of the influence of the supernatural ambient at that instant.

not death-dealing to the future personal project of life. Indeed, we have proceeded *per sic et non* in dividing sin, in the situation under discussion, into "mortal" and "serious."[8]

We submit that the distinction proposed is not merely notional but real.[9] It is true that personal "mortal" sins (in our sense) occur: St. Paul had no trouble identifying them in his reading of the Old Testament and in his observations on the pagan world in which he lived — at least to the extent that any man may judge. But in the present development of culture and of spiritual awareness and of sensitivity to moral values in modern man, particularly in a Christian country and in a more or less moral environment of life, we hesitate to think that in every

---

8. The case will be raised of a man who has not sinned "mortally" (that is, has not made this determined anti-God choice) but now sins "seriously," that is, here and now makes this particular choice of a serious sin — suppose that he is killed suddenly, in an auto accident, would he be saved? We would hope so. Modern insight into the mystery of death stresses that in dying the whole personality is exposed in its very center, and that man then enters a situation in which he is totally aware as a person of the implications of covenant in his life. He can see then what he really is, and he will respond accordingly. **Qualis unusquisque est, talis finis videtur ei.** But the position he has taken in merely "serious" sin, and the character he has assumed by committing it, do not really tell what he is in the deepest center of his personality. They are rather false symptoms of it. Precisely because his sin was "only" "serious" and not "mortal," we would hope that he preserves a real state of personality which, when unveiled to him in his final decision, would lead him to repentance and to God. Salvation should not be thought the matter of chance which another approach might make it, but rather the mystery of a personal and human encounter with God over a whole life climaxing in death.

9. Would our "serious" sin be mortal in the classic sense that it is death-dealing to the entitative habit of sanctifying grace in the soul and the virtue of charity? If it is, then there is still an "overshadowing" of the person by the influence of the grace-ambient in which he is, and through which his sin is not "mortal" in our sense. We agree that in the accepted patterns of approach, in the current categories of classification, it is more probable that the habits in question would be lost. But we would wish for a new classification of the traditional data in the light of more modern insights into the psychology of the human person in his life commitments. This is beyond the scope of the present essay.

act which ordinary people would spontaneously classify as seriously sinful the dynamic virus of truly "mortal" (in our sense) sin is found. We think that modern men do indeed at times commit "mortal" sins, but that very often their sins are merely "serious."[10]

In the same situation we are discussing, a third case is possible. We may be dealing with a merely apparent, not a real, self-realization against God, with a merely apparent, not a real, violation of the covenant bond. It is the case of an occurrence which is judged to be objectively serious, but whose grave moral and theological significance has not impinged on the personal sensitivity of the man involved in it. He does not personally react in the situation as if such grave values were implied. His assent in conscience to the gravity of the situation is not "real." This can happen even when he knows that something is forbidden to him, even "seriously," by what he calls "the Church," and when he goes ahead and does it all the same. His full personality as he stands in covenant before God is not uncovered in his own presence, the center of his freedom is not called into play in a covenant-breaking situation.

In this case, of course, we are dealing with something which is neither "mortal" nor "serious" sin; we shall have to call it "subjectively nonserious." The fact that it appears to be like serious sin from an external standpoint comes from the limitation of insight that restricts all external discernment of personal conscience. It is not forbidden to think that in the mercy of God

---

10. The distinction we propose between "mortal" and "serious" sin does not seem to be identical with the classic distinction between sin ex **malitia** and sin ex **infirmitate**. It seems that either "passion" or "malice" can be the dominant factor in the creation of the crisis situation of what we call "mortal" sin. It seems, on the other hand, that in the actual commitment of "mortal" sin a certain "malice" is always present. Perhaps we have not looked sufficiently at the total situation, but rather isolated the two "acts" — sin from weakness and sin from malice — without relating them to one another dynamically. It is interesting to compare our proposals with the insightful remarks made many years ago by Ch.-V. Héris on this point, in the collection **L'Enfer** (Paris, 1950).

such a case happens not infrequently in the lives of ordinary people.

Apart from the situation of relative but fully-personal involvement in a covenant crisis, there are other situations in human life when the person is partly aware of his mystery as a person, and is called upon to deploy his personal freedom in a way that partly shows his deeper attitudes. The whole self, the center of personality, is not engaged as such. And yet the person is using a certain freedom in deploying a *particular act* in a particular direction at this moment, without however involving the basic orientation of his whole self to God. We may call it a "peripheral" awareness of person, a lesser and passing level of personal manifestation and action. We have then actual personal guidance and control of the act, but not a realization of the person, the self, as such. Covenant bonds are not radically in question. In such a situation what can happen?

The person can truly deploy his act against objective moral norms. It could be, sometimes, with a personally free awareness and allowance of the contributory role of that particular deployment towards a seriously compromising situation ultimately involving the totality of the person. There is a certain real engagement of the person here, and he takes on a certain character as a certain type of man — a certain type of "sinner," if it be legitimate, as it is, to extend the use of that word to these inferior cases. We could never call him a "sinner" in the strong and direct sense in which we used the term above, in the case of the "mortal" sinner. But there is a certain personal entering-into the sin situation in this case, a certain personal permitting it to color at least the fringe areas of one's personality and personal freedom. The epithet, in an understood sense, is sufficiently justified.

This is what we will call "venial" sin, for want of a better word. "Venial" is the usual word to cover these minor cases, and this is the full-blooded case of such sin.

On the other hand, the case could occur in which the person might deploy his peripheral freedom in the situation we now have in mind, and do so *without* any personal permissiveness of a pattern which might lead to a covenant crisis in the proper sense.

In other words, there would not be the full-bloodedness of what we have just called "venial" sin. The inner character and significance of the deed that is done, and the position that is taken, are inhibited from the very outset from assuming their true and proportioned structures and orientations. It is really a question of a very superficial taking of position, without much import for the life pattern of the person. *Peccatum levissimum, sed peccatum in quodam sensu.* We would like to call it "light" sin — not even "venial" in our terminology.[11]

It is almost impossible to give concrete examples of these distinctions in general and in the abstract. We are dealing with the problem of formal subjective guilt, with "sinning," which is always particular and concrete. We would need to get down into the concrete situation and conscience of a particular person, his own assessment of values, his life horizon, his awareness of his personal freedom, and see exactly what *he* was doing in a definite instance. From this angle every sin ever committed is absolutely unique. We would submit nonetheless that the distinctions we have offered at this level are not simply notional but real: people do act, do sin, in these ways.[12]

As we concluded above, so we must conclude here that a third case is possible in the situation we describe. It is something that might look like a "venial" sin or a "light" sin, but would not really be so at all. It is only an *apparent* control-deployment of an act

---

11. The distinction we propose between "venial" and "light" sin is not identical in concept with that made between "deliberate" and "semideliberate" venial sin. Deliberation is not the formal point of our distinction, admittedly in a different frame of reference. Often the deliberate-semideliberate distinction is taken to be one of intensity in conceptual awareness and aroused interest in the situation as felt by the person explicitly — to that extent it is of little relevance to our discussion. We concede, however, that a greater real intensity in the person is found in "venial" sin than in "light" sin — to this extent the two distinctions might overlap in the concrete.

12. This may throw light on the concrete approach to the problem of "imperfections": concretely they will often reduce either to venial-light sin or to acts of the virtue of prudence. In the latter case they are not "imperfections" but the pathway of a unique person in virtue.

against objective moral norms, subjectively and formally there being no imputation óf sin at all.

We think here of a case where the objective morality of an occurrence is highly wrong, but its moral significance does not impinge on the control-reactivity of the person. It does not get "through" to him, he does not react to it, it does not mean anything to him. The fact that he acts one way or the other has in the concrete no proper meaning as an expression of his personality.

We think also of a case of mere violation of culturally-accepted behavior patterns which perhaps are often spoken of as "moral" standards and are said to involve "sin," but in which nonetheless there is no true enshrining of objective moral law. They are mere general standards of behavior and not moral standards at all; nor do they appear to the person as such. The violation of such standards is not in itself sin.

To this total analysis of the two situations and the various cases within each of them we must add the position of a person who does not and cannot grow into the maturity of personal freedom and its expression, and this not because of any personal fault or because of past deeds, but simply because of the moral insensitivity of the human community and environment in which he lives. Cramped by it, he is simply unable to live positively his covenant relations with God in personal love. There is something objectively wrong with the situation but, in relation to the acts we consider, there is no question of imputability to the particular person. This brings out once again that Sin is a much greater and more communitarian mystery than the mystery of a "bad human act."

It is indeed a terrible distortion when grown, adult people (lay, clerical, or religious) fret their lives away about minor details that at most are "light" sins, and never grow personally to live and love and use their freedom positively in service of God and others. It is not only a serious pastoral problem; it is a grave distortion of right moral outlook.[13]

---

13. Here we might add a word on the relative unimportance of one or

SUMMARY AND SCHEMA

The following schema may express what has been suggested concerning the variant incidence of formal sin in human life:

1) In the whole course of life consummated in the death-experience:

Sin

2) In situations of relative but truly personal awareness during life:
   A) in authentic self-realization against God:
      a. entraining a sin-course unto sin-death:

Mortal Sin

   b. not entraining a sin-course unto sin-death:

Serious Sin

   B) in merely apparent self-realization against God:

Subjectively Nonserious (*Sin*)

3) In situations of peripheral awareness during life:
   A) in authentic control-deployment of an act, against due norms:

---

other sinful act in a past human life now truly lived in covenant with God. Looking at the matter post-factum, we can divine that in the providence of God many persons would not be put in a situation where they would really love Him with a wholehearted covenant commitment except as a rising out of a real failure in their past history. A spirituality that would particularly rejoice and take pride in having never blotted one's copybook in some respects is not particularly Christian or particularly humble. If in fact such grace has been granted, it is a great gift of God's mercy; if it has not, to one who now loves it is not a matter of great agitation. Many people do not sufficiently evaluate that "horror of all sin" which they instinctively possess.

     a. with a permissive attitude to the possibility of a
     crisis situation:

Venial Sin

     b. without a permissive attitude to the possibility of a
     crisis situation:

Light Sin

   B) in merely apparent control-deployment of an act,
     against due norms:

Subjectively No Imputation of Sin

Our suggestions, thus seen in the schema, depend on the following tenets:

1) Sin (in the biblical sense) can happen only in the framework of *human life* in its totality, not in the framework of any single human act.

2) Human life in its totality is the mystery of man's personal *awareness* and loving commitment to the God of covenant in love; it is a growing mystery, consummated only in the *death-experience*.

3) During life, the final awareness of covenant values is prepared for by *moments of relative awareness* in the person's spirit; they are, as it were, the preradiance of the final encounter with God.

4) Situations of such relative awareness are two in kind: *truly personal*, when the person, at a given stage of his growth, is exposed and called upon to show *himself* fully in reaction to the situation, and *peripheral*, when the person merely deploys an *act* without implicating the heart of his inner self.

5) In all such situations the person can be involved in two different ways: by *entering*, or not, into the *train of life* naturally set up by the deed performed (in this the influence of *ambient* on the person's psychology is paramount).

6) There is the ever-present human danger of interpreting the *merely apparent* position of the person for a *real* one.

Perhaps the original questions could be reformulated in the light of our answer. Perhaps we have really asked and sought to answer: What is the meaning of human life in relation to the biblical mystery of sin?

ASSESSMENT

Diagnosis

In a concrete case, diagnosis of the various strata of sin is difficult and, from the point of view of a confessor, often in the last analysis impossible. Usually the confessor is presented with (*a*) material normally judged to be grave, (*b*) a certain conceptual perception of this normal standard by the person, and (*c*) a conceptualization by the person of what seems to him to be the "state of free choice and full consent" required for serious sin in confession. There still *could* be a large gap between these points and a real personal assent to a truly grave crisis situation in sin. In the language of the average penitent, "he knew it was wrong and he did it, he consented to it." That is all the confessor is told. It is about as much external evidence as he will get.

We do not think that there is any metaphysical link between the case described and "mortal" or even "serious" sin. We do not think judgments of this nature are mechanical; we think they must respect the mystery of each human person. We agree, however, that for the most part, a confessor, when presented with the case described in ordinary circumstances, would normally proceed as if he were dealing with either "mortal" or "serious" sin and not with "venial" or "light" sin. This is, at the most, a working practical assumption, to be tested against the personality and moral sensitivity of the man, if and as known to the confessor.

But then how could the confessor pick the difference between "mortal" and "serious"? It is an even more delicate matter, and the best evidence to work on is a knowledge of the personal attitudes of this particular man. We would go as far as to suggest that the difference in the concrete, from the point of view of formal guilt, between "mortal" sin, "serious" sin, and even "full-blooded venial" sin are probably not the same in different personalities, with different gifts of personal awareness, different backgrounds and environments, different patterns of life and different vocations. In this sense we concur with the suggestion of some recent authors that the ultimate difference between mortal and venial sin lies in the imperfection of the act, i.e., the subjective involvement in the action.[14]

We need to recall that there is a shade called "gray" between "black" and "white." In some way, deep down, the person himself knows what he does; but if he does, he is not always able to express it to others, or even to be clear in his own thoughts about it. We concur again with a recent suggestion that he cannot possess absolute certainty of his mortal sinfulness, any more than he can possess absolute certainty of his state of justification; and we think that the signs by which he might come to a reasonable assurance, in peace, on the latter point are much easier to discern than the signs that might lead to a reasonable conclusion in the former.[15]

In the sacrament of penance the final judgment on these things does not matter very much. At least it does not matter nearly as much as a past age of moral theology thought. The main point is not a matter of neat accountancy, with columns clearly marked black and red. The main point is that here and now the person is sorry for whatever sinfulness has entered his personality in his deeds, and is humbly using the present grace

---

14. Cf. B. Häring, **The Law of Christ** 1 (Westminster, Md., 1961) 363. Cf. Charles E. Curran, "Masturbation and Objectively Grave Matter: An Exploratory Discussion," **Proceedings of the Catholic Theological Society of America** 21 (1966) 95-112, at p. 100.

15. Cf. J. Fuchs, art. cit., p. 294.

as a source of new life. Then whatever the exact classification of what he did, it is all working unto good for the person who is now caught up once again in the love of God. The confessor need not be anxious, if externals of the past are presented as they ought to be, if the present is indicative of humble love, and the prognosis is for new life in Christ and the Church.[16]

Formation

Persons must be formed for life and love in God. A positive formation to the grandeur of personal awareness, in covenant with the living God, is of itself the best way to assure the absence of sin.[17] This formation aims (1) to help people grow as free persons and to live; (2) to deliver them from slavery to false behavior patterns without true moral and personal significance (some are in need of a messianic deliverance); (3) to educate them to be sensitive to true moral significance in every situation and in every action; (4) to free them from superficiality on the level where "venial" and "light" sins can happen; (5) to insert them deeply into the ambient of divine love, given to them in Christ through the Church and penetrating the deep recesses of their being; (6) to deepen the intensity of their commitment in love to their own personal vocation in life; (7) positively to help them create situations in which their basic love-gift to God is exercised and deepened; (8) positively to give them a sense of mission to help others to such a mature and sinless personal love.

---

16. The question will be asked in the light of our suggestions: Are "serious" sins (not "mortal") to be accounted as necessary matter for the sacrament of penance? The prima facie answer is affirmative: this is the sense in which the usual legal formula has traditionally been taken. One would also acknowledge the relation of this question to the problems of justification and the classification raised by our discussion.

17. One practical point: we would wish preachers to abstain from the dictum "such and such a thing is always a mortal sin." It is much preferable to say "it is always seriously wrong." A renewed examen of conscience for the Christian is urgent, with emphasis on personal attitudes.

The living of covenant in this way and the violation of covenant do not go together. "He who is born of God cannot sin."

Catechetics

We introduced this study with a reference to the common
catechetical theme presenting sin as "saying no to God." We saw
that sin means much more than this; and we saw that this "much
more" is not found, fully at least, in what ordinary people do
when they say they "commit sin." We have come full circle. We
are back to our starting point. We see now the value in the catechetical formula. The formula, it seems to us, is sufficiently personal, sufficiently flexible, and sufficiently meaningful to be very
useful in conveying to the ordinary person a sense of what he
does in the ordinary things he calls his sins. To this extent we feel
it deserves retention. But if taken alone and as the chief message
concerning the meaning of sin, the formula is inadequate. We
need to give people a broader horizon of the mystery of iniquity;
we need to form them to view their lives (and their vocation) as
a whole, to be lived in the presence of the covenant God in growing personal awareness and response. Only in this background
can the formula perform its limited but useful role.

PART TWO: THE MYSTERY OF FORGIVENESS

Chapter Six

THE SACRAMENT OF PENANCE:
AN HISTORICAL OUTLINE

M.-B. CARRA DE VAUX SAINT-CYR, O.P.

Since only things that change have a life story, it may appear
surprising to speak of history in connection with a sacrament.
When confronted with an immutable reality, the historian must
remain silent. Such a supposition, insofar as human institutions
are concerned, is purely chimerical, for time serves not only as
an exterior form for man's institutions but is an essential part of
them as well. In a single movement, time passes and institutions
disappear. But can we apply this law to an element of the order
of faith? Strictly speaking, God has no history; he "is" (*Ex* 3, 14),
purely and simply. The Church's Founder assured her of per-
petuity without decline: "Thou art Peter, and upon this rock I
will build my Church, and the gates of hell shall not prevail
against it" (*Mt* 16, 18). As for the sacraments, it is a solemnly
defined truth that they come from Christ himself as a whole, a
system structured forever.[1]

The reaction expressed above grazes the truth as it is expressed in dogma. Indeed, all the sacraments were instituted by

---

1. Council of Trent, Session VII (1547), canon 1.

Christ. The Lord himself imparts the value of eternal life to human actions, just as he destined and bequeathed them to his Church. The words that accompany the first eucharistic office — "Do this in remembrance of me" — assume great importance in this consideration (*Lk* 22, 19; 1 *Cor* 11, 24-25). However, one must not exaggerate this article of faith to the extent that it would directly result in begging the question. We certainly do not hold that the ceremonies constituting the administration of the sacraments, such as we ordinarily see them, can be traced in every detail to Jesus Christ. The truth of this statement can be verified today simply by observing the present considerable diversity. Although there are differences between the Eastern and Latin liturgies, the essential elements are rigorously identical in both cases. This is absolutely legitimate.

Thus we come to grasp an important point: the sacraments are immutable in their substance, for it was Christ himself who fixed once for all the central core. But the outer shell (or perhaps we should say the pulp, the flesh which contains the center) can vary according to the needs of time and place. And, indeed, this change has occurred in keeping with the cultural milieu where the Church has taken root.

This opens a perspective which enables us to trace the lifeline of a sacrament, to write its history in the sense we have indicated. The importance of this possibility is enormous, not simply because human curiosity must be slaked, but because the Church's way of doing things at a particular place and time casts a revealing light on the mysterious reality that makes up each sacrament. Different ways of administering a sacrament can reflect diverse aspects of the treasures of grace it contains. Thus history can provide effective enrichment in the process of our growth in faith.

Having thus cleared the way of a common but prejudicial objection, we can now state our aim: to sketch with large strokes the history of the sacrament of penance from its origin to our day. This rapid development can be divided into two unequal parts. First we must call attention to a basic difficulty present at the beginning of Church history when the very possibility of sacramental penance after baptism was challenged. Matters then appear to have stabilized and a particular rite for the administration of the sacrament was universally instituted. Let us refer to the sacrament at this stage as "ancient" penance, "solemn" or "public" penance. The perplexing period marking the transition between the terminal phase of the Roman Empire and medieval Christianity saw public penance fall into disuse and replaced by a new sacramental discipline, private penance, still in force today. During this period the bonds uniting Eastern and Western Christians were stretched to the breaking point; they finally ruptured in 1054, at the dawn of the second millennium in the life of the Church. This date marks the point where our examination will narrow to a consideration of the Latin West only.

PENANCE AFTER BAPTISM?

Our Lord manifestly instituted the sacrament of penance on the occasion when, after his resurrection, he breathed upon his disciples, saying: "Receive the Holy Spirit; whose sins you shall forgive, they are forgiven them; and whose sins you shall retain, they are retained" (*Jn* 20, 22ff.). The Fathers have universally agreed that, by such a striking action and by such clear words, the power of remitting and of retaining sins and of reconciling the faithful who have fallen after baptism was communicated to the apostles and to their legitimate successors. It was with good reason, therefore, that the Catholic Church denounced and condemned as heretical the Novatians, who obstinately denied the Church's power to remit sins.[2]

---

2. Council of Trent, Session XIV (1551), **Decree on the Sacrament of Penance**, ch. 1. This text constitutes a sort of preamble to the exposition of the Catholic doctrine on the sacrament of penance. It serves to introduce the refutation of the Protestant denials as the immediately subsequent text shows: "That is why the holy Council, which approves and accepts the authentic meaning of these words of the Lord (Jn 20, 22), condemns the fallacious interpretation of those who, in order to combat the institution

The Council of Trent presented the authoritative and traditional doctrine. When affirming the Church's perpetual teaching on the point, allusion was made to the first great crisis in the Church caused by the sacrament of penance. This difficulty arose in the third century.

The Rigorist Crisis of the 3rd Century

Toward the middle of the century, the Church suffered the triple blow of three persecutions: that of Decius (250-51), that of Gallus (253), and finally that of Valerian (257-58). Occurring after a long period of tranquillity, the oppression struck the Christian communities as a violent shock. While martyrs and confessors were not lacking, it appears that the weak who denied their faith through fear of torture were, unfortunately, more numerous. When the crisis had passed, the ecclesiastical authorities were confronted with a considerable number of apostates who solicited pardon. Some were even arrogant in demanding their reintegration with the Church. As early as 250, St. Cyprian at Carthage and the presbyterial college at Rome (the pope, St. Fabian, having been one of the persecution's first victims) were obliged to find a solution to the perplexing situation. After mature deliberation, enlightened by extensive· correspondence between the two Western metropolitans, indulgence won out on both sides. The renegades were to be reconciled to the Church but, naturally, not before undergoing penance, and severe measures would be adapted to the individual case in question. The solution was far from satisfactory. At Carthage, around a certain Felicissimus, there gathered a group, among whom Novatus, a priest, was particularly prominent. Complaining that Cyprian was too rigid, this same group broke from the Church, thus

---

of this sacrament, apply them falsely to the power of preaching the Word of God and the Gospel of Christ." See also ch. 2, "The Difference between the Sacraments of Penance and Baptism" (Denz. 895) and canons 1 and 2, including the very precise definition of faith (Denz. 911-12).

creating a schism. Rome, at least in the beginning, had opted for indulgence. A more reserved attitude then appeared, coinciding with the rising influence of Novatianus, a priest in the presbyterial college. When it was finally possible to elect a new pope, Cornelius, he adopted Cyprian's line of conduct. Then Novatianus, vexed and disappointed at not having been raised to the episcopacy, broke with Cornelius, leading an important group who pretended to be scandalized by an indulgence smacking of weakness. They organized themselves into a schismatic Church around Novatianus. Now consecrated bishop, he assumed the role of the legitimate pope and, strangely, joined cause with the partisans of Novatus. Under the confusing name of Novatians or Novatianists, the dissenters were to maintain for several centuries their stubborn opposition in the name of an ideal of intransigent purity.

Analogous incidents had already occurred early in the third century. At Rome, Pope Calixtus I had admitted to penance Christians guilty of grave and scandalous faults, thereby supplying a cause for schism in the Roman community. In Africa, at the same time, Tertullian, the first great Christian writer of the Latin language, was expressing exalted opinions of the Montanist sect. Having broken with the Church, he bitterly railed at the practice of promising pardon for sins of the flesh, the alleged action of a bishop who was highly placed. This was, perhaps, Aggripinus of Carthage.

Concretely, the Church in this moment of her history was confronted with this question: Was it possible for the Church to accord pardon in the name of God to a Christian who had fallen into serious and scandal-producing sin after baptism? The dispute centered around three sins designated by the rigorists as "unforgivable": apostasy, homicide and adultery. The concern was not to determine whether God was capable of pardoning these offenses, but rather of establishing whether the Church had the power to forgive them. By way of summary, we can say that the issue amounted to a challenge of the very existence of the sacrament of penance, at least in certain cases.

The Full Significance of the Question

At the risk of overemphasis, we shall put the matter bluntly. This well-known quarrel did not merely represent a distant event of minor significance or one more example of theological quibbling. The faith of the Church was at stake. With recent re-examination of the problem, the danger reappears. The editor of a new edition of the curious work, *The Shepherd* of Hermas, wrote concerning the quarrel:

> A dozen years ago a coherent theory was imposed on the majority of critics. It can be summarized as follows: baptism remits former sins, but the primitive Church then demands a perfect life from the baptized. If one were to sin seriously after baptism, no additional terrestrial recourse is possible; he can only await God's judgment in total uncertitude, if not in complete certainty of damnation. There is no such thing as post-baptismal penance. The irremissibility of sins committed after baptism is affirmed in the passages of *the Epistle to the Hebrews* (4, 4-8; 10, 26-31) and in several apocryphal texts. This intransigent, rigoristic position represents the common opinion in the Church between the years 100 and 140. Reflective minds might have guessed that the outlook could not be maintained indefinitely.[3]

It would then appear accurate to conclude — and historians of dogma with liberal tendencies have not failed since the time of Harnack to take this step — that the sacrament of penance was unknown to primitive Christianity of the first two centuries, or, more precisely, that a single kind of penance was known: baptism. The sacrament we know today would thus have been "invented" by the Church under a very different form around the year 200. Such a position manifestly contradicts Catholic teaching as it was solemnly defined at the Council of Trent, for if the foregoing hypothesis is granted, penance is not a true sacrament.

---

3. R. Joly, **Sources Chrétiennes 53** (Paris, 1958), pp. 22-3.

Theologians and Catholic historians have been energetic in refuting the foregoing assertions. As a rule, agreement in presenting the following interpretation has been fairly general. The Lord Jesus himself instituted penance as a sacrament distinct from baptism, but, to the extent that the paucity of documental and historical evidence permits us to perceive, the sub-apostolic age experienced certain doubts in the matter. Hesitations, scruples and apprehensions were widespread, engendered by the strong rigoristic currents abroad in various areas within the Church and flourishing in heretical sects such as the Montanistic adventure. This sect, in full-blown development at the end of the second and the beginning of the third centuries, was the most representative of the rigoristic type. The rapid intervention of several Roman pontiffs and of men such as St. Cyprian (at Carthage) was required to dominate the crisis. Rigorism, far from being a primitive doctrine, represented no more than a kind of temporary and localized blackout of the ecclesial conscience.

ANCIENT PENANCE

The reader may feel that the difficulties just described are false and may question why historians resort to oracular pronouncements when it would suffice to refer to the documents of the very early Church in order to judge events in the true light of evidence. Unfortunately, such documents, at least clear and unequivocal ones, do not exist. Only the naïve are astonished by this vacuum, for it is an historical truism that the closer one moves to origins, the scarcer evidence becomes, and if documents do exist they are prone to be imprecise. This is true of the period we are discussing. Christian writings between the time of the New Testament and the third century are extremely scant. As is to be expected, none of the existing records give us a complete exposition of the Church's doctrines and practices. Furthermore, pertinent allusions are difficult to interpret since living conditions and social milieus were so different from those of the present day. Man is too prone to imagine spontaneously that the problems existing around the years 80, 100, or 150 of that era were, on the whole, more or less the same as those confronting him in the twentieth century.[4] This is a prodigious error and a fact to be borne in mind as one ponders clues provided by the New Testament or the earliest patristic era.

At the New Testament Level

We shall momentarily neglect the Gospel texts themselves in order to focus our scrutiny on the concrete evidence provided by apostolic writings. Among other things which strike the investigator are the discordant themes of the *Acts of the Apostles*. Alongside the almost idyllic picture of the primitive communities sketched by St. Luke (and some believe that simplifications contribute to the idealistic impression given in *Ac* 2, 42-47; 4, 32-35; 5, 12-16), serious transgressions in the case of several isolated individuals are not concealed, as in the episode of Ananias and Saphira and the even more curious one of Simon the Magician.[5]

---

4. Some very pertinent remarks have been made on this subject by E. Amann in his article, "Penance," in **Dict. theol. cath.** XII, 757: "We reason too much when we study the past, arguing from the practices which are in vogue today. In our nations of ancient Christian civilization, the baptism of adults is of very rare exception, and the practice of the sacrament of penance is quite naturally determined by this state of things. We have a little difficulty in understanding the primitive communities in which the great mass of baptized persons (and these baptized persons are not the great mass of Christians) have received the sacrament of initiation only as mature adults, sometimes quite aged, and, in the ancient times at least, in conditions which suppose a true and profound conversion. So that if we realize the moral situation of these communities, of those especially which are small, held well in hand by the authorities, we can understand that the necessities of penance were felt less keenly then than in later epochs. There is a correlation between the delayed admission to baptism and the practice of penance which has not always been sufficiently perceived, a fact which Saint Augustine particularly called to our attention (Cf. **Confessions** I, 9, 17)."

5. **Ac** 5, 1-11; 8, 9-24. We will note here that, contrary to Ananias and

However, the account of Paul's activities with the generous and picturesque community of Corinth affords the most refreshing instruction. The apostle was obliged to reprehend grave excesses, and on such occasions he struck with force. When a Christian went so far as to lead a common life with his father's second wife, the sanction was immediately imposed: the delinquent was ejected from the community and Christians could have no further relations with him. It was a real excommunication, not only from participation in the sacred liturgy but from fraternal life as well. The decision can be compared to certain scriptural passages.[6] St. Paul cites, for example, a precept from Deuteronomy which commanded, in the interest of the holiness of God's people, that the "perverse be excised from the community." In the old law the expression had the sense of a condemnation to death, but the epistle completely modified this perspective: the separation from the holy People of God was a penal measure with medicinal effects. While still imprecise, these various attitudes are extremely suggestive of the later practice of penance, and one has the impression of finding in them the elements of the early features of penance.[7] However, we must insist that, despite manifest similarities, nothing permits the scholar to

---

Saphira, Simon the Magician felt himself called to penance as a result of a severe rebuff from Saint Peter. Certainly, no sacramental reconciliation of the inventor of simony is described here, and we must not think of the sacrament when reading the admonition: "Repent!" But the attitude of the prince of the apostles hardly favors the rigorist concept of "irremissible" sins. Could we go farther and see, in the intercession required by Peter of the guilty one, a veiled allusion to a liturgical usage which would ulteriorly have marked the "deprecative" form of absolution on the part of the bishop when the sacrament later became more prevalent?

6. We are reminded here especially of **Mt** 18, 17.

7. Cf. 1 **Cor** 5, whose final verse (13) quotes **Dt** 13, 6. The meaning of this whole passage is made clear by 14, 1-2, the first part of which repeats the prescription of the "law of sanctity" of **Lv** 17, 1ff. (also 19, 27-28). In both, the motivation is clearly the same: "Sanctify yourselves and be holy because I am the Lord your God" (**Lv** 20, 7); "Thou art a holy people to the Lord thy God, and he chose thee to be his particular people of all nations that are upon the earth" (**Dt** 14, 2).

assume that he has discovered the sacramental practice of reconciliation as it will function later.[8]

Primitive Patristics (from 100 *to about* 150)

Much of what has just been said also applies to the first Christian writings which follow the New Testament. While it is difficult to grasp the precise import of certain elusive passages, one can, nevertheless, discern a distinctive climate: the demanding nature of Christian life. Nothing can be added on this subject to the declarations of St. Paul who had previously exhausted the subject (*Rm* 6, 1ff. and parallels). However, one can find traces of mercy, and this trait is very much in the tradition of the Gospel.[9] In fact, there would be very little to say about this

---

8. If the guilty person for whom Paul recommends pardon in 2 **Cor** 2, 5ff., is the incestuous man of 1 **Cor** 5, a further step would be made in this direction, but nothing authorizes such a supposition. The succession of events to which the two letters to the Corinthians refer is quite involved: the actual state of the affair seems quite uncertain. A first letter to the Corinthians, called "precanonical," is thought to be lost; our present "second letter to the Corinthians" perhaps combines several distinct primitive communications, or at least fragments of these. For further discussion, see the **Introduction** to the Pauline epistles in the **Bible de Jérusalem**.

Let us add here that there is nothing to be drawn from **Jm** 5, 16 concerning the sacrament of penance. The mutual confession of sins recommended here is a traditional practice among the Jews; it recalls the liturgies of penance in Judaism (as, for example, in **Ps** 106, **Dn** 9, 1ff., and so forth).

Without complete silence on this point, we could be dispensed from a lengthy discussion of difficult New Testament texts which have certainly brought water to the mills of the rigorists. Let us recall briefly that the impossibility of salvation which seems affirmed here is not established on the side of divine mercy or on that of the powers of the Church, but from the point of view of the dispositions of the sinner: whoever does not wish to renounce his sin or who through apostasy rejects the proposed grace cannot hope to accede to pardon as long as he remains in these dispositions.

9. In this connection, St. Clement of Rome's **Letter to the Corinthians** (end of the 1st century), ch. 57, certainly does not qualify as the witness of a precise fact manifesting the usage of sacramental penance, but at least it is a valuable index to a prevailing spirit.

period if it did not offer us the curious figure of Hermas and of his unusual work, *The Shepherd,* destined for an astonishingly brilliant career.[10]

In this work, it is not a question of scattered remarks on penance or observations gleaned from considerations devoted to other subjects, for the principal theme of the work is an invitation to penance. Nevertheless, several factors complicate the interpretation of a work which one would imagine, in *a priori* fashion, should illuminate our subject. Prudence must be exercised in summarizing the message of Hermas, and lack of agreement among scholars concerning its value can serve as a prudent warning to the incautious. Accordingly, it would not seem rash to conjecture that the most obvious message of *The Shepherd* of Hermas was that, in virtue of a revelation accorded the author which was to be transmitted to the Church, an exceptional penance might be granted Christians who had been baptized for many years. Of course, the post-baptismal penance could be accorded only once, and it was not to be administered to newly-baptized Christians or the catechumens awaiting baptism. The latter were to preserve without stain the faith they pledged to God and to Christ. These precise requirements suggest the unusual nature of the measure. Indeed, some have interpreted the action as a kind of jubilee. In any case, this type of penance was mercifully offered as a last chance. It seems clear that Hermas desired to combat rigorism, but the way he went about it fails to provide satisfactory evidence of an ecclesial penance which has become institutionalized and accepted custom.

In the interest of brevity, we shall not pursue the problem of *The Shepherd* of Hermas. It is certain that shortly after its appearance, and undoubtedly by 250, ecclesial penance was well established.[11] It eventually triumphed over the last hesita-

---

10. Cf. R. Joly, **op. cit.** This contains a rather recent (1958) discussion of the question and many useful references.

11. The first truly strong and explicit testimony is that of St. Cyprian of Carthage (see Amann, **op. cit.,** pp. 775ff.). In the history of the doctrines and rites, the cases of spontaneous and instantaneous generations are highly unlikely; we would then be led to give value to rather fragmentary testi-

tions, including those springing from the three irremissible sins
(apostasy, adultery and homicide). But in the light of Hermas'
remarks, would not ecclesial penance appear to be an innovation? If so, the genuine defenders of primitive tradition would
be the rigorists, and it would then be imperative to reject penance as a sacrament.

The True Interpretation of the Facts

It becomes readily apparent that the controversy is a sterile
one, for the problem has not been properly stated. Protestants
who deny, and Catholics who defend, the sacramental nature of
penance appear to unconsciously share an excessively rigid concept of the institution of a sacrament by Christ. There seems to
be a constant tendency of the human mind to represent the
truth under a simplified form and, most particularly, to attempt
to clarify an historical affirmation bearing on the distant past
by clothing it in the trappings of contemporary custom, as in
the case of a practice which is to have the force of law. Modern
man immediately envisions a clear, precise, juridical act drawn
up after the model of a present-day legal document and duly
executed before a notary. While we never fail to mock such
naïveté in others, we ourselves succumb to it far more often than
we realize.

In defense of the sacrament of penance, one must note the
evidence imposed by reading the Gospel. Of primary importance
is the power over sin of Christ, this man who is the Son of God.
An outstanding example of his force is visible in his cure of the
paralytic: "In order to convince you that the Son of Man has
the power to forgive sins on earth. . . ." Such is the purpose of
the episode (*Mk* 2, 1-12, particularly verse 10; cf. *Mt* 9, 1ff. and

---

monies met during the first half of the 3rd century and to see in them indications of a practice on the lines already fixed. The doctrinal quarrels of
the period touching on this point have naturally had to play a role in
this sense.

Lk 5, 17ff.). Furthermore, this liberation from sin is one of the great benefits resulting from the incarnation of the Son of God, and the Gospel presents this incentive as the chief motivating force of his terrestial mission. There is no doubt that Christ transmitted his power to the Church. She can forgive sin. She does so, first of all, in baptism, according to the very formal precept received from Christ. But does the power to baptize exhaust the Church's power to pardon sin? Nothing is less evident. Granted, the verse from St. John (20, 22), evoked by the Council of Trent to confirm the institution of the sacrament of penance by Christ, has a very general implication. But, in order for Christ to institute a sacrament of pardon for sin other than baptism, it sufficed for him to will the delegation of his own power over all faults to his apostles. And when it happened that circumstances placed a baptized sinner before them, they were not caught off guard but were aware, when forgiving, that they were carrying out the order received from the Master. It was indeed Christ who was responsible for the gesture of pardon which they offered.

In this regard, if there was one striking feature in the conduct of the apostles, it was the self-possession and authority they exhibited in resolving the problems confronting them. It suffices to recall the actions of Peter or Paul whereby they irremediably committed the Church's action in the future.[12] Indeed, the Twelve were far from timid. They displayed calm assurance in executing their powers, even when it was a question of unusually revolutionary acts. It is in this light that one must ponder Paul's reaction when confronted with scandal at Corinth; he energetically intervened to make a natural, spontaneous decision: "After all, I think that I, too, have the Spirit of God" (1 *Cor* 7, 40). This exercise of apostolic power was so

---

12. We are reminded particularly of the attitude of Peter toward the first pagan converts, Cornelius and the people of his household (**Ac** 10), and that of Paul in regard to the question of Jewish observances. It is true that several times the decisions seemed dictated to them from above through visions or dreams inspired by the Spirit. In any case, the apostles were very sure that the Spirit would not deceive them (cf. **Ac** 15, 28).

spontaneous, so self-possessed, that it does not occur to the witness to recognize therein an institutional operation, even if only
in its early stages.

The phenomenon just described explains the impression of a
vacuum which is discernible in the very early Church after the
disappearance of the apostles. Of course, life continues, but a
certain drifting, a drop in tension, is perceptible. While this
decline has been established by historical verification, it is even
more obvious today. This fact permits us to point out to the
reader that there was a unique, untransmittable dimension of the
apostolic function. With the passing of the apostles, revelation
was closed and the essential structures of the Church were fixed
forever. They were the founders and their role is irreplaceable,
for they participated "once and for all" in the event that was
Jesus Christ.[13]

But could not the obscurities and scruples which beclouded
the history of penance during the second and a large part of the
third centuries have resulted from the groping attitude then
prevailing in the Church? There was hesitation even on points
clearly established by Christ. Indeed, the Lord prescribed that
we should pardon "seventy times seven" (*Mt* 18, 22), but, on
the other hand, should not baptism signify a complete break
with sin: "We have died, once for all, to sin; can we breathe its
air again" (*Rm* 6, 2)? On this precise point, the ecclesial mind
will require time to assess the tone and significance of the heritage
received from Christ through the intermediary of his apostles.

It must be pointed out that the significance of this hesitation
is not at all clear. Did the Church question her own power to
remit sins committed after baptism, or did she simply refrain

---

13. Cf. **Heb** 7, 27; 9, 12, 26, 28; 10, 10. What we have just said naturally does not mean that in our eyes the Holy Spirit would have abandoned the Church at the death of the last apostle, or that henceforth Christ
would be less present within her (**Mt** 28, 20). However, the remark has
value, we think, on the human plane of ecclesial consciousness; there is no
longer the assurance of a Peter or a Paul; the hesitations which history
observes manifest that this consciousness gropes its way before being able
to explain itself clearly.

from using the power, judging such an action inopportune? The few extant documents were not concerned with this distinction, and they probably were not even aware of its existence. In actuality, the distinction is a relevant one. However, since the point remained obscure, the denunciations of the rigorists as well as contrary interventions remain disappointingly ambiguous.

The matter is further complicated, no doubt, by the unsatisfactory relations between Scripture and tradition. The text of *Jn* 20, 22, being manifestly unclear, has long caused debate. From what quarter did the light, which permitted the profound meaning of this passage to be grasped, finally come? From the Holy Spirit, of course, but working in and through tradition. But here again, the term "tradition" must not be taken in too formal a way. St. Thomas uses the happy expression *familiaris apostolorum traditio.*[14] How is one to understand a "family" tradition coming from the apostles, a tradition transmitted familiarly by the Twelve? For our part, we would willingly see a certain note of spontaneity, of naturalness, arising from the conduct of Peter or of Paul: convinced that the Spirit was guiding them, they provided a solution with serene self-possession. Such a gesture, even if its full implication is not recognized, orients the Church's action and manifests the meaning of such and such a word of Christ.

The Ancient Penitential Rite

After the very basic question — does the Church have the right and the power to remit sins committed after baptism, through the force of the Holy Spirit received from Christ? — let us now consider, in the light of the affirmative response which

---

14. Cf. **Summa Theol.**, III a, q. 64, a 2, ad 1: "All that which is a necessary constituent of the sacrament was instituted by Christ who is both God and man." It is true that Scripture does not always tell us that, but the Church holds it **ex familiari apostolorum traditione**. It is thus that Paul wrote to the Corinthians in regard to a question of discipline at the eucharistic repast: "The rest I shall set in order when I come" (1 **Cor** 11, 34).

was finally formulated, how the discipline of the sacrament was organized. The inquiry takes us to the third century, since the solid evidence we possess on this point dates from about 240 or 250.

However, it is fitting to first locate our examination with respect to a famous quarrel encumbered with misunderstandings. For a long time it has been common knowledge that the ancient discipline differed considerably from the one employed today in the administration of the sacrament: penance formerly was public, whereas now it is private and secret. Several scholars have spent a great deal of effort, time and talent attempting to establish that our private penance was actually practiced in the ancient Church. It is now clear that this labor has not succeeded in achieving universal agreement. But must a sacrament always be found under the same forms throughout the ages to guarantee its continuity? In any case, no one believes that public penance entailed a rite demanding a detailed confession of sins before the Christian community.[15] A quarrel over words has helped obscure the issue here.

We must now describe the ancient rite. This will not be difficult because we are sufficiently well informed to be justified in sketching only the conclusions of many historical inquiries. What

---

15. The detailed accusation of faults was made secretly to the bishop alone or to the priest he had appointed for this function. A letter of St. Leo the Great to the bishops of Campania (459) shows that in certain places the practice of making penitents confess their sins publicly had been introduced. This pope protested: "For the penance which the faithful seek, do not let them read publicly the detailed list of all their sins, since it is sufficient to indicate to the bishops alone in secret confession the state of their conscience." It is regrettable that the commentary which accompanies the text contains a manifest contradiction. "The penitential discipline in the Church did not include only the public confession of sins; among others, the text of St. Leo the Great shows that secret confession of sins was sufficient for those who sought penance. His letter shows that at Rome secret confession was of almost immemorial usage." The error lies in this: public penance was not opposed to a detailed and secret acknowledgment of sins to the bishop; it included it, on the contrary, as its first requisite. From this one cannot argue for the coexistence in antiquity of a private and a public penance.

interests us is not the detailed description of the rites but the lessons that can be sifted out from the vision of things reflected by the rites.

Consider the case of a baptized person who had fallen into grave sin and irremediable scandal (we shall return to the latter feature). Either spontaneously or by dint of public pressure and the indignation of his brothers, the person formulated his confession. The bishop, as head of the Christian community, accepted it and endeavored, by an attentive examination of the sinful conscience, to determine the guilt and the dispositions of the penitent. After this, he prescribed the treatment indicated by the illness in question.

First of all, the guilty one was cut off from participation in the sacred mysteries (the eucharistic service and community prayers), completing the break he had initiated by his sin. "Expel the wicked man from your midst," St. Paul had already said in adapting a prescription of *Deuteronomy* (1 *Cor* 5, 13; *Dt* 13, 6). Since the Church is constituted by the holy People of God in communion — a community life with the Father by the Son in the Holy Spirit — the sinner cut himself off from the community. However, the "excommunication" was not complete. Despite his sinfulness, the penitent still remained a child of the Church, one of her members, and he was not disowned. Although he was not permitted to take part in the assembly's eucharistic celebration, he had to attend the liturgy of the Word which preceded it.

The situation was dramatic. Driven from the ranks of the faithful the day he began his penance and consigned to the rear of the church, he had to remain there, wearing coarse clothing, chains and ashes. When the faithful entered, he was required to prostrate himself, soliciting their pity with tears and exclamations. In response, the entire community prayed for him, joining its penance to his. To state it another way, the prayers and penance of the guilty one were assumed into those of the community. The latter were precious in Christ's eyes, for the Church as his bride had been rendered spotless through purification by his own blood so that he might present her, resplendent, to himself (*Eph* 5, 27). The bishop — the leader of the people, king, priest and shepherd, like Jesus Christ whose place he took — concluded the intercession by a prayer which gathered all the elements (Collect); then, extending his hands over the penitent, he invoked upon him the grace of the Spirit himself who is, in the words of the liturgy, "the remission of all faults."[16]

The ceremony was repeated frequently during an interval which often was quite lengthy, depending on the fervor and sincerity of repentance displayed by the guilty one. Indeed, the humiliations which he assumed and the rough asceticism to which he submitted himself under the auspices of the Church (fastings, macerations, prayers) were, in the ancient mind, a cause for repentance to ripen in the heart from the contrition whose first flush was felt at the instant of the preliminary confession. It was up to the bishop, as shepherd and experienced doctor of souls, to judge when repentance had sufficiently softened his heart and turned it permanently toward the love of God. What a realistic and virile approach! As soon as he judged that the desired result had been obtained through divine grace, the pontiff admitted the penitent to full reconciliation.

As Easter approached (on Holy Thursday or Saturday), the rite just described was repeated for the last time, with only the bishop's prayer over the penitent differing. Instead of being sent away, this time the penitent was reintegrated into the community of the faithful. The prelate, or one of his deacons, led the forgiven one to his ordinary place. There, in the midst of his brothers, he once again took his place for the eucharistic offering and communion of the Lord's body and blood. The faithful recognized that his sin had been taken away and he was reinstated in the communion of the divine life which is the Church. However, he had to submit to certain conditions. We shall say a word later about these "after-effects," but we must now return to our rough sketch in order to trace its essential lines. The structure of the so-called "public" penance can be reduced to five headings.

---

16. Cf. the **Postcommunion** for Pentecost Sunday.

Exceptional Penance

The unusual nature of this procedure was its most striking feature. Today, confession, along with the eucharist, is the sacrament most frequently administered by the Church and the one most frequently received by her members. The assiduous reception of penance is an excellent indication of the Catholic's fervor. The contrary was true in ancient times when the faithful rarely confessed. The sacrament was given only to sinners. While it is difficult to summarize in a few words the history of a discipline which developed over two or three hundred years, certain guidelines stand out. Only sins that had grave public repercussions were liable to penance: the famous triad of "unforgivable" sins — apostasy, homicide and adultery. These played a veritable role of catalyst. Other offenses were gradually added to the list, and during the third and fourth centuries the number of sins requiring public penance had considerably increased. While it would appear that this list eventually came to approximate our present-day catalog of "mortal sins," the two were never identical. As in the case with venial sins, certain more serious offenses were remitted by means other than sacramental penance during the early period of the Church's life.[17] The situation can, ironically, be described by saying that, while the reception of penance characterizes the "good Catholic" today, yesterday it stigmatized the weak one.

Public Penance

As the name suggests, the type of penance we shall now con-

---

17. We could add that the ancient discipline had to involve more than a case of a delicate conscience; we must picture a murderer or an adulterer coming to confess his crime to the bishop. The submission to penance, either to the public authorities or their counterpart, was to risk attracting suspicions to oneself if not denunciation. This, even if the hypothesis of a detailed confession to the whole community is excluded, as it must be, is not demanded at all for public penance.

sider was indeed "public." Preliminary ceremonies denounced the guilty one before the entire community. Of course, only the bishop (or a priest delegated by him) received the detailed account of sins, but everyone was very much aware that so-and-so had joined the ranks of the penitents, and they knew, if not the exact sin he had committed, at least that it was one of the three (or slightly more) which appeared on the famous list. In many cases, the offense undoubtedly was already a matter of public knowledge and even of notorious scandal. Consequently, the public character of reparatory penitence caused no particular problem — except, of course, that it was extremely harsh. In any case, the epithet consecrated by usage is fallacious. It would be more accurate to call attention to the "social" side of the discipline. In fact, our modern concept of publicity will almost certainly distort our comprehension of the situation. The essential point is that Christians had a keen sense of the ecclesial community and they were extremely sensitive to any fault, no matter how secret, which was prejudicial to the People of God. Considered within this framework, it was normal that reparation should take the form of penance to be performed before the entire Church.

A Striking "Dramatic" Feature

There is danger of giving the expression "dramatic" an entirely misleading interpretation. When historians call attention to the "dramatic" side of the ancient rite of penance, they wish to stress the fact that symbolism played a more important role than it does at present. To grasp the meaning of this symbolic action, one must remember that the principal actor was not the penitent sinner but the Christian community.

Hence, one feature, the assembly's role, stands out: the local Church, the faithful grouped around their leaders, the bishop and his clergy, priests and deacons (and, accessorially, lesser ministers). If we wish to characterize the place held by the Church, we should say that the penitent's role before her symbolized her role before God. Before the offender was admitted to penance, he was separated, rejected from this remnant of God's people, from the holy assembly which offered the eucharistic sacrifice of the new and eternal covenant through the hands of its pontiff. The exclusion of the "perverse," the serious sinner, from its bosom visibly ratified the spiritual situation which he brought about by his sin. He became a stranger to God's holy people, to the mystery of reconciliation between God and men effected by Christ. The Church kept her distance from him because he had spiritually detached himself from her. One cannot serve two masters; no alliance between God and Satan is possible. The community bore in mind the fundamental demand repeated after Christ by Peter: "Just as he who called you is holy [he is obviously speaking of God], you also must become holy in your conduct as it is written: *You shall be holy, because I am holy.*" The Church was conducting herself as the holy and immaculate bride of the Lord; she remained beside the Father and his holy Son who said to the Jews: "Which of you can convict me of sin?" (*Jn* 8, 46).

But this bride of Christ, free of every stain and fault, did not cease, therefore, to be a mother for all her members to whom she had given birth to the Lord in baptism. If the Christian in question had separated himself from her by sin, he nevertheless remained a member and son for her. This status resulted not only because of the baptismal seal impressed on his soul forever, but also because his sins had not killed the faith within him. His vow, furthermore, marked his readiness to ask God's pardon. Thus the Church assumed Christ's role; she who is without sin placed herself in the ranks of sinners, assuming their offenses in order to carry them in her flesh on the wood of the cross and to destroy them by her death. After having taken her distance with respect to the guilty one, the Church mercifully approached him. The penance, supplications and tears to which she had condemned him, she now made her own, praying, beseeching and mortifying herself with him. This act provided an astonishing sign, for the same penances and austerities would or would not have the value of pardon according to whether or not they were carried out in keeping with the bishop's judgment, and in union with the Church over which he presided. In modern theological language, the sacramental value of penance resulted from its ecclesial character, for it was imposed by the Church, executed in keeping with her prudent judgment, and assumed by the community in its own prayer and expiation.

When the time of reconciliation finally arrived, the community was represented. Indeed, it found its very fulfillment in the gesture of the pontiff who led the penitent into the midst of his brothers. The estranged one had again become a dynamic member of the Church, enjoying the plenitude of his rights (participation in the eucharistic offering and praising the Father through the Son in the Holy Spirit). He had once again entered into living communion with God, for he was again in union with the Church.

A second trait renders the preceding one even more precise. The Church, as we have just observed, played the role of "mediator" analogous to that of Christ, her spouse. However, her role was more than analogous, for she indeed assumed the role of Christ himself, with her attitude visibly reflecting his. But what do we understand by the term "Church"?

We are now speaking of the local Church, the concrete Christian community on pilgrimage in a determined place. She, the mother of this Christian penitent and sinner, was this distinct assembly of virtuous men and women grouped around a bishop who, at the very center of the community, took the place of God the Father or Jesus Christ. Since the sinner had offended both God and herself, it was, quite naturally, from her that he sought help, intercession and reconciliation. The explanation should come as no surprise, for how was the Church, the bride of Christ, the mystery of grace and abode of the Spirit, to render herself present in concrete dimensions of human existence if not through the mediation of the local communities which were her members? The universal Church was thus present in the local one, the latter playing the role of a sacrament in respect to the former, rendering her present as a member and providing access to the entire body.

What was this local Church, and of what did she consist? She was a community of believers. To say believers is to say faith, and it was indeed the Word of God received in faith and sealed by baptism from which this group of men evolved. "Love of Christ has assembled us as one," sings the liturgy, and John the Evangelist further clarified the thought: "We have come to know and have believed the love that God has in our behalf" (1 *Jn* 4, 16). But remember: this group was a community and not just another chance get-together or unorganized crowd. A Church, a Christian assembly, differed from a troupe of strollers; it was not a mere crowd vibrating with the same drive. The Church's common soul, loving faith in the Lord Christ, became incarnate, assuming a social structure and constituting the fundamental presence of Christ. "Where two or three are gathered for my sake, there am I in the midst of them"; "I am with you all days, even unto the consummation of the world" (*Mt* 18, 20; 28, 20). This presence was accomplished according to various levels of density. One portion of the flock or of the People of God was grouped around a shepherd and a father—the bishop—surrounded by his priests, the latter aided by their "companions in service," the deacons. We thus have the living reflection of the Twelve assembled around Christ, drawing to him the crowds to whom he will send his disciples to break the bread of the Word, or the more mysterious bread — the miracle announcing the eucharist (cf. *Mt* 10, 1ff. and 14, 19ff.).

We wish to stress that the entire Church intervened to take an active part in the sinner's reconciliation with God. The entire community participated: not only the bishop with his clergy, but also all the people in whose midst he took the place of God. The entire Church, including the simple faithful, exercised the sovereign intercession, an intercession certain to be answered since the community assumed the role of the celestial high priest: "We have an advocate with the Father, Jesus Christ the just, and he is a propitiation for our sins, not for ours only but also for those of the whole world" (1 *Jn* 2, 1-2; *Heb* 7, 26; *Jn* 11, 42). Did this mean that everyone — bishops, priests, deacons and faithful — was on the same level, equally harnessed to the divine work of pardon as horses to the plow? Indeed not! There was an order among this people, with the foundations and superstructure in keeping with the diverse functions required (*Eph* 2, 20; 1 *Cor* 3, 10ff.; *Eph* 4, 10-12; 1 *Cor* 12, 28). Their respective roles were rendered visible in the penitential procedure. The sinner's act of accusation was made to the bishop as father and shepherd. He judged the sin and assessed the penitent's contrition with a view to rendering a medicinal penance (cf. *Ez* 34, 1ff., especially 34, 16). All prayed for the guilty one, but the bishop alone presided, assembled the prayers into a formula (Collect) and imposed his hands on the sinner as a sign and guaranty of the restoring work of the Spirit in the penitent's heart. The bishop did not preside in virtue of delegation by the community, but rather through that of the imposition of hands which he himself received from his predecessors in the priesthood. He thus joined in the act whereby the Lord installed the Twelve as shepherds of the flock purchased for his Father by his own blood (*Ac* 20, 28). With this final clarification we feel that the obscure features of the early penitential rite have been clarified. It is fitting to stress the fact that the undeniable grandeur of the rite sprang from its awareness of the ecclesial dimension of sin and the mediatory function of the people of God in the ministry of reconciliation.

"Laborious" Penance

The traditional modifier "laborious" is employed to indicate the distinction between "second penance" and the "first," namely baptism, the sacrament of adhesion to Christ, the seal of the faith which is born. The baptized person is dead to the old man which he formerly was and is reborn to the life of a son through a mysterious relationship with the Lord's paschal mystery. The repentance required of the catechumen was a complete break with the world in order to turn toward God. In a sense, it was an entirely new beginning. The catechumen was to perform no other work than that of receiving grace in his heart through faith (*Jn*

6, 29). Before being reborn with the risen Christ, he was incapable of expiating his former faults. Once he was entombed in death with Christ through baptism, expiation was no longer limited to him alone. On the contrary, the Christian sinner had to work out his repentance in a manner which both expressed his sorrow and stimulated him to greater heights, while simultaneously offering reparation to God the Father for the friendship shattered by sin.

There is no doubt that this reparation, or "satisfaction" as theologians call it, played a major role in the early sacrament, constituting its most visible feature, and this for a double reason. In the first place, it imposed a satisfaction that was extremely demanding because of its length, the severity of fasts and the macerations required. The sacrament also entailed "after-effects" for which the penitent was responsible for the rest of his life. Whereas a present-day penance might require you to say a decade of the rosary, equivalent satisfaction formerly involved a sentence of a completely different degree of severity. Furthermore, the order this "satisfaction" occupied was reversed. While we now perform our penance (the decade of the rosary) *after* having received absolution, the latter could not formally be given until after the fulfillment of the former, and as a consequence of it. The satisfaction or reparation voluntarily undertaken by the sinner, under the control and discretion of the Church (the bishop, to be precise) constituted, if we may employ the expression, the "test" of the penitent's sincerity and contrition. It manifested his sorrow while nourishing and fulfilling it. The ancient Church would have found it scandalous to reconcile a sinner before he had given adequate proof of his contrition and before he had been sufficiently punished for his crime. The practice does not spring from a juridical view of affairs, but from a realistic vision of *human truth* which is indispensable to an authentic love of God. Man is not an angel, and he can only love God with his spiritual and carnal heart — with his will, of course, but also with the sensitivity of a flesh and blood being.[18]

---

18. Cf. the insistence of the precept of charity in Mt 22, 37 and other similar passages.

The After-Effects of Penance

We have made several allusions to the problems that continued to weigh on the penitent after his reconciliation. These after-effects were of an exterior order and varied according to time and place. The basic notion involved a certain dishonorable status, from which arose the custom of refusing holy orders to a former penitent. Other consequences were even more chafing in the Christian's daily life. The punishment gradually came to be standardized and, in time, it amounted to inflicting the penitent with one of the more severe types of "monastic" regimens. Besides fasts, humiliations and macerations, the penitent was sometimes obliged to abandon certain trades after completing his satisfaction and always before its termination. The married were obliged to observe continence during penance. Once having passed the way of the *ordo poenitentium,* that special "class" of the faithful — the pardoned sinner and those submitted to penance — was held to obligations which practically led to a monk-like existence *in* the world.

Conclusion

To characterize this penitential discipline in a succinct formula demands stress on the fact that it constituted an *exceptional regimen.* The extraordinary measures employed adequately manifest its severity. Such circumstances did not result by chance. The primitive Church, in the vigor of her young faith and in her God-centered hope, made the Lord the very focus of the life of the faithful. The intransigence of this exclusive charity occasionally led to a certain disparagement of "this world." Hence, the primitive Church considered the serious sin of one of her members a monstrosity. Attention was called to the crime by setting up for its cure a procedure that was exceptional in its demands and its rigor.

The penance just described disappeared at a given moment in history. We need only refer to its end in passing, since we shall be obliged to return to the matter when presenting the discipline that replaced it. At any rate, from the fourth or fifth to the tenth centuries, the old rite was swept away in favor of the prevailing type of penance. Introduced and propagated by the Irish monks, it rapidly spilled across Europe. Our significant task is to scrutinize history in order to discern the reasons for this upheaval. What caused the change?

A preliminary response would entail taking into account the theory that old-style penance disappeared because massive invasions shattered the cultural and social universe of the lower Roman Empire where primitive Christianity, that of the Fathers of the Church and the first great councils, had flourished. Under this theory, the overthrow of the sociological structures can explain the change in discipline; the Christianity of Athanasius and Ambrose disappeared because the empire of Constantine and Theodosius collapsed; the death of this Christianity was brought about not by the extinction of Christian people, but by the breakup of the disciplinary regimen it had forged.

However attractive the solution just described may appear, and despite the element of undeniable truth that it contains, the taproot of the evolution obviously remains untouched by such political considerations. While there was a very definite sociological background to the transformation penance underwent, it was not the great invasions but the wholesale conversion of the empire preceding them that explains our transformation. To put it bluntly, we can say that the old-style penance did not die under the blows of the barbarians but rather collapsed under its own weight.

Diagnostic Difficulties

A definite judgment in the matter is difficult since the two events occurred almost simultaneously. The empire was converted during the first quarter of the fourth century; the barbarian invasions broke loose in the early years of the fifth century. A careful analysis reveals the influence of Christianity gaining visibly from the year 200. Afterward, the barbarians became a threat to the Roman world. Furthermore, the most valuable evidence we possess concerning the transitions from one type of penance to another comes from regions where the old world, the *ancien régime,* continues to survive vigorously in habits and customs. These same regions were submerged by invasions and, politically speaking, they were included in the barbarian kingdom. Such overlapping of trends complicates the task of tracing the causes of the event under examination.

How to Settle the Question?

Perhaps we can support what was said above, that the very success of primitive Christianity led to the disappearance of ancient penance. The fact is easily explained. We possess the most accurate information about the regions of Gaul and northern Italy where the old-style world survived most successfully. It is obvious in the case of Provence at the beginning of the sixth century, and we are abundantly documented on this area, thanks to the works of Césaire d'Arles and the canonical decisions taken under his inspirations, pastors appear to have been driven against the wall. On the one hand, the list of sins calling for public penance had become much longer. There was even a tendency to consider a series of slight offenses as the equivalent of a serious sin requiring sacramental absolution. Penance had simply become more universal. Many bishops stressed this point when addressing their flocks. The latter, as a rule, appear to have been unmoved by the exhortations, and their conduct is understandable. If they submitted to penance and subsequently fell back into their bad habits, they would be excluded definitively from the life of the Church, for the principle of a unique penance remained steadfast, despite the discreet action of Roman pontiffs who were constant in their wish that the moribund (*in extremis*) not be abandoned without reconciliation and viaticum. When this point was finally won (and it was not easily conceded), other penitents upon a second fall continued to be excluded from the Church until their deathbed confession. Understandably, the great mass of Christians were no longer docile in accepting the after-effects of penance. Very few were inclined to abandon commerce or a military career, or to adopt the practice of perfect continence, or to become monks or to lead a monklike existence in the world.

Another situation affords an even more piquant detail: the very bishop who vehemently exhorted his flock to enroll under the penitential banners was the first person to recoil if too many of the faithful took him at his word. Young people — men and women in the flower of youth — hesitated to submit to penance, even when they should have done so, since youth, as everyone knows, is the age of passion. A young man would be foolhardy to assume that, once absolved, he could continue to live continently; therefore, he felt it would be imprudent to attempt such a feat. Local councils gradually discouraged the practice. At this point, the difficulty was how to determine the age suitable for penance. The delicacy of the situation was perceived by St. Avitus of Vienne, after a droll episode involving a certain gentleman from Grenoble named Vincomal. The latter's bishop, unsure of general principles in counseling potential penitents, maliciously sent the gentleman to the metropolitan. The moral of the story seems to be that when all is said and done, youth is more a question of temperament than of gray hair, since the latter does not necessarily rule out a gay heart and warm blood. Penance was not recommended even to the elderly who had a penchant toward fast living, for a relapse was almost certain in such cases.

What conclusion can be drawn from this state of affairs? A large part of the community came to live on the sacramental borderline, or even in a state of sacrilege. Many people were certainly in need of penance but they did not dare present themselves through fear of the sacrament's harshness, or because the bishop foreseeing the possibility of a relapse, did not wish to admit them. Thus the *ordo poenitentium* involved frequently only the most fervent Christians for whom penance was a pious practice rather than a necessity. The extremely devout did not fear penitential austerities and were eager to embrace a quasi-monastic existence. Since registration on the penitential lists was an impediment to holy orders, the clergy was recruited from among the very pious. While the situation may appear logical when viewed within an immediate framework, it is extremely illogical when placed in the general context of ancient penance. The sacrament, far from being the refuge of notorious sinners, became a devotional practice of the pious, engendering a kind of third order or secular institute.

Reasons for the Anomaly

Obviously, the situation was singularly paradoxical and could not persist. Some attempt to explain the enigma by contending that the ancient regimen of penance was conceived by and for small communities of fervent Christians. In their view, the institution reflected the life conditions of small but intensely religious groups. While grave sins were held to be possible – the most primitive Christian experience in the Pauline community of Corinth was on record to remind posterity of human weakness – serious falls were nevertheless regarded as an extremely remote possibility. Furthermore, the very system of self-accusation (or the possibility of being denounced) and the machinery set up for the culprit's amendment and re-entrance to grace point to the operational structure of a fraternal organization united by a common faith and hope, whose members knew each other well enough to feel mutually responsible for each other's personal welfare.

This solidarity was certainly strengthened by the sociological pressure on the minority from the surrounding "world," foreign and hostile in its paganism, but seductive in terms of power and culture. Christian faith was condemned, it would seem, to a daily regimen requiring courage and even heroism. Life required that one go straight to the heart of the matter without concern for trifles. The radical choice of God and Christ was expressed spontaneously in the conviction, already abroad for a considerable time, that Christ's return was imminent. The old-style penance participated in this climate of ardent tension so characteristic of the period of "interim morality" (to employ an expression coined to convey the notion that the time of terrestrial pilgrimage remaining for the Church to complete could be no more than a provisional interval). Despite the excess apparent in this vision of the situation (and it becomes more obvious when systematized and made to serve as a key for the general interpretation of all the events of primitive Christianity), the approach nevertheless contributes insight into the truth and consequently enables us to grasp the spirit of ancient penance.

It is less astonishing, then, that the penitential institution appeared inadequate before the pastoral perspectives presented by the massive thrust of converts. With Christianity in the process of becoming a major force within the city, it is conceivable that the conviction of the masses, however sincere it may have been, did not constitute heroism. Even before, when the empire rallied to Christianity in the second century, and when long periods of tranquility saw considerable progress among the Christian masses, such encouraging developments were invariably followed by the disheartening phenomenon of persecutions giving rise to numerous apostates. When the crisis had passed, the renegades sought pardon in haste. They were sincere believers, but they were not heroes. This pattern of developments explains the perplexity of a figure such as St. Césaire d'Arles, when confronted by a flock which, while not wishing to forget heaven, was emphatic in refusing to renounce the world completely. The ingenious artifice, which consisted in deferring baptism or penance until one's dying moment, was a manifestation of a prevalent attitude. For practical purposes, it proves that the old system was a failure in many ways. Yet, in taking leave of the old rite, it would be unjust not to call attention to its demanding grandeur and the simple but powerful beauty of its ceremonies, so expressive of the holiness of the People of God and so indicative of their union.

6

How Modern Penance Grew

Our hero's life story reads like a fairy tale. A young Christian was captured by pagan pirates and carried into slavery in a foreign country. He escaped and went to live near a pious bishop who both initiated him to monastic discipline, recently introduced from the Orient, and elevated him to the episcopacy. Freshly consecrated, our young bishop returned to the land of his former captivity, charged with the mission of implanting the Church there. Upon his death, it was conceded that he had been more than successful in the difficult task. However, this narrative constitutes neither novel nor legend; it is the authentic life story of St. Patrick, apostle and patron of Christian Ireland.

What interests us in the episode are the very broad powers given to Patrick for the transformation of the far-off land into a Christian kingdom. In the middle of the fifth century, at the moment when the old world was reeling under the onslaught of the barbarian invasions, Ireland appeared to be an extremely remote European frontier. The missionary bishop could rely on no other forces than his own. Patrick's conduct proves that he was deeply influenced by his prolonged residence near Bishop Germain d'Auxerre, the great promoter of the monastic movement in Gaul. Such a formation would account for the way the Irish monasteries were founded — and they rapidly became numerous and prosperous. Contact with Bishop Germain is also reflected in the organizational aspects of Patrick's administration. The monastery served as the nerve-center of the diocese, with the abbot as bishop ordaining certain of his monks for the pastoral needs of an area.

The most outstanding feature of the Irish Church was a new practice of penance, for Patrick and his disciples never implanted the calssic discipline, but forged a new one by grafting the sacrament onto a practice of the monks of old. The latter, more commonly known as the fathers of the desert, had inaugurated what has come to be known as spiritual direction for the formation of novices and the spiritual welfare of the faithful. In keeping with the custom, an elderly, experienced monk received the younger man's manifestation of conscience, carefully listening to the account of temptations and faults in order to counsel, to reprove and to correct. There was no trace of a sacrament in the beginning, since neither the senior monk nor his younger colleagues were priests. By a stroke of extraordinarily bold genius, Patrick revived the venerable custom and made it the rite of sacramental penance in which the senior monk was the priest and the penitent opened his conscience to the former, receiving from him not only efficacious spiritual direction, but pardon for his sins as well.

Characteristics

Patrick's decision was of cardinal importance. In keeping with the practice of the ancient discipline, public penance thus became *private*. Penitential expiation was no longer executed before the entire community, for now the penitent accused himself secretly to the priest. To these major innovations, two others of even greater significance were added. On the one hand, it was no longer a question of a unique penance, because the sacrament, far from being incapable of reiteration, now had no fixed limit. On the other hand, the famous penitential "after-effects" disappeared, a logical sequence to the preceding development. These changes show that penance was no longer an exceptional measure. Thus administered, the sacrament was not reserved to a determined category of serious sins. Patrick's innovation permitted the Irish monks to emerge from the blind alley where shepherds elsewhere in Christianity continued to be blocked. Furthermore, the sacrament thus gained its full extension and was put on a more suitable basis in keeping with the humble conditions characteristic of the daily life of the ordinary Christian. The historian can thus join St. Patrick in remarking somewhat familiarly that the sacrament of penance had at last found its "cruising speed."

We must admire the vigorous good sense and lucid realism which the apostle displayed when confronted by this most per-

plexing problem. Completely alone in the beginning and confronted by rough tribes addicted to brutal habits and destructive
vices, but who were nevertheless frank, he had the discernment
to extract the greatest value from his treasure, the sacrament of
penance. It was no longer a question of the exceptional reconciliation of an occasional fallen member of the redeemed remnant
in its thrust toward *parousia,* but rather a matter of the exercise
of the sacrament of mercy: that of the slow, gradual conversion
of the Christian, combined with an effective means of forming
the Christian's conscience, while gently and patiently pushing
him along the road to holiness.

There was now no question of the bishop being tainted with
laxity, since harsh satisfaction was required. This in turn demanded another innovation: instead of withholding absolution
until the penitent had completed his penance, pardon was accorded immediately after the self-accusation. To understand this
change, it suffices to remember that the Irish monk-priest was
a kind of itinerant pastor who went from one parish to another.
This situation gave rise to picturesque details. Since ancient
Christianity attached great importance to the maintenance of a
degree of proportion between the gravity of the fault and the
severity of its expiation, and since each of these good Irish
priests could not be an accomplished moralist, a memory aid
was drawn up for the confessor as insurance against disorder.
This aid was called a *liber poenitentialis* (a penitential book) or
simply a "penitential." The confessor had merely to total the
penances due, and he was probably instructed to make adjust-
ments in those cases where the total would surpass the normal
man's possibilities to fulfillment. A candidly ingenious system of
commutations (a shorter but more severe penance in exchange
for one which was less oppressive but longer) was invented to
circumvent this difficulty. However, when some quick-thinking
but less pious Christians began to divide their penitential works
among the poor who were duly stipended for their service, the
Church quickly condemned the introduction of this division of
labor into the sacramental system.

Spread of Irish Penance

The situation could have remained static — Ireland following the new-style penance and the rest of Europe the old — if the robust piety of the Celtic monks had not led them to envisage an astonishing ascetical exercise. Being excessively attached to their homeland, exile was the greatest misfortune they could imagine. From this attitude sprang the idea of voluntarily going abroad for the love of Christ. Thus was born the *peregrinatio pro Christo,* or what we may call the "pilgrimage for the Lord." It was through such inspiration that one of the Irish monks, Columban, disembarked about the year 600 in Merovingian Gaul where Christian customs were no longer flourishing. The saint was particularly shocked by the state of penance which had fallen into oblivion. The old rite had ostensibly continued to disintegrate. The Franks were not acquainted with the Irish practice, and we can imagine that they were not prepared to accept it easily, but Columban was undaunted. He immediately set about to re-evangelize the country and his efforts produced excellent results. Several monastic foundations remain even today as landmarks of his course and as testimony of his influence: Luxeuil in the Jura, Bobbio in northern Italy where he died and Saint-Gall in Switzerland, named after a disciple who was responsible for its establishment. The Merovingian lands (in addition to Gaul and Switzerland, they included sections of the Rhineland and of Thuringia) and northern Italy were soon won to the new custom. Other countries held back, such as Visigoth Spain where Arian invaders and their king had been converted to Catholicism. The latter development resulted in a curious brand of Christianity, strongly organized under the direction of national councils and the metropolitan of Toledo. The Spaniards, having remained faithful to the ancient usages, rejected the Irish innovations with disdain. It seems that a certain conciliar statement which had sharply attacked the new practice of penance and branded it as "repugnant," was directed at the activity of a certain Celtic monk who toiled on Spanish soil. In any case, the

Arabs destroyed the kingdom in a single battle in 711 and immediately took over almost the whole of Spanish territory.

One would expect Rome, always solicitous to maintain tradition, to have resisted the new-style penance. However, by the end of the eighth century the Eternal City was absorbed in a great work of reform carried on in close association with the powerful king of the Franks, Charlemagne, who was soon to become the emperor of the West. This shrewd statesman possessed unusual organizational skill, and he was soon fired with the double ambition of converting his kingdom into a first-class State and of restoring Christianity to its full splendor. His liturgists toiled to achieve unity in customs and religious rites, even as their colleagues struggled toward a common goal in more profane domains. Unity amounted to adopting the usages of Rome. However, it sometimes happened that certain local customs, Gallic or Germanic, slipped in to contaminate a Roman ritual in one detail or another. In the case of penance, while the Carolingian liturgists practiced a kind of syncretism, their first concern was to restore the ancient rite, the only one officially known at Rome. But the new style, having become ingrained habit, could not be eradicated by mere decree. Thus, by the time of the late Middle Ages, the ancient practice and the Irish rite had achieved a juxtaposition, their respective jurisdictional areas being sharply defined according to the well-known principle: "A public sin requires public penance; private sins, private penance." Apparently the effort to restore the old rite smacked of undue concern for tradition.

When examining the penitential practices of the era, a word must be said of the frequent use of excommunication, since it was often inflicted on those who were guilty of serious faults. The penalty must not be confused with the sacrament of penance, even though, in its exterior forms, excommunication somewhat resembles the first step of solemn penance. Given the possibility of employing other punitive measures and leaving aside the learned classifications of canonists and theologians, it seems a fortunate thing that private penance continued to figure prominently and finally dominated. Public penance had become a remnant of the past, bereft of meaning in the daily life of the Christian faithful.

Final Developments

Renewal of Christian life and thought following the Gregorian reform prepared the way for the great centuries, the twelfth and the thirteenth, which were so significant in the life of the Church. This period saw features of private penance become stable in two sectors.

In the first place, during the first decades of the thirteenth century, the form of absolution, expressed until then in the form of a prayer (the deprecatory formula of which the *Misereatur* following the *Confiteor* may be cited as a typical example), was changed to the indicative form *Ego te absolvo*. The reader should be aware that we are limiting our consideration to the practical level. Leaving aside the subject of indulgences and that of general absolution, it is relevant to remark that all these developments exerted a mutual influence, one upon the other.

The second innovation of importance came from the Fourth Lateran Council in 1215. Innocent III, in his presiding role, promulgated the following decree: "Each member of the faithful of both sexes who has reached the age of discretion must confess his sins at least once a year to his own parish priest, and accomplish, within the measure of his means, the penance which is imposed. . . ." This decision was certainly instrumental in bringing frequent confession into common usage. Most opportunely, the foundation during the same epoch of the first mendicant orders, Franciscan and Dominican, was to provide devoted propagators of the practice.

It was a golden age for theology; in addition, a parallel evolution occurred simultaneously, involving the application of principles. The importance of sacramental absolution and the Church's power, known as "the power of the keys,"[19] gradually

---

19. Cf. Mt 16, 19.

came to be held in greater esteem. Emphasis had formerly been placed (and quite properly so) on interior repentance inspired by the Holy Spirit, but this was done at the expense of the priest's role, for he was merely to witness the pardon accorded by God in the name of the Church. The timely reaction tended to underline the true power of the sacrament and the decisive role played by the priest when giving absolution in God's name.

Conclusion

We shall not pursue the history of the sacrament further, since its main outline has now been adequately sketched. If one reflects on the outstanding features of this history, he cannot avoid being impressed by the two very different forms of administration which the sacrament assumed. Has the time arrived for yet another change? To be candid, we must admit that penance is under attack today because of its individualistic and inhospitable character. Many of our contemporaries are ill at ease when they approach the confessional, and they are generous and sincere Catholics. This discomfort, or even repugnance, is experienced by more people than one might imagine. The sentiment cannot merely be classified as pride or some other vice; that explanation is too often made with an unconcern as gratuitous as it is unjust when objections are raised.

A certain number of the faithful, especially priests who are keenly aware of developments, may reflect with nostalgia on the former rite of public penitence. However, caution must be exercised in this matter. While it is impossible to deny the grandeur of the former rite, certain weaknesses were nevertheless inherent in it. First of all, we must remember that, in the long run, the practice proved unworkable. Is a stronger argument needed? As compared to the former practice, the private and confidential character of today's sacrament, even if it appears formidable to some, does correspond to a refinement of conscience, to a sharper perception of the uniqueness of each personality and the respect which is due it. In addition, the fact that we can approach the sacrament for our daily sins, that it is indefinitely reiterative, represents a considerable progress over its ancestor.

Aside from the efficacy of the grace proper to the sacrament, other advantages of the present-day rite include the powerful aids in the formation of conscience and the fostering of spiritual growth. We must admit that our present practice has an Achilles heel, in that the penitent scarcely senses the presence of the Church, the People of God whom he acquired for himself by Christ's paschal victory. While this loss neither affects the essential core of the sacrament nor threatens its validity, the symbolism of the gesture has unfortunately become so withered that one scarcely recognizes penance as the sacrament of the community. The faithful do not sense the Church's presence except naïvely from the fact that the confessional is erected there; they have no acute awareness of the living Church of which the structure is only a symbol. Although the penitent recites the prayer, "I confess to Almighty God," and asks pardon "of all the saints," does he realize that it is a question not only of those in heaven but of his brethren as well? It is very doubtful, and even if the penitent does have a vague awareness of these elements, the role of the People of God has become insignificant and accessory.

In view of the changing man which the contemporary world is producing, should Vatican Council II have prescribed a revision of the penitential rite with a view to rendering it more expressive? The task is a delicate one, but it would seem to demand attention. The Church must ever examine her conscience in a spirit of ceaseless rediscovery of the unfathomable riches which she carries within her.

Chapter Seven

THE ECCLESIAL DIMENSION OF PENANCE

PAUL ANCIAUX, O.S.B.

There has been much talk in recent years of the ecclesial dimension of the redemption. When we apply this idea to penance, we probe the sacramental significance and importance of Christian penance; we come to grasp the relation between the mystery of the Church and the sacrament: we see how penance must be consecrated, confirmed, and brought to perfection through the Church. In this study the Church will signify the whole Christ, the fullness of Christ understood and realized in his Mystical Body, the hierarchy and community of the faithful.

Our study has two parts: (1) we will seek to understand how the Church is the foundation of the sacrament of penance; (2) we will show how the efficacy of this sacrament admits of an ecclesial dimension. Through such considerations as these, we come to a better understanding of our faith in the mystery of the Church and pinpoint its sacramental reality; for the sacraments are, in fact, the efficacious celebrations of the mystery of Christ seen as the working out of the redemption through the Church.

Church Foundation

Confession is man's expression of a conversion of heart, by which he returns to the God who calls to him in Christ. Christ's own preaching begins with a call to such a conversion: "Repent, for the kingdom of heaven is at hand" (*Mt* 4, 17).

Sacred Scripture contains a revelation of the mystery of sin, of human weakness and cowardice of a kind that may on first contact discourage the faithful. Sin is like a shadow in salvation history, a shadow that grows darker as the light of God's love enters the world. The mystery of iniquity can only be understood at the foot of the cross, for only he who has been struck with God's love as manifested in the risen Lord could have the courage to repent and abandon his sins. Why has the modern world lost the sense of sin? Is it not because faith in the love of God the Father has been lost? Those who have not faith in a Savior do not have the courage to call themselves sinners. They are forced to deny sin, to create a theory of morality in which sin does not exist.

To understand the stages in the evolution of the theology of sin we must first become aware of the progression of the revelation of the mystery of sin in salvation history. Old and New Testaments alike insist that sin has at once a social or community as well as a personal dimension.

The social bearing of sin in Scripture is better understood in terms of the covenant between God and his people. Men are not only created in God's image and invited to share his life, but they are called to a new community in Christ, who redeemed them from sin, sin that destroys unity among men. The more we insist upon man's utter subjection to sin, the more God's love appears; or, to put it another way, the better we understand Christ's redemption, the more sharply do we see the true dimensions of sin. St. Paul has stressed the darkness of sin as an antitype to the mystery of Christ's redemption. All are saved by the grace of God in Christ just as all have sinned in Adam.

Sin, Personal and Social

Revelation indicates how the personal and social aspects of sin are essentially related. God has called each man to be a member of the human race and to help in the building up of the family of men. He gathered his people, reunited them in the Qahal of the Exodus and in the Church of the new dispensation. Sin, the refusal of God's call, not only undermines man's relation to God but breaks down the relations among men themselves. Called to help build up a community of love, man is attracted by the double goal of love of God and of his fellow man. Sin is a refusal to love and, by its very nature, a disintegration, rupture, discord. The love which dominates *salvation* history makes its way to the heart of the individual (personal vocation), calling him to establish the family of God's people (community vocation).

The divine plan can be carried out only through Christ, the head of the new humanity. In God's new covenant with men, man's faith in the Lord Jesus is ratified by incorporation into the Church. Baptism, the sacrament of faith, signifies a man's entry into the community of faith, the Mystical Body. The Christian vocation, the mission of the baptized, has an ecclesial dimension: to take part in the work of Christ, the redemption of all men.

This community dimension of the Christian life gives us an insight into the real significance of the sacraments. Considered from too individualistic a point of view, they are frequently reduced to mere instruments of grace, guaranteeing eternal salvation. But the sacraments can have their full meaning only in the light of the New Covenant. They are the foundations of the Church, destined to structure and build up the Christian community for the working out of the redemption. They can be understood only in relation to the Church because they are ecclesial realities, acts of the Church, engaging the whole Christ, head and body, hierarchy and faithful.

Church and Sacrament

Let us consider this ecclesial dimension as the foundation of the sacrament of penance. When one of the faithful confesses, he comes to the Church to win by its mediation full reconciliation with God. As a member of the Church, a man submits through his faith and his baptism to the penance imposed in confession. The repentance of the baptized person who confesses is the first part of the sacramental action. By the intervention of a minister of the Church acting in the name of Christ and the community, this conversion is brought to completion and sealed with absolution.

Penance has traditionally been called second baptism because the first conversion to Christ is confirmed by the sacramental action of baptism. Penance, then, as a reaffirmation of this conversion, supposes in the penitent, besides the baptismal character, a faith in Christ and the Church expressed in the humble confession of sins.

This faith in Christ, supposed in every confession, is the foundation of the sacramental action. This action takes place in an atmosphere of faith in Christ, who instituted it and whose power underlies the efficacy of its grace. Christ is the true *actor sacramentorum;* it is he who encounters sinful man in the sacraments, to re-establish or deepen a man's union with God and his neighbor. Such, moreover, is the profound meaning of the teaching about the institution of the sacraments by Christ. It is not a question of the invention or of the precise determination of external rites, but rather of the origin of the saving power of the sacraments in the Church.

Ecclesial Actions

In the evolution of its external form penance showed elements which are common in the history of humanity: conversion and expiatory confession. The typically Christian content of, and the efficacy proper to, the sacrament of penance depend entirely on the will and the activity of Christ. According to a juridical formula, Christ is said to have merited all graces and to distribute them fully in the sacraments of the Church. This juridical formulation is often understood in such a way that the sacraments are reduced to quasi-magical channels of grace. This view must continually be corrected by the personalist and existential dimension of the sacrament: Christ as the basis of the sacraments, the vivifying spirit, the mediator between God and man. By his Incarnation and the mysteries of his life, the Son of God becomes Lord in the power and fullness of the Holy Spirit. The essential relation between Christ and the sacramental actions of the Church should be realized in its full import. Christ is the foundation of the sacraments to the end of time. Patristic and theological tradition make clear that the merits of the minister do not explain the efficacy of the sacraments, but the efficacy is explained by the power of the Lord who acts through the minister. He, however, must have the intention to do what the Church does and must celebrate the rites according to the prescriptions of the Church.

The sacraments are ecclesial actions, expressing an active presence of Christ who gives life to the relationship between minister, priest, and penitent faithful. In carrying out the work of uniting men with God and their fellow men, the priest represents both Christ and the community of the faithful. The community aspect, this intervention of the community through the ministry of the hierarchy in the sacrament of penance, was much more clearly expressed in early forms of ecclesiastical penance (or penitential discipline). Then it was clear how the whole community had to support each of its penitents through prayer. If the intervention of the whole Church in favor of repentant sinners is less obvious in the rites today, it is no less essential. The repentance of the sinner is supported and guaranteed by the fervor of the whole group. The sacramental reality of penance supposes and expresses the communion of saints in Christ.

Priest's Role

The priest not only represents the community but acts in the Lord's name as a member of the hierarchy, charged with a particular mission and endowed with special powers. By the priest's intervention the promises of Christ are guaranteed, and the penitent receives the pledge of a full reconciliation with God through restoration to the ecclesial and Eucharistic communion.

A sinner's conversion can be perfectly achieved only within the Church, for he returns to God by the priest's ministry and by this ministry his liberation from sin is achieved. Here we have the answer to a common objection: If sins are forgiven by repentance, why confess them? Why does the Church impose confession to reconcile the sinner? If we answer that the sinner receives "more" grace, we ignore the principal point of the sacraments, the specific character of sacramental grace.

The complete understanding of why we need confession and absolution is to be found in the part the Church plays. Tradition and the fathers are clear on this point, though its complete formulation has been slow to develop. St. Thomas expresses this truth in the following way: Christ as doctor of souls acts in two ways: he calls to the sinner interiorly through the Spirit; he completes through his minister what he has begun in the sinner's heart. The intervention of the minister "brings about" and "completes" the sinner's conversion so that there is full reconciliation with God and liberation from sin. But how is this completion to be understood?

Efficacy of Penance

To grasp the sacramental dimension of the efficacy of Christian penance and the importance of the Church's intervention, we take into account specific aspects or perspectives of the New Covenant. We must consider the characteristic meaning of the grace of the New Testament, which cannot be received in its fullness except in the Church through the sacraments of the New

Covenant. Baptism is the culmination of the initial conversion to Christ by incorporation into the Church, the Body of Christ, the People of God. By baptism a person is united with Christ not only interiorly by faith but "corporally," as St. Thomas says. This corporal union is founded upon the ecclesial union and celebrated in a particular manner in the Eucharist.

In confession the sinner addresses himself to the Church. He confesses to the priest because he sincerely believes he encounters Christ through the Church just as it has been the Church who has suffered harm through his sins. He submits to the penance of the Church in order to re-establish communion and restore unity. It is important to help the faithful realize the full meaning of their coming to Church to confession. By approaching the confessional a person affirms his state as a sinner in the process of being redeemed, his willingness to repent in the Church, and his faith in ecclesial mediation. By his penitential confession the baptized asks the aid of the community, against whom he has sinned, and the intervention of the minister in the name of Christ and the Church. By his repentance he expresses his desire to take his place in the community again, to live more faithfully as a Christian, and to participate more deeply in the life and mission of the Church. As the external penance is an expression of the interior, the interior is made efficacious and guaranteed through the Church.

In the light of these general perspectives, we may ask what is the efficacy of confession and absolution in perfect and in imperfect contrition.

Perfect Contrition

We note that for St. Thomas perfect contrition was not determined by its motive as such, but by the presence of sanctifying grace (ontological perfection of penance) and by the intensity of the conversion (psychological aspect). This intensity does not function at an emotional level but on the level of that spiritual activity that we refer to as the setting a basic goal or making a profound choice with regard to sin or God. Penance achieves its true meaning when a man regrets his sins as an evil separating him form God; he loves God above all created things. This psychological aspect of Thomistic theology corresponds to the modern concern with the fundamental goal or final end to which all actions and tendencies are more or less consciously directed. In the measure that his fundamental choice corresponds to the necessary orientation of human existence toward God and man, a human being is justified by divine grace. But if one subordinates his life to a created value, preferring it to God, he is so basically disordered that he cannot receive grace.

Already Sacramental

It is true that the sinner receives sanctifying grace when his repentance is sufficiently intense, but can we say, then, that the efficacy of the sacrament is somehow anticipated? Authentic repentance, including as it does the determination to confess, is already sacramental in the sense that it is the first step in the sacrament just as absolution is the final one. The grace received as a result of perfect contrition is already sacramental although it is not complete. The full sacramental grace can only be had through the mediation of the Church and by one's genuine reinstatement within the community.

The sacramental grace of penance affords a quality, a richness, a fullness of sanctifying grace that can be had only within the Church. The sinner is again able to participate in the typically Christian actions of the sacraments, to take part in the work of redemption as a member of the body of Christ. The necessity of confessing a mortal sin before going to communion is not a meaningless vestige of former ecclesiastical practices; rather it brings out the true meaning of reconciliation with the Church. This reconciliation with the Church is the sacramental reality (*sacramentum et res*) and brings full reconciliation with God.

Only by stressing the ecclesial dimension of sacramental

grace, the theological virtues, and the Christian life, will we be able to bring the faithful to see that the necessity of confession is a genuine corollary of the necessity of baptism. A misunderstanding of the ecclesial nature of the sacraments is manifest in some of the faithful who, when they hear that pagans in good faith have grace, wonder why anyone should be baptized. But the sacraments are realities which have meaning only in the mystery of Christ. They are continuations of the action of Christ in his Church to incorporate the believers in his redemptive work and have them take part in the building up of the kingdom of God.

We begin to see that sacramental grace is more than just an increase of sanctifying grace. It is a new and more intense participation in the community of love in Christ and a deepening incorporation in the mission of the Church. The quality peculiar to sacramental grace is found only in union with the Church through those specific acts of the Christian community, the sacraments of Christ. We can also better understand how confession is the perfection of the perfect contrition of the Christian. Perfect contrition, manifesting its desire to do God's will by submitting to ecclesiastical penance, is the beginning of the sacrament within the Christian, and the priest's absolution perfects it.

Imperfect Contrition

Between the case of a sinner who only pretends to be sorry and the man with perfect contrition, we have the case of the sinner whose sorrow, though sincere, is not of itself deep enough to obtain sanctifying grace. What happens in the confession of such a man? A little reflection will show us how complex the reality and efficacy of the sacraments are. We must, in fact, distinguish many aspects in this living process of conversion from the state of mortal sin to the effective realization of one's reconciliation with God and the Church.

The tradition formulated by St. Thomas and the Council of

Trent teaches that a sinner can go to confession if his sorrow is sincere even though in itself it is insufficient to receive sanctifying grace. If the person acknowledges his faults and indicates an intention of doing penance and avoiding sins in the future, he will obtain the grace of pardon by this sacramental action. Imperfect contrition is, in fact, a disposition sufficient for obtaining sacramental grace by confession and absolution.

By its nature confession is the expression of the conversion and repentance of the sinner. By the avowal of his sins, he is invited to hate them and to set aright his fundamental goal by placing God above all things. The Church helps the sinner's initial good will of submitting to ecclesial penance by reinforcing him with the prayer and sacrifice of the community and the minister who acts in the name of Christ and the Church. The priest's advice ought to encourage the penitent and help him find the means of deepening his sorrow. The penance the priest imposes is meant to sustain and deepen the penitent's sorrow. If the priest decides the penitent is sincere in his contrition and resolution of amendment, he gives him absolution, thus reconciling him with the Church and allowing him to take part in the sacramental acts of the Christian community. He is encouraged to live the life and mission of the Church in the service of God and love of his neighbor. By thus involving himself more and more in the Christian life, he deepens his conversion. Confession and absolution have been typically Christian means and guarantees of his full reconciliation with the Church and with God. Through the mediation of the Church, the sinner, involving himself more and more in the Christian community, perfects his repentance and accomplishes his complete conversion.

Such reflections in the area of the efficacy of Christian penance invite us to consider confession as an essential part of the Christian life. Too often the sacraments are isolated, cut off from their foundations and reduced to a practical formalism that smacks of magic. Confession, like the other sacraments, is part of the whole Christian life. It is the first expression, the first sign of the return of sinful man to God and his brothers through the

Church. The sinner comes to the priest because he wants to be reconciled with the Church by taking up with renewed fervor his place in the community. This Christian way of life, this conversion to God, is achieved through the Church and expressed chiefly in the sacramental actions. By the sacraments, in fact, Christ realizes the redemption among men of each age and makes the New Covenant between God and men.

Chapter Eight

CONFESSION: PSYCHOLOGY IS NOT ENOUGH

LOUIS MONDEN, S.J.

The Confession of Sins

Among the deep-seated causes of the present crisis in the sacrament of penance, the confession of sins as it is practiced today
is a very specific difficulty. If so many people reject sacramental
confession and long to cast off their sinfulness in a direct meeting with God, the reason is not so much that they no longer feel
the need for a visible sign. Confessing one's guilt is an archety-
pal experience, one so deeply anchored in the very structure of
the human psyche that the need for it will never disappear. But
modern man no longer sees in the confession of sins as practiced
in the sacrament of penance a real "signifying" of his guilt. And
that authenticity has vanished because the materiality of the sign
has been so much stressed, endowed with such autonomy, that
it absorbs the whole attention, leaving no scope for the "signification."

Awareness of the psychic complexity of the sinful action may
force us to experience the confession of sins more authentically
as the sign that it is. The priest in the confessional is no public

attorney looking for an exact reconstruction of the crime, nor is
he a psychiatrist who must decide how accountable the defend-
ant is or a psychotherapist who must rid the penitent of his
complexes and his unconscious inhibitions. He is one who, in
God's name, utters God's releasing word over the sin. What he
must know and what the penitent must tell him is not an adequate description of the sinner's situation, a perfectly true insight into the extent of his sinfulness. What the penitent tells
him is only a sign of what he tells God. The confession of sins
is a sincere signifying, to the extent of his insight and according
to certain rules prescribed by the Church, of his being a sinner
before God. Hence he confesses more (or often, unknowingly,
much less) than what he expresses in words. The sins he confesses are only a sign and a very imperfect expression of what
God forgives him. And the priest's judgment, his human meeting
with this sinfulness, is only a sign — often a very imperfect and
shadowy sign — of the merciful salvific judgment of God, which
is not tied to the limitations and mistakes of our human judgment. Both penitent and priest may be wrong in their judgment
about the confessed sins; in fact they often are — much more
often than our textbooks of moral theology suppose. If both are
in good faith, this mistake does not matter at all, for God forgives not what has been confessed, but what has been signified
by the confession.

However various the forms in which the sacrament of penance has taken shape within the Church over the centuries, they
all have one point in common: they always comprise a "signifying" confession by the sinning member of the Church, not only
of his sinfulness in general, but of the sins he personally has
committed. Hence the Council of Trent declares that by divine
disposition this "signifying" belongs to the essence of the sacrament (although the expression *jure divino* had not yet acquired
the meaning we assign to it today and was often used for ecclesiastical and even for civil laws).

The very detailed norms for that signifying were first laid
down by the Council of Trent and have since been impressed
upon the faithful: all mortal sins must be confessed with species

and number and also with any circumstances which might modify the nature of the sin. Yet, despite every tendency toward rigidity, even textbook teaching retained enough feeling for the "signifying" function of confession to acknowledge the right of confessor and penitent to deviate from the material completeness of the confession if that completeness would impair the signifying function instead of promoting it. Thus, in the case of the scrupulous penitent, whose anxiety about completeness threatens to smother the religious meaning of the confession of sins. Also for sick or dying persons, whose state of exhaustion makes it desirable that the whole attention and all available spiritual energy should be devoted to a contrite resignation rather than a painstaking effort of memory. Or, again, for the penitent whose relationship to the confessor (member of his family, close collaborator, superior) is such that the human resonances of the confession of some sins would clash too disturbingly with the religious meaning of the act. Should the penitent himself stand in a sinful relation to the confessor, the Church even forbids confession under the most severe penalties, because in such a case the sign cannot possibly reach the required integrity of signification.

Might not a return to a more authentic experiencing of the sign-value of the confession of sins mean for countless people not only a release but also a growth toward religious authenticity? Might they not recover with greater integrity the meaning of confession as a salvific meeting with Christ within the Church, if their examination of conscience were centered in Christ's welcoming love rather than in themselves? The objection to the examination of conscience expressed by a profoundly religious man — "They think they will forget themselves by dint of looking at themselves" — can be met and answered only through such a reorientation of the sacrament toward God.

On the priest's side, too, might not many a confession be better if the questioning were inspired not so much by an anxious solicitude for a materially complete enumeration of sins as by the need to allow the penitent to express as authentically as he can his personal awareness of sin? The questioning might then become more discreet, with a more sensitive respect for the person; it might become the exception rather than the rule, and it would not, as often happens now, destroy rather than promote the authentic sign value of the confession of sins.

Might this not also supply an encouraging solution for the countless "Easter only" confessions of people who are so under-developed religiously that what may perhaps be a vivid awareness of sin can hardly pierce the crust of psychic inhibitions, human respect and secretiveness, and whose confession can be as awkward, yet as eloquent, a sign as the clumsy gestures of their friendship or the stammering words of their declaration of love? It might equally be a welcome solution for the confession practice among non-Westerners; for some highly cultivated Asiatic peoples, for instance, whose whole way of thinking and whose feeling for symbolism is offended by confession in the Western manner.

It is especially in the devotional confession that the problem of the acknowledgment of sins would be considerably aided by a stronger emphasis on the religious sign-value. Where there are no mortal sins to be confessed, there can be no material norm for the confessing of sins. It is guided exclusively by the desire to express, as integrally as possible, the need of meeting the risen Christ with one's burden of sin. The recurrent complaint, "I don't know what to say," or "It's always the same," does not necessarily point to shallowness or lack of self-knowledge; it may equally well be the expression of religious sincerity and a deeper realization of human complexity. The more we experience our sinfulness, the more we also notice the inextricable blending in us of the wheat and the cockle which are to grow together until the final harvest; the more difficult, too, it becomes to express in facts and figures all that is unutterable and unfathomable in ourselves: our inner disorder; the labyrinthine ways of evil in our soul; the tacit compromises with our own cowardice or the conniving acquiescence in that which leads into sin; our refusal to commit ourselves and our pretexts for sloth; our running away from God into dissipation and our attempts to ransom ourselves with devotional practices; the way we ration our generosity and our love of neighbor. The difficulty lies deeper than we generally admit.

The solution for this difficulty should amount to more than technical devices. We are often advised to "personalize" our confessions. This expression is ambiguous. It is often interpreted as a psychological scrutiny, a more exact analysis of our actions. That easily leads to a "psychologizing" of confession, which, to my mind, may have very harmful consequences. When we read some — especially Dutch — books and what they present as a model confession we sometimes wonder whether we have to do with a confession or with a psychological pep talk, and we ask ourselves what function, if any, the final absolution might have in all this. The whole attention is directed toward the subject himself, and if, after a while, the results of confession are no longer psychologically noticeable — this is almost unavoidable in the event of a deeper religious development — the devotional confession will readily be discontinued as devoid of value.

The personalizing of the confession of sins should be attempted not so much along the lines of a psychological clarification of what must be said as in a renewed stress on a more authentic and profound realization of the sign-value of what is said and on the quality of the awareness of sinfulness which expresses itself in that confession. When someone in his examination of conscience, without any effort to fathom his actions in their deeper psychological motivation, succeeds in living his past in religious recollection, out of the deepest root of his being-for-God, there is a good hope that the connaturality of his faith and love with the divine exigency proposed to his life will begin to function as a power of discrimination which will existentially, not psychologically, sift the authentic from the unauthentic elements of his spiritual life.

That line of demarcation will be more difficult to verbalize than a psychological analysis. There are great individual differences in this respect: some are more eloquent than others; some are extroverts, others introverts; there are many other factors at work. Hence, in the concrete confession of sins, this inner realization will be expressed quite differently by different penitents — by some in vivid terms, by others in plain, or even in stereotyped, hardly ever changing formulas. Possibly, as the inner life grows stronger, the same phenomenon may occur for the confession of sins as happens in prayer: it becomes increasingly poor in ideas and in words, it condenses its fullness in a seemingly commonplace expression which nevertheless is for the person in question filled with the plenitude of his experience of life and of God. An attentive listener will be able to detect, within the poverty of such a confession, the unmistakable note of religious authenticity.

When this innermost need of God's saving and purifying presence, the meeting with Christ who has risen and triumphed over sin, is always experienced in living authenticity, less importance will be attached to the psychologically visible results of frequent confession. The routine of an ever returning, almost changeless symbolism will then express and nourish the growing vital intimacy with God, just as the monotonous routine of common life and of loving communion between husband and wife serves as the growing and living symbol of all the seasons of married love. Quite often — more often than psychologists tend to believe — this regularly repeated coinciding with his true self and with the core of his relation with Christ will lead a man even psychologically into decisive moments of break-through and prepare the way for a gradual integration even of his psychic immaturities.

The Address of the Priest

The same difficulty the penitent has in the confession of sins attends the address of the confessor. This address, too, is an intra-sacramental event, and not, in the first instance, an occasion for moral or psychological counseling. What absolution will accomplish in the sinner is anticipated liturgically in the priest's address. It is therefore a sign of the concrete appeal of a merciful God, creating a new life, but also inviting, urging, demanding; of a God who is to meet, in Christ and in the Church, this concrete sinner in his concrete sinfulness.

The priest may use this religiously very intimate moment to give practical advice, to propose certain things, to help develop insight into the problem created by the situation. The function of spiritual direction and moral counseling may be exercised on the occasion of confession.

Yet this function has nothing to do with confession as such, even though historically it has often been associated with it. Furthermore, the priest will not, in most instances, have gathered enough information from the penitent to give safe psychological guidance without endangering the religious character of confession through a long conversation mainly profane in content. A directive given with the best intention, but based on inadequate information, may have exactly the opposite effect, and the penitent, who mistakenly includes it in the sacred content of the sacrament, will often be afraid of disobeying it, lest he should refuse to do what the sacrament itself demands. Thus innumerable conflicts of conscience originate in the platitudes uttered too hastily for complex situations by a well-meaning confessor. Aversion to a conversation forced on him in confession, anxiety about a too human curiosity trying to pry into his intimate affairs, put a damper on many a Christian's enthusiasm for the sacrament of penance and make him unwilling to use it.

Modern man wants to receive this sacrament again in its religious integrity, and we must satisfy his need. This makes it desirable that confession and eventual spiritual direction should be carefully kept apart wherever possible, and that psychological counseling should take place outside the confessional.

From this point of view the restoration of a collective liturgical celebration of confession which, while maintaining the present practice of confession, links it once more with the valuable elements of ancient tradition is to be welcomed as a step forward. Here the danger of psychologizing is reduced to a minimum. The biblical context and the atmosphere of prayer deflect the examination of conscience from excessive attention to self and lead it into a God-centered perspective. The ecclesial dimension of sin and forgiveness is emphasized in a strong and releasing manner. And the priest's address becomes the message of God's merciful word, in the presence of which man cannot help taking up his position on the religious level. The results of this renovation point to an often amazed rediscovery by the faithful of the ecclesial and sacramental meaning of confession, which appears to have been pushed into the background in their former practice of the sacrament.

The "firm purpose of amendment"

Can the same principle of sacramentality that frees confessor and penitent alike from an atmosphere of psychologizing self-analysis be applied to one more function of the absolving priest, that of ascertaining the dispositions of the penitent, especially the authenticity of his contrition and his so-called "firm purpose of amendment"? At first glance it looks very much as if in this area the personal psychological intuition of the priest should prevail. Yet, here too, only a purely religious attitude can safeguard the reverence due to the penitent's intimate life and to the hidden nature of the action of God's grace.

As the Church's representative, the priest who celebrates the sacrament of penance is obliged, as in the case of every other sacrament, to see to it that it is conferred in a valid and worthy manner. When he is faced with manifest bad faith or a mocking of the sacrament, he is confronted by the penitent himself with the impossibility of accomplishing his mediating task, and the refusal of absolution will only note this impossibility and prevent a useless profanation. In all other cases he will have to consider the very fact that someone comes to the sacrament as a very serious presumption of sincere contrition and of a decision to break with sin. A mere psychologically justified suspicion that contrition is not sufficient or the will not resolute enough has so much chance of being wrong that it would be unwarranted to let the granting of absolution depend on such an uncertain insight. The expressions and formulas which the penitent uses are mostly borrowed from what he has heard in catechism lessons and sermons about perfect and imperfect contrition, about the motivation for contrition, and about the conditions of an authentic purpose of amendment. Yet these formulas often hide a personal experience of a quite different nature from what they mean in scholastic terminology. "I can't really be sorry for it" may mean, for instance, that he cannot overlook the beautiful human aspects of a sinful adventure, while previous education has taught him so consistently to identify what is humanly repellent and shocking with what is sinful that he is unable to distinguish the sinful from the beautiful aspect of the adventure with any degree of clarity. "As soon as I get the chance, I'll do it again" may be a clumsy way of expressing the combination of sincere will with a feeling of at least temporary powerlessness for good. In both cases an anxiety is expressed which can only derive from a sincere will for good, and is a guarantee both of the contrition and of the firm resolve. I still remember the conclusion of a long conversation I had — "I should like to confess all the things I have told you, but I'm afraid that I have no real contrition. Actually I don't feel at all sorry for it. I want to go to confession only out of a great anxiety." "And what, in the prospect of hell, are you so much afraid of? Pain or something?" — "Not at all, that leaves me cold. But never again to know oneself loved by God. . . . I can't bear the thought!" "Wouldn't what you have told me be an act of perfect contrition?"

The priest will often face the task of kindling and deepening a contrition which is still wavering and immature. If he tries to effect this through the psychological shock of a sharp rebuke or by insisting on the gravity and ugliness of the sin committed he will, as a rule, only evoke self-defense or hurt the penitent uselessly. Real contrition derives from love, not from horror of the evil in us. Making the penitent aware of God's love, inviting and waiting for him, tapping the religious sources of contrition, will offer much greater hope of a real inner change. What good can be expected from using the word "crime" or even "murder" for an abortion? Will not the awareness that God loved that burgeoning life, that one's own anxiety or egoism has been put above God's love, and that God's forgiveness means precisely an invitation to a greater and more selfless love for others in the future, penetrate more deeply to the "heart" and give hope of bringing about a more real conversion than words which render the anxiously hidden but deeply burning sense of guilt even more oppressive? Would not an engaged couple who have gone astray find more strength if they were made to realize that they have loved each other not too much but, in reality, too little — not with the fullness of love which God's love asked from them — more than if they are rebuked for their sensuality or threatened with a loss of future married happiness?

As for the firm purpose of amendment in the case of regular and almost changeless relapsing into the same sins, it presents penitent and confessor with a twofold question: whether the deeper groping underlying that series of sins is striving toward God or away from him, and whether the steady return of the same sins may not indicate that the root of the evil lies elsewhere than in the sins themselves, so that only an effort made on that deeper level might bring about a steady improvement.

The first question brings us back to what has been said of the basic option, and especially of the indispensable role of time in the breakthrough of that option across all that man is and has become psychophysically. Between abstract knowledge of one's situation or of the solution to a problem and an insight which has become existentially real there is a gap which cannot be bridged by reasoning and arguments, but only by a hidden organic process of maturation, in patience and over a length of time. The process is rather like that of a hidden spring seeking an outlet through all the resistances of the soil, until suddenly it spurts freely, as spontaneously as if it had just come into existence on the spot: so the path of a decision, taken in all sincerity but still not well enough rooted in life, strives toward the moment of a breakthrough, when man can commit himself entirely in the resolution he has made. The same series of sinful acts, remaining apparently unchanged may, in two different persons, or even in the same person at different moments of his existence, have a totally different value as a symptom. It is true that the priest may use his psychological power of insight to find out whether, under the sinful symptoms, he can make out the first

faint indications of an impending deliverance. He may sometimes, or even frequently, see the same unchanging sin turn from
negative to positive through a gradual reorientation of the deeper
directedness.

But equally often he is in danger of being wrong and of taking for ill-will what is only a temporary helplessness on the part
of the penitent — or perhaps even his own impatience for a solution. The penitent who tells his confessor: "I'm giving up, I'm
not going to fight anymore, I can no longer believe that God is
helping me" does not expect the confessor to attack his ill-will,
he is expecting some answer from God's mercy to what may
sound like rebellion but is in fact an urgent and generally hope-
ful prayer for help. Experience shows only too clearly how often
a religiously unauthentic answer from the priest, and even more
a stern rebuke or the threat of refusing absolution, has had fate-
ful consequences for the religious life of a penitent.

Once more, the only solution which respects the sacramentality of the confession can be found in a purely religious testing,
by the penitent himself, of his good will as manifested in words
against his inner essential directedness towards God. His firm
resolve is not a merely autonomous psychological decision but an
answer to God's merciful forgiveness, a readiness to allow the
risen Christ, the conqueror of sin, to cure him of his sinful attachment. If the priest wants to promote this readiness, his dialog
with the penitent may not be the meeting of his personal insight
with the penitent's actual self-knowledge, but his attitude must
be as integrally as possible a referring to Christ's invitation, which
overcomes all sin. Then the penitent's answer can also come
from his deepest readiness, which will act as a power of discrimination revealing either the sincerity of the psychological decision
or the self-deception in it. The priest's psychological power of
insight can be useful, because it may help him address the penitent in a religious language attuned to his dispositions. But it
should not induce him to allow that address itself to turn into
psychological counseling.

This gives us an answer to our second question also. If the
root of the evil is deeper than the confessed sins, the power of

discrimination deriving from the inner directedness toward God, precisely because it surges out of the innermost layers of the personality, will offer more hope, as it breaks through to the surface, of meeting and illuminating the hidden resistances than would a premature and unavoidably superficial probing for psychological drives and unconscious motivations.

The Sacramental Penance

This perspective likewise puts the sacramental penance in a truer light. Penance aims at reparation. It is true that, once forgiven, the sins need no longer be atoned for. But their consequences in the psyche and in the environment; the person himself with his weakened will, his greater attachment to evil; the sedimentation of the past in habits, reflexes and memories; the wrath and the pain of those who have been injured — all this demands, even after forgiveness, an effort at reparation and renovation. Classical theology calls this the *reatus poenae*, remaining in the sinner after confession. The sacramental penance is not the fulfillment, but the sign of this attempt at reparation. And the fact that it is not chosen by the penitent but imposed by the confessor is an expression of the fact that it is not an autonomous will of redress but an answer to the love of the risen Christ, the conqueror of sin, calling man to a new life. Hence in the penance too it is not the material act which is most important, but its value as a symbol of Christ's desire for renovation and of the sinner's willingness to meet that desire. The "proportion" of the penance with the sins committed, which is demanded by textbook theology, cannot be a real, but is only a symbolic proportion. A materially exiguous penance may, in some cases, have a more intense value as a symbol than a more extensive expiation. There is furthermore no objection to some intervention on the part of the penitent in determining the penance. A dialog may help in finding the best-adapted sign, or the penitent himself may be entrusted with the task of determining the sign which will appeal to him most. All this supposes, of course, that this looking for the sign occurs in the religious perspective which is so purely situated by the prayer recited by the absolving priest: "May the passion of Our Lord, Jesus Christ, the merits of the Blessed Virgin Mary and of all the saints, and also whatever good you do and evil you endure bring about the remission of your sins, the increase of grace, and the reward of everlasting life."

The "proximate occasion"

A delicate point in the formation of a firm purpose of amendment is the resolution to avoid the proximate occasions of sin. That notion of a "proximate occasion," too, has become so rigid during the last century that it has turned into a computation of probabilities and become synonymous with "serious risk." Ratings of movies, appraisals of books and of plays, are classic examples, and everybody knows how absolutely these only very approximate norms have been applied and are still being applied. Whereas the proximate occasion is in fact nothing but a concrete situation in which the occurrence of sin may be foreseen with moral certitude, always assuming that objective and subjective factors shall be taken into account — and not only objectivated subjective factors such as ability, habit, and so on, but the whole concrete situation of the person in question — in practice only the objective probability was considered.

Would the priest not safeguard confession more integrally as an encounter and as sign if, instead of deciding with his own fallible insight what is a proximate occasion for the penitent, he helped the penitent himself to decide out of his religious directedness toward God's will and invitation, what risks he may take or should avoid? As long as the penitent shows good faith, the priest shall trust him. Should he reach the conclusion that the penitent, more or less consciously, is deceiving himself, then he can frankly but religiously raise the question of good faith: "Do you really think that God does not ask this from you?" Or even: "Are you wholly sincere before God?" But only in a case of

evident bad faith might a refusal of absolution be justified, because in that event the religious meaning of the sacrament itself
is endangered.

From all that has been said it is clear that the function of
psychological judgment, so risky in view of our modern realization of the inextricable blending of freedom and determinism, is
being reduced to a minimum in the sacrament of the remission
of sins, and that, far from endangering the religious meaning of
confession, this raises it to a new level of integrity. The psychologically talented priest, even the professional priest-psychother-
apist, may use all the subtle power of his empathy and his scientific skill in the confessional, provided that he uses them in the
service not of a psychological but of a religious event. And one
who is less talented psychologically can be a confessor inspired
by grace and bestowing grace through the purity of his religious direction.

As a "holy simpleton" the Curé of Ars was far from being
a psychotherapist, and from the reports jotted down about him
it is evident that his advice contained nothing which was humanly profound or sensational. Nevertheless, the railroad station
of Lyons had to provide a special ticket-window to sell round-
trip tickets to Ars, exceptionally valid for eight days because
one generally had to wait that long before entering the confessional. There can be no other explanation than that the whole
manner of this psychologically unskilled priest whose holiness
made him an expert in God's ways and whose saintly life
spoke louder than his words, had such connaturality with
Christ's redeeming love that it was capable of penetrating all
illusions and complexes to bring the very depths of a human conscience into dialog with that love.

Chapter Nine

CONFESSION AS A MEANS OF SELF-IMPROVEMENT

JAMES F. FILELLA, S.J.

In a recent survey of Christian attitudes and practices (sacrament, etc., 1967), it was found that Catholics had acquired a greater appreciation of the role of the holy Eucharist in their devotional life, having made it much more central and meaningful, and had become more chary and cold about the practice of the sacrament of penance. It appears that many among the faithful nowadays harbor some doubts and misgivings about the efficacy of confession to bring about a real and lasting change in their lives, as they would have reason to expect from a sacrament instituted by Christ for the absolution of sins and the strengthening of the Christian against temptation. It is true that all believing Catholics accept the sacramental power of confessions made to a priest who has faculties to absolve sins and to confer special graces enabling the penitent to resist temptations and grow in the spiritual life. Furthermore, many fervent Catholics will testify to the psychological benefits of a good confession. Still, the unfortunate fact is that far too many among the faithful have to admit that their weekly or monthly confessions have degenerated into a routine and fruitless performance which at times may appear to border on ritualistic compulsion.

Many causes can be assigned for this apparent inefficacy of confession. Some originate from the religious apathy of lukewarm Christians; others may be due to the mechanical and impersonal manner in which confessions are often made; and still others may be psychological in nature. It is to this last aspect of the crisis affecting the practice of sacramental confessions that we wish to turn our attention in the light of Mowrer's views on the matter.

Mowrer has for a number of years been concerned with the failure of psychoanalysis and similar psychotherapeutic techniques to effect lasting cures among mental patients. He seems to attribute the cause of this failure to the *secrecy* and nature of confidentiality with which the patient's expression of his shortcomings is protected. The following statement is an expression of this viewpoint —

> If "secret confessions" to psychiatrists and priests had really a good record of accomplishments, we should be glad to be spared the embarrassment (of having to resort to more public forms of confession). But the record is *not* good. . . . After all, secret confession is a contradiction in terms—secrecy is what makes confession necessary. . . . Should we actually expect much to come from letting a priest, psychiatrist . . . or some other specialist hear our sins. . . ? (1966, p. 114).

Mowrer's contention is clear: he holds that confessing one's sins to a person who is professionally bound to secrecy defeats the very purpose for which confessions are made. Instead he goes on to propose that the only solution is to be sought in confessing one's sins to people with whom one is intimately and personally associated and who "really matter," that is, to the "significant others in one's life," or to "the ordinary people in one's life." Mowrer seems to think that the efficacy of confession as a means of self-improvement comes from admitting to oneself and to others in public and without secrecy what one really is.

In the following pages we shall try to explain Mowrer's integrity theory of human behavior in order to be able to understand better, in the second part of this essay, his views on the effectiveness of confession. Finally, in the third part, a few critical remarks on Mowrer's position will be added by way of conclusion.

I. MOWRER'S PSYCHOLOGICAL THEORY

In many of his writings, Mowrer professes himself a devoted churchman (of no specific Christian denomination) and a disillusioned psychoanalyst. His ideas are very personal as a result of his frank and objective re-evaluation of the so-called contributions of psychoanalysis and behaviorism to the understanding of man. The publication of his study of anxiety (1950) marked his departure from orthodox psychoanalytic views, and his drift away from it has gathered momentum ever since. It is upon this latter part of his psychological career that we shall draw to present his views on the relevance of secret confession to the task of self-improvement. We shall examine his position in three stages.

Mowrer's Reversal of Freud's Theory of Neurosis. Freud formulated a theory of neurosis that created a number of moral ambiguities. Strictly speaking, the theory had been framed in psychological terms: neurotic symptoms were looked upon as the result of a relentless emotional state of tension initially caused at an early age by a traumatic incident or sequence of incidents, which the patient could not resolve at the time, and whose effects could not be fully suppressed thereafter. The whole explanation was put beyond the scope of morality; for neurotic symptoms were interpreted as the natural manifestation of a mental *illness*, i.e., an ailment with a psychological cause rather than a physiological one. The neurotic person is to be treated like a *patient*, i.e., a person *suffering from* an emotional illness over which he could have little control, and for the origin of which he could hardly be held responsible. The treatment to be followed by the patient, however, seemed to imply taking a course of action with some moral consequences. Freud's explanation would lead one to believe that the emotional ailment was perpetuated by the unresolved conflict between the unconscious need to express the instinctual drives of sex and aggression residing in the Id and the "moral dictates" of society enforced by the super-ego or "the voice of one's conscience." The therapeutic task, then, was to consist in the re-education of the patient under the neutralizing presence of the doctor by teaching him the practical way of expressing the repressed forces of the unconscious against the irrational demands of the super-ego or conscience.

Mowrer openly expressed his disagreement with this view of neurotic behavior and its treatment. He held that "anxiety comes, not from acts which the individual would commit but dares not, but from acts he *has* committed but wishes that he *had* not" (1950, p. 537). In his opinion, the goal of therapy was not "that of attempting to close the painful discrepancy between a person's moral aspirations and his performance by lowering the level of moral aspirations" but that of "helping the patient become a better person, i.e., to improve and *raise the level of his performance*" (1961, p. 224).

Mowrer's view of human behavior and its disorders is deeply moral. Instead of mentally sick people, he would rather speak of neurotics (1953, p. 82) and of psychotics (1959, p. 1) as *sinful* people who have had "a hidden history of serious misconduct which has not been adequately redeemed." For Mowrer, guilt is the central problem of mental disorders — "real, palpable, and indisputable guilt" — and the way out is none other than that of a simple confession, i.e., admission of one's misbehavior without any palliative, pretexts, or alibis.

Mowrer's Integrity Theory of Man. The growing dissatisfaction with Freud's views on neurosis and its treatment, and on the psychological nature of man, induced Mowrer to review his position and formulate an Integral View of Human Nature and Human Behavior (Mowrer, 1965). The gist of Mowrer's integrity theory can be expressed in the following statements:

a. Man has the power to choose to act or not to act.
b. If he chooses to act, then he may select one or another of many possible options.
c. Man has to be held responsible for his choices.
d. In this manner (by making choices) he becomes the creator of his own destiny.

It is obvious from the above statements that the distinctive characteristic of human life *as human* is man's responsibility for his choices and his actions. In practical life, then, an individual begins to live as a human being when he makes himself assume responsibility for his conduct. This may be a very difficult step in one's life — probably the hardest choice a person has to make. It is difficult indeed; but inescapable if he is to lead the life of a truly *human* being.

Human integrity in practice means at least three things: doing the right action according to the dictates of one's conscience with knowledge and freedom (i.e., responsibility); secondly, owning up to one's mistakes if in any thing he has gone wrong; and thirdly, making amends for one's misbehavior in an effective, tangible manner. In short, man shows a genuine sense of responsibility by doing right as well as by admitting to his own wrongdoing and trying to make restitution.

Two points call for a short comment at this juncture. First of all, what seems to be the actual cause of psychologically abnormal behavior is not the moral mis-conduct as such, but the fact that having acted wrongly, *one tries to cover it up*. A morally wrong act is not of itself the cause of pathological behavior. The real, true, and specific cause of neurosis is the fact that the "sinner" reacts to his wrong-doing in an oblique or tangential manner: by explaining it away, by hiding it, by ignoring it, or by denying it to himself and to others. In other words, neurotic behavior is due to the desperate attempt at *disowning* what actually forms an *integral* part of a person's past and, therefore, of his life.

Seen in this light, a neurosis appears to be the persistent effort to annihilate the act itself after it has been performed: it is a futile wishing that it had never taken place. Obviously, this is an impossible task. By trying to do the impossible, the neurotic person begins to behave in the repetitive, symbolic, relentless way which is typical of a neurosis. The behavior in itself and in its social surroundings appears abnormal, odd, irrational and meaningless, when in point of fact, it signifies the predicament the neurotic person finds himself in.

The second comment to be made on the integrity theory of man's behavior is Mowrer's emphasis on the *social dimension* of human responsibility. The reference to the social dimension recurs so often that it has to be taken as an essential and vital characteristic of Mowrer's system. One of the more explicit passages is the following:

> Therefore, in light of the total situation, I see no alternative but to turn again to the old, painful, but also promising possibility that man is preeminently a *social* creature and that he lives or dies, psychologically and personally, as a function of the openness, community, relatedness, and integrity which by good actions he attains and by evil action he destroys" (1961, p. 44).

Mowrer seems to imply in all his writings that no man acts truly in a responsible way (i.e., integrally human) if he does not, directly or indirectly, take into account the *social* relevance of his actions. Failure to do so is the basis of sin and the most propitious disposition to remain in sin.

To Return to the Concept of Sin. Mowrer seems convinced that the failure of modern man to see in sin one of the most powerful forces of social and psychological destruction is leading the whole of mankind to the brim of a major human catastrophe. Hence his insistence on the moral roots of many of the psychological disturbances affecting men. He has defied (1960) scientific opinion, and has insisted that however unwelcome and unpleasant the word sin may sound to scientists, the word must be retained in order to bring unambiguously to light the essential moral nature of human acts.

In keeping with the social dimension of integral human actions, Mowrer's thesis is that sin constitutes a denial of the human nature of man, which tends to perpetuate itself in the persistent effort the sinner is forced to make in order to misrepresent himself to himself and to others. We have already seen how this blind persistence is at the root of neurotic symptoms and cannot help but result in the total alienation of the sinner from himself and from the rest of society. It is in this situation of total isolation that sin reigns supreme.

Echoing Bonhoeffer's saying that "in the darkness of the unexpressed, sin poisons the whole being of a person," Mowrer comments:

> Sin demands to have man *alone*. As long as man is in community, in free and open touch with others, he will have a vivid sense of the consequences of wrong acts which gives him the strength and wisdom not to commit them—or if he does, to move rapidly towards their rectification. But if he has committed himself to the path of hypocrisy, of being with people but not *of* them, he does not have this advantage and is almost certain to get into moral predicaments of one kind or another (1961, p. 216).

This is a challenging statement: sin is presented as the quintessence of self-centeredness and selfishness. It separates man from society and continually reinforces this social division by "possessing" the sinner, and taking him away from the community of human beings. Like the legendary vampire, sin attacks its victims and "sucks their blood" when they are alone and completely helpless. Sin creates social isolation and thrives in isolation.

What should be the proper course of action for an individual who is guilt-ridden and fully in the grip of sin? The answer is simple: he should pause, take a good look at himself as he *really* is, and then get down to the business of "confessing" — i.e., owning up with courage to his past misbehavior with the full realization that it cannot be changed, and then go on to try his level best to counteract the effects of his past evil actions by proper restitution and by resolving to do better in future. As sin grows

in strength and in social isolation, it loses its grip in the presence
of deeply established and dynamically healthy human relations.
For Mowrer the best antidote to sin is a healthy community of
persons, and the most effective method of counteracting the effects of sin is to re-establish the social connections which sin has
destroyed. This brings us to the core of our problem, namely,
the problem of confession.

II.   MOWRER'S VIEWS ON THE EFFECTIVENESS OF CONFESSION

Confession is looked upon by Mowrer as the life-line which
will bring the sinner back to the community of the living. The
moral and social view of human responsibility and the anti-social
nature of sin have led Mowrer, step by step, to this conclusion.
We shall now try to explain the theoretical justification of confession against objections which have been raised to it.

Theoretical Justification of Confession. In Mowrer's view, confession is the first step in the return of the "wanderer" to the community of his fellowmen. Thus, confession is the best "medicine"
for the all too human tendency to deny responsibility for the
evil acts one cannot fully approve of in one's past life. Let it be
clear, however, that confession is the *first* step—not the only
one. Many more have to follow: to be effective, confession must
be placed in the whole context of repentance, namely, self-knowledge, self-accusation, penance or restitution, and the resolve to do
better.

In this cycle of acts, the specific value of self-accusation or
confession lies in its *socializing effect.* After all, talking to one
another is the most concrete and unequivocal external sign of the
inner disposition to relate to others. It is true that speech can be
used to erect and buttress an edifice of hypocrisy and empty
formalism, but the connotation of the word "confession" seems to
stand in direct opposition and contrast to such dubious use of
speech, and emphasizes the complete frankness in human communication which excludes all pretense and misrepresentation.
Confession is the frank and candid disclosure of what is most in-

timately our own: our aspirations, our thoughts, our secret desires, our hidden actions insofar as they fall short of the ideal before us. Confession is the *ultimate* in human communication and self-disclosure.

The effects of confession are of necessity social through and through. Admitting to others the seamy side of one's self releases unsuspected forms of energy and sets under way a process of rehabilitation in our relations with others. A good confession is the first in a sequence of acts which constitute the total cycle of complete and effective repentance and reform.

The emphasis on this dynamic approach to confession as a part in the cycle of actions leading to personal reform is the best answer to a number of objections that have been raised against it. To the objection that verbal confession of one's own shortcomings may exacerbate unconscious guilt feelings beyond control, and may in extreme cases precipitate suicidal episodes, one can reply that this may be just as true of confessions made in complete secrecy, i.e., isolated from society. Such confessions are more a symbolic sequence of words uttered on the occasion of being before another person than a real desire to reveal oneself *to* another. Within Mowrer's system, and many clinical and social psychologists would concur with it, it is only confession *to* another, truly and really meant, that restores the socially centered gravity in the life of a person and thus tends to neutralize and desensitize the feelings of guilt. Such fruitful confessions reestablish the social moorings a person needs to make a program of repentance effectively realistic.

Another objection raised against the psychological value of confessions comes from its verbal nature. It can be framed thus: How can a mere verbal self-accusation be sufficient to restore the order destroyed by sin? Or, as Mowrer himself puts it: "People do not 'talk' themselves into sin; they *act*. By the same token, I do not believe anyone ever talks himself *out* of sin' (1961, p. 78). Again, this objection can be solved if one sees confession as a necessary but not sufficient condition of repentance, i.e., if one looks upon confession as the first, and only the first, in the sequence of acts which constitute the dynamism of repentance.

A third and more serious objection originates with the very nature of the life process. Life is irreversible: one cannot change what has already taken place, nor can one wish any part of one's life out of existence. Once done, it is done for ever. How can, then, confession be of any use? Would it not be better to forget all about it, and act as if nothing had happened? How can the admission of what one cannot approve of in one's life be of any use to regain one's balance and live a better life?

The answer to this objection is to be sought in the fact that confession is of no use unless it represents a "change of heart." Human life is much more than the mere sum-total of the acts performed by an individual in the course of his existence. It has a qualitative value as well. Human life is to be judged in the light of the general orientation a person has toward himself, toward the world, toward others and toward God; and also with reference to the degree to which his actions in everyday life reflect this orientation. The quality of a person's life is to be estimated by the intention with which he performs well-ordered actions in an effort to reproduce in himself the totality of what is expected of man.

Now it is true that we cannot change the nature of our past acts after they have been performed; but we *can* change the prominence and meaning they have in the general orientation of our life and the effects they have on us. If our present orientation to life remains more or less the *same as* the one we had at the time of performing the evil actions we are ashamed of, then these civil actions continue to lord it over us unchallenged. They are still alive as integral parts of our sinful life, even if we do not commit them again. On the other hand, if our orientation to life *has changed,* then the evil actions have ceased to occupy the position of pre-eminence they once had, and they have been relegated to a marginal position *with no existential presence* in our life.

This is probably more than Mowrer would be prepared to say; but it is, I feel, very much in keeping with his approach to the whole problem. Against this background it should be easy to appreciate one of Mowrer's favored ideas: the value of open confessions as different from and substitutes for the secret type of confession prevalent in psychiatric and religious circles.

Secret vs. Confessions. Confessions made in secret seem to be deficient in what is, in Mowrer's view, most precious in confession, namely, its social and socializing character. Secrecy seems to deprive confessions of their psychological and social vigor to effect a real improvement in the life of an individual. Mowrer is very explicit about this aspect of his theory—

> I am persuaded that healing and redemption depend much more upon what we say about ourselves to *others, significant others*, than upon what others (no matter how highly trained or untrained, ordained or unordained) say *to us*. It is the truth we ourselves speak rather than the treatment we receive that heals us (1966, p. 114).

This is a significant passage. What Mowrer is saying is that not any type of confession will do in order to effect a real change in the person's life. He seems to be excluding four types of confessions as being practically ineffective. The first group is the type of confession in which someone *does* something over us (e.g., absolution by a priest). The second type of ineffective confessions are those in which someone *reassures* us of our innocence (e.g., psychiatrists of the psychoanalytic schools). The third type of confessions excluded by Mowrer as useless are those in which someone *says* something to us (e.g., advice given by a priest, social worker, or teacher). Finally there is the group of confessions in which everything remains in an atmosphere of *neutrality* (e.g., some forms of non-directive therapy and counseling). Secret confessions of any type are, in Mowrer's view, a psychological contradiction for they destroy with their secrecy what they have tried to achieve by means of confession. At its best, secret confession is nothing but an extension of one's inner problem without the socializing effect true confessions should have.

Instead, Mowrer advocates a form of open confession, in which the intimate self-disclosure is made *to* a person who is really *present* in the social life of an individual, i.e., to a "significant other" in his life. The value of confessions to the "sig-

nificant other" resides in the total disclosure not only of the nature of the evil actions, but also of the identity of the evil-doer.
It is in this concurrent disclosure of one's self-identity as well as
of the acts, that confession becomes meaningful and socializing.

Mowrer (1966) has emphasized that such confessions are to
be primarily *about oneself*. Some people are likely to think that
any frank conversation is a confession. This is not the case. One
can be very frank about others; but this hardly qualifies as a
confession. It is only when the only culprit one can be absolutely
sure about (i.e., oneself) is exposed by means of self-accusation
that confessions become open and have the salutary effects to be
expected from them.

This is not an easy task, to be sure; but it is extremely *simple*.
There is nothing complex or complicated about it: all one needs
is the courage to go against one's pride. No special linguistic skill
is required. Mowrer points out that it is far more complicated
to explain how sorry we feel than merely to state the cause of
our sorrow.

The results of open confessions in Mowrer's opinion boil
down to the invigorating or strengthening effect they have in the
life of an individual. Confessing sins to significant others is not
just a matter of getting reassurance or of being exonerated of past
failures. It is much more than this. It is a kind of drawing full
benefit from the resources available in a group of people. It is a
sort of sharing in all the good qualities of all the members in a
group. "One is weak," says Mowrer, "because one does not allow
the strength, concern *and discipline* of others to operate to advantage. . . . With striking regularity, persons who become deeply
open with a group find that their 'will-power' is mysteriously
strengthened" (1966, p. 116).

A sincere, genuine admission of one's shortcomings and sins
in public has an irresistible effect on others: it mobilizes their
interest in us, gives us something concrete to work on, and puts
everything in its proper perspective — with the result that all
members of a group seem to be happy to help us in our struggle
for self-improvement. It has been Mowrer's observation (1966, p.
116) that whenever a patient in group therapy begins to be more

self-critical, more responsible and open to others, the response and support he gets from others is much more personal, encouraging and effective than if he had merely asked for assistance.

Practical Problems. Mowrer is well aware that the practice of open confessions is bound to create serious problems. How far should one go? What should one reveal? To whom? In what circumstances? These and similar questions begin to emerge as soon as one contemplates the possibility of making open confessions a regular policy in one's relations with others. A few remarks on this aspect of the problem seem to be in order.

a) *To whom?* In the light of what has already been said, it is clear that what matters is to reveal oneself to the *significant others* in one's life. Mowrer (1966) enumerates the following by way of example: family members, friends and acquaintances, and working associates. The following principle may be helpful to decide practical cases: "Tell it to whom you would most dread having your story known."

b) *What?* The answer is simple: what you are most ashamed of — even your most personal thoughts. Mowrer (1966) carefully distinguishes between passing thoughts and thoughts on which one dwells, and which often are the pattern for later actions. "The best way of bringing an end to it (deliberate thought) is to submit oneself to the discipline of absolute candor."

c) *When and Where?* The choice of the best conditions in which open confessions may be made with profit is a difficult problem. It is obvious that no one should go about in search of "victims" to pour the filth of one's life on, however significant they may be. The situation itself must be significant to justify an open confession.

d) *Individually or in a group?* The goal of open confessions is society itself. Consequently, they must be made in a group. However, to the uninitiated this may be an unsurmountable obstacle. In this case, he may begin by making a confession to one or two significant persons in his life. With experience, he will learn that the fullest beneficial effects come from a group.

To conclude, Mowrer's insistence on the salutary effects of openness and frankness is understandable in the light of his in-

tegrity theory of human nature and behavior. He is a firm believer in the integral view of man in himself and in his social
relations with others. He must be true to himself and to others.
In this basic concept of human integrity we find the final reason
why open confessions are to be preferred: they represent a bal-
anced blending of two fundamental virtues — frankness in our
dealings with others, and courage in having others know us as
we really are not only when we have been fair and kind to them,
but also — and above all — when we have wronged them. Whenever any one of us has not lived up to his responsibilities as a
human being, there is only one solution to the problem: to subject
himself to the chastening effect of the discipline of *absolute
candor.*

III.   CRITICAL COMMENTS

At this juncture, a retrospective view of the main ideas of
Mowrer's theory of human behavior will convince the reader of
its basic soundness. His integrity theory of human nature and
behavior has much to recommend it. Its emphasis on the cen-
trality and pervasive nature of human responsibility together
with its dynamic approach to human relations, has had a healthy
influence on the approach of many psychologists to the understanding of modern man. Its formulation of the genesis of neurotic behavior in terms of its moral roots is challenging indeed. Its
insistence on the beneficial effects of frankness and openness in
social relations has been a welcome change from the excessive
importance accorded to patient-to-doctor and doctor-to-patient
relationships in other forms of therapy. Looking at it as a whole
one cannot but be impressed by the refreshingly sound view of
human nature proposed by Mowrer. A few critical remarks will
help us see it with even deeper insight and appreciation.

The Moral and Psychic in Mowrer's System. Mowrer's reformulation of neurotic behavior went a long way towards the renewal of a number of key concepts in psychology which had just
been taken for granted under the influence of psychoanalysis and

behaviorism. It strengthened the shift of emphasis from a quasi-mechanized impulse-theory of anxiety and neurosis towards a more rational explanation in terms of responsibility, intentionality, freedom, and meaningfulness which had already begun to gain acceptance among many psychologists.

However, the zeal to prove the intimate connection between the moral and the psychological spheres in man's behavior led Mowrer to a confusion between the two terms with small gain for either one. In many of his statements it is not easy to determine precisely whether he is speaking of the moral effects of a misdeed, or of the moral effects of a psychologically defective action, or of the psychological effects of moral misbehavior, or of the psychological consequences of a psychologically defective action. Nowhere does Mowrer come to grips with the problem of whether a morally evil act is also always, or often, or sometimes, or never a psychologically defective act.

This clarification is important and badly needed in the type of discussions Mowrer has given rise to in his theory of human behavior. Had it been made, it would have brought into prominence what, in our opinion, is Mowrer's main contribution to the understanding of man's behavior: the need for frankness and candor in our daily social intercourse with other human beings. We feel this to be Mowrer's main contribution, for it is against this background that one can understand his insistence on open confessions and his explanation of neurotic behavior.

The confusion between the sphere of the moral and of the psychic in Mowrer's thinking seems in a way to be fully accepted by him. In one of his addresses he has said: "Irresponsibility, wrongdoing, immorality, sin: what do the terms matter if we can thus understand more accurately the nature of psychopathology?" (1961, p. 48).

But terms do matter! After all, it is mainly through the proper use of terms that issues are clarified; hence, our objection to Mowrer's confusion and his failure to see the importance of defining the differences between the moral and the psychic in man. That they are both aspects of human behavior is beyond dispute; that they both interact in the concreteness of human activity is clear, too. But equally clear should have been the realization that one is not the other.

The practical outcome is that, whenever Mowrer speaks of the need for confession, it is difficult to tell to what aspect he is referring. Does he speak of the need for a *penitent* to have his sins forgiven? This is a moral-religious problem. Does he speak of the need for a *neurotic* to speak to a significant person in his life and thus recover his sense of balance and his genuine personal integrity? Then this is a therapeutic goal. Does he mean the need for an *ordinary normal individual* to unburden himself and thus create a better set of social conditions for improved human relations? Then this is a psychological and social task. That one or two may take place together is no reason for not distinguishing one from the others.

Again, the same basic confusion prevails in the treatment of guilt. There are many facets to the state of guilt, in which the moral and the psychological are intimately interwoven. It is difficult from Mowrer's writings to find out whether he is referring to moral guilt as a result of a morally evil action deliberately perpetrated (sin of commission), or of moral guilt due to not having done something one ought to have done (sin of omission), or of the self-dissatisfaction one is likely to experience for not having chosen an action which later on may have been better than the one selected (for instance, not having studied medicine and having studied law instead, when in later life one realizes that medicine would have been right for him). This may sound like unnecessary hair-splitting; however, it is our surmise that the psychological experiences involved in these three types of "guilt" may not be the same. It may turn out to be more concrete for sins of commission, more vague but no less disturbing for sins of omission, and much more diffuse for psychic "unforeseeables" or unlucky choices. Maybe, after careful study, wide individual differences in the experience of guilt will be found. In any case, this is a matter that cannot be settled by "fiats" or by keeping the whole thing in a state of confusion.

Raising such questions moves us into the field of the unexplored. It is relatively simple to make a moral code of things one ought to do — a code that has been written and re-written by most moralists throughout the ages. It is not so simple to prepare a moral code of things one ought not to omit — this is an aspect of morality over which moralists are now showing much concern. But it is well-nigh impossible at this stage to prepare a *moral* code of what we should not loath doing for our psychological, social, economic, and technological development and well-being! Who is prepared to point out whether a psychologically defective act has or has not become a morally sinful act; and if so, when? And yet, regardless of the moral verdict one may pass on such actions, the whole matter of the *psychological outcome* of psychologically inadequate or morally wrong acts remains to be discussed. Are we prepared to grant that even if a psychological immature or inadequate action is not morally sinful, it will not lead to the formation of a psychologically defective reaction-pattern or neurosis? This is not a question of illness or immoral acts — it is a psychological problem. And to state it in terms of pathology as Freud did, or in exclusively moral terms as Mowrer has done, is to avoid coming to grips with the psychological nature of a psychological problem.

Evaluation of the Open Type of Confession. On psychological grounds and especially in the light of the findings of social psychology, Mowrer is justified in stating that "There is a steadily mounting evidence that nothing provides such radical relief as having no secrets, at least no shameful ones, *from anybody*" (1966, p. 117). There is no doubt that frankness, openness, "the discipline of absolute candor," and "self-transparency" do have an unsuspected beneficial effect on the personal life of an individual, be he sinner or saint. As regards the usefulness of confession as a means of self-reform, the point at issue is whether the good effects of social life, which are obvious from the psychological point of view, go beyond the psychological sphere into the field of the moral and the religious. Can we say that a man is likely to become less of a sinner and more of a saint, the better he is integrated into the life of the group?

The answer to this question depends on many factors, theological, social, and psychological. Mowrer and most psychologists with him assume that social life has a balancing effect on the life of an individual, so that moral life becomes not only possible but even easy. Mowrer is very explicit about this: he feels that a socially integrated life is the best antidote to sin. In a passage partially quoted above, he has this to say:

> Through secrecy one is shielded from group sanctions, so it is not surprising that, while practicing secrecy, one is commonly helpless in the face of temptation. One is "weak" because one does not allow the strength, concern, *and discipline* of others to operate to advantage. Confession indicates willingness to live under the judgment of others (1966, p. 116).

In other passages, Mowrer (1961, p. 215; 1966, p. 116) has suggested that the so-called *will-power* of philosophers and spiritual writers may be nothing more than the social strength of knowing that one belongs to a group. In any case, he seems to propose that the beneficial influence of group life on an individual consists in the deterrent effect of living "under the judgment of others," and in the strengthening assurance that others are concerned and sympathize with his problems.

Our personal opinion in this difficult matter is that we should stress the good effects of being personally integrated with a group in the form of a closely-knit community, with no implication as to whether or not such beneficial effects are to be identified with what philosophers meant by "will-power," or spiritual writers and theologians by "divine grace." It is our conviction that instead of looking for ready-made equivalents, we should foster an attitude of bold exploration into forgotten or not fully recognized aspects of this extremely complex problem of how to effect a personal reform after a confession has been made. The issue Mowrer has raised regarding the psychological effects of open confession is one of these forgotten or by-passed issues. The social strength he is talking about is a new variable, which has not received sufficient attention in moral and religious writings. It is this aspect of human life and self-reform that is coming to the fore at present. We should be bold to explore it fully without confusing it with what other people mean by will-power or divine grace.

The Religious Dimension. The mention of divine grace brings us to the last critical remark on Mowrer's theory. We wish to draw the reader's attention to a source of ambiguity in Mowrer's writings, and to what we consider a glaring lacuna in his thought. Nowhere in the treatment of guilt or atonement is mention made of the religious implications of man's misdeeds and his reform. "As a churchman" Mowrer believes that "the concept of God is vital or meaningful" (1961, p. 110); but his treatment of sin, guilt, atonement, repentance and similar topics fails to take cognizance of the *psychological* repercussions of "this vital concept." Is this omission intentional? Was his reference to God a sort of a concession made to the type of audience he was addressing when he made this remark? Was he merely paying lip-service to a "concept," not daring to face up to the practical implications of the "vitality" of God's relationship to man for the psychological well-being of men?

Mowrer is oviously free to consider the religious dimension and its Christian contents as something "metaphysical" and "with no empirical verification"; but if he wishes to give assistance to Christian men as members of a society, and validly analyze all the elements that go into the making of their psychological troubles and deficiencies, he cannot ignore the psychological experience created by the belief in this "ultra-empirical reality." From the psychological point of view the act of personal commitment to God in the fellowship and union with Christ is of momentous consequence. It is an entering into a *new community,* in which there are not two independent sets of relations (social among men and religious between God and men), but one single relationship, religious and social *at the same time,* between God and the community of men in and through Christ, the God-Man.

Who is, then, the Significant Other *par excellence* within the Christian Community? The answer is simple: the Mystical Christ, the People of God organized into a community by the presence of Christ. Without this clarification, it is difficult to understand the Christian experience of sin or of forgiveness.

Seen in this context, confession as practiced by Christians is the Sacrament of re-entry into the Community of those living in Christ. The priest is the official (meaningful and significant) representative of the Church, who in his official capacity *listens to* us who disclose both our identity as sinful Christians and our sins as the acts through which we have severed our connections with the living community of the faithful. He too, in the official capacity, *speaks to* us, welcoming us into the renewed participation in the redemptive and unifying action of Christ, *if* we are ready to work out our salvation within the Christian Community through penance and by a life more in keeping with our vocation as Christians. It is in this listening and speaking to the penitent by the priest as a significant representative of the significant Other (Christ) and others (Christian Community) that the social nature of confession is forcefully brought out into bold relief. In the Christian Community *there is no such thing as a completely secret confession: all confessions are open in the deep meaning of the word.*

The above statement should not be interpreted as if nothing could be done to bring out much more forcefully the social nature of confession. It has been mentioned only to put the problem in proper perspective. After all, the social value of an open confession can be realized only if we have the right understanding of what openness actually means. From the analysis of the concept itself, the psychological outcome of open confessions has to be measured not by the number of people, but the significance of the people to whom we reveal ourselves.

The actual meaning of significance has never been fully developed by Mowrer. This requires further study. It appears that the social significance of a person in one's life is to be clarified by the degree to which a person induces us to break through our self-centeredness and selfishness. An individual becomes socially significant to us to the extent to which he succeeds in drawing us out of our own selves and brings us into contact with the members of a community. In addition, it is our opinion that the significance of a person in our lives is to be determined also by the seriousness of purpose and selflessness with which he receives our confession. If there is the slightest suspicion that the other may use the knowledge he has of us for his own selfish interests, his significance as a socializing agent in our life wanes to the point of complete extinction.

Within the Christian perspective and vision of faith, the person who can most effectively bring about in us the change from self-centeredness to social openness and dedication is none other than Christ himself, especially under the mysterious "effacement of his personal individuality" in the reality of the Church. Confessions are not made to the historical Christ who lived as an individual two thousand years ago; but to Christ alive in the Church. This emphasis should restore sacramental confessions to their full social meaning in the practical lives of all Christians.

IV. CONCLUSION

The critical remarks we have made will be sufficient to show that the problem of confession as a means of self-improvement is not a simple matter. We personally feel that much of what Mowrer has said about open confessions can already be put into practice within the present framework. After all, the obligation of secrecy binds the priest alone, not the penitent who can always benefit by his frankness and openness towards the significant others in his life. We may be sure that a little less fuss about personal weaknesses would do us a lot of good both individually and collectively, while we keep the form of self-accusation to be made in confession in view of receiving sacramental absolution as it is practiced at present, even with the strict secrecy by which the priest is bound. After all, even in the event of having open confessions on a wider scale than it is now possible, it will always be the duty of the priest never to "remind" those under his care of their sins or defects, however public the confessions may have been. It is to be expected that the need for mutual respect

202   *The Mystery of Sin and Forgiveness*

will always remain as the basis of society, the best and most tactful expression of which may often be found in an attitude of discrete silence.

Mowrer did well in insisting on the moral origin of psychological problems and disorders. By doing so, he has guarded us against the facile tendency of many (priests included) of explaining cases of abnormal behavior exclusively in terms of illness rather than in terms of the desire to hide the sinful character of some of our actions. It is unfortunate, however, that in his zeal to counteract this tendency towards over-simplification, he was not sufficiently careful to distinguish between the moral and the psychological aspect of man's conduct; nor was he duly mindful of the religious dimension of man's life.

REFERENCES

Mowrer, O. H. **Learning theory and personality dynamics.** New York: Ronald, 1950.

Mowrer, O. H. **Psychotherapy: theory and research.** New York: Ronald, 1953.

Mowrer, O. H. Religion as thesis and science as antithesis. **The Hanover Forum,** 1959(1), 5, 37-46.

Mowrer, O. H. Sin, the lesser of two evils. **Amer. Psychol.,** 1960, 15, 301-304.

Mowrer, O. H. **The crisis in psychiatry and religion.** Princeton: Van Nostrand, 1961.

Mowrer, O. H. Learning theory and behavior theory. In B.B. Wolman (Ed.) **Handbook of clinical psychology.** New York: McGraw-Hill, 1965.

Mowrer, O. H. Integrity theory: a self-help approach. **Psychotherapy: theory, research and practice,** 1966(3), 114-119.

Sacrament de Penitence Aujourd'hui. **Informations Catholiques Internationales,** Feb. 1967, 282, 17-24.

Chapter Ten

COMMUNAL PENANCE: A LITURGICAL COMMENTARY AND CATECHESIS

GABRIEL-M. NISSIM, O.P.

"I prefer to confess directly to God," people are saying widely nowadays. Our answer is much less apt to be accepted because of current practices.

A questionnaire recently showed that people's theological ideas correspond exactly to what shows up in the actual usage: individualistic, monotonous, juridical. It is not enough to improve our teaching; we have to lay the axe to the root of the practice. And we have good hope of success, as is shown by recent bold improvements in the Mass.

Are we disquieted by those who ask us why they should any longer come to confession, or just silently do not come? By rights we should be more frustrated by those who keep coming to confession, just clinging to a comfortable routine dinned into them from an infancy catechism class. Guided by a sound instinct, some parish groups have bypassed talking about it in order to show by action what the real sacrament of penance is. In togetherness situations like army camps or scout outings they have set up "penance liturgies" which are proving widely popular, and succeed in deepening the sense of sin and pardon not only in the faithful but even in their priests.

A justification and a theology of this practice would be in place. But our goal here is more modest. We will just describe such an operation, as we have seen it working itself out over some time. We will add how well this corresponds to what we can learn by looking a little deeper into Vatican II on Liturgy or even into the commonplaces of sacramental theology textbooks. Thirdly we will reduce this to the simple terms of what can be put forth in a catechetic homily. Needless to say, our task throughout will be to allay the anxieties of those who shudder "this smacks of novelty."

Conviction Expressed

We will distinguish between the external rite and the "opting" or expression of inner conviction which underlies it. The rite must include an entry, a liturgy of the word, and the conferring of the sacrament. Entry of the priests — as many as possible are required — in alb and violet stole will be accompanied by a chant of repentance or of joy at the pardon of God and followed by a repentant moment of silence and a collect-prayer aloud. The liturgy of the word should be brief: a single Scripture reading, a homily not too long to leave room for some more moments of meditation, and another Psalm.

Still part of our Scripture meditation should be what used to be called the "examination of conscience." Instead of "Did I do this? Did I do that?" the leader can put it in prayerful and even joyous form: "Forgive us, Lord, for the times we have all been hypocritical," or "How kind of you, Lord, to keep calling us to you in spite of the number of times we have lied to you and to each other." At each "item" the group will join in by echoing not the negative but the positive and constructive verb: "Lord, forgive"; "We do thank you, Lord." And needless to say, the faults singled out for repentance should flow more directly from Scripture and from the urgent social and creative burdens it imposes.

For the sacrament itself, everyone will stand — or we might even get them to kneel, a "tradition" which is genuine. "May the Lord be upon your lips," says one priest as invitation to the *Confiteor*. Then the fathers take up a position in different parts of the room. Some priests who wish to should come to confession first. Then the lay participants who wish to come — no one has to — should be "marshaled" by sensitive laymen: not just for traffic-control, but to emphasize both God's initiative and invitation; and the communitarian character of the enterprise. Each one who confesses will receive his absolution with the same privacy, and in a certain small proportion of cases also a more lengthy word of guidance, though the circumstances of the rite make this feasible only as a "normal exception."

Separate Absolutions

Whatever tedium may be involved in these separate absolutions can be left to an alert chant-leader to dispel. But really this "delay" is an important activity of witness and meditation for a notably large category of the Christians who will be present. Many of them may have faith and desire yet not be able to receive absolution because of a situation they are involved in. The anonymity of their participation gives them fullest opportunity to share the sentiments of their comrades without pressure or embarrassment.

The rite ends with the priests all standing together with their spokesman, who recites the formerly optional invocation. "May the passion of our Lord Jesus Christ . . . and whatever good you do and evil you endure be cause for the remission of your sins, the increase of grace, and the reward of everlasting life." He then imposes collectively a penance to be done individually, and invites the assembly to express their joy in pardon by a recessional song.

Such a ceremony should take place no more than three times a year, chiefly in Lent and Advent. It should be organized in groups of several churches within a locality at varying times, so as to fit best the convenience of the laity and guarantee that a maximum number of priests will be present at each to hold bottlenecks down to a minimum. There are advantages in taking peer-groups together; but there can also be great mutual influence by mingling the teen-agers occasionally with their elders.

Community Acts

To take part in a ceremony like the above is a way of "opting" or voting with our feet. It expresses that awareness of what the rite really means which is the community's proper part in the "handing on of sacred tradition." This in no way cuts the ground from under the bishops, who alone have the right and duty to decide the how and when of that reform of current confessional practice which is unmistakably imperative. We cannot convey a theoretical understanding of what penance means without embodying it occasionally in a concrete dress-rehearsal. The very word "sacrament" is a curious rendition of the Greek *mystery,* and mystery can never be expressed in all its dimensions by mere explanatory words; it must be lived to be learned. The liturgical decree of Vatican II is speaking really of *sacrament as such* when it requires that one particular sacrament like the Eucharist be celebrated with ever more public and community participation.

Thus for example when it says that the collective should take precedence over the individual in all those cases of Mass *and* sacraments "supposing" community participation, we are given guidance about the future of confession even though its present form could not be said to "suppose" cooperation. One obvious pastoral benefit would be to revive the dormant sense of ecclesiality in many Catholics. They can discover by concrete action that there is no such thing as an approach to God except through the mediation and in the heart of the Church, and in the

Church's dynamic movement which is Christ's own. And specifically the power to forgive sins was given to the Church and as a sign of renewed association with the ecclesial community and through them with God. Just as it is mother Church as a whole which brought us to the birth of faith by baptism, so it is the Church in its entirety which pardons us. How can this be perceptible otherwise than in a communitarian rite? The Council itself tells us that the local community somehow holds the place of the Church established visibly in the universe.

Ministerial Role Is Central

The congregation does not compete for the power of jurisdiction belonging to the priest, nor does it lessen his jurisdiction. On the contrary, the congregation underlines the priest's jurisdiction all the more. Here, as in other things, the ministerial priesthood and the priesthood of the baptized are ordered to each other. The Church mediates grace through the priest, through the power he has received directly from Christ, with the bishop, and in dependence upon him. The priest's mission is to serve the church by visibly expressing the ecclesial function of reconciliation and by making this function efficacious, that is, by exercising his office sacramentally. There are so many profound theological truths in this that it would take a long and ponderous sermon even to touch upon them all.

Far more telling is the effect of just turning it into a drama. The simple and humanly warm steps of the ritual outlined above really translate for us these dogmas: (a) the grace and pardon of Christ is given in and by the Church; (b) everyone bears before the Church the guilt of his own faults, manifested not by a detailed accusation but by his simple presence and *Confiteor;* (c) penance like baptism is linked with the Eucharist as that "going to be reconciled with your brother which must precede laying your gift at the altar"; (d) the pilgrim church itself is in constant need of its own repentance and reform.

Sacrament Is Dialogue

From another angle, no sacrament should be administered without embodying its own need of "instruction in the word." Sacrament is not magic but dialogue, dialogue between a free God and a self-yielding man. Again what the Council says about "restoring Scripture readings to sacral celebrations," even if meant proximately for the Mass, applies with even greater and more obvious need to a sacrament like penance whose meaning is not so palpable without such formal instruction. Just as in Jesus himself there is no distinction between word and sign, word and human experience. Word reconciling us in peace with God; so too this representing of the gift of peace must be experience suffused by explanatory word.

Even our self-accusation should be scriptural. Not only our private conscience, but the word of God looming over us reveals to us our sin. The prophetic function of the charismatic community, so downgraded in the administration of penance as in other current Church practices, can at least be supplied from chosen Scripture readings. These show up our own sinfulness to ourselves better than that sterile and monotonous repetition of little lists of trivialities which we have depressingly come to regard as the normal confessional "accusation." Chants and prayers too should piece out the mini-rite surviving in the *Confiteor*. And almost more important than sorrow should be the *thanks* which now scarcely finds expression in the penitential ritual at all. Such thankful joy, which frankly does not fit the psychological posture of individual remorse, finds an altogether natural expression in the collective community joy "at one sinner's doing penance," given voice in the homily or chant.

Recent centuries' cudgeling of the "minimum necessary for validity" has all but obliterated that humus from which comes food for growth, "the penitence of the man's totality and of the Church." Here we have in one unitary experience: (a) change of heart tangibly effected by repentant and deep-resounding prayer; (b) acknowledgment that God's grace took the initiative to bring the penitent to where he is standing; (c) the conviction prominent in tradition that this grace is upheld by the intercessory prayer of the Church; (d) attestation of the known fact that formerly both penitent and minister wrestled long in foodlessness and prayer both before and after the brief instant of the rite itself. Words sung or spoken to bring forth these convictions must not be seen as a mere appetizer to kill time while waiting for the sacrament to get under way in earnest. They contribute organically to effect the communitarian sanctification; so importantly indeed that they justify limiting Scripture readings.

Choice of the Scripture reading, which is the way of letting penitents know what sin is and of what they should accuse themselves, may be suggested by some concrete problem known to be creating difficulty in that group. Or it may be some general lesson on mercy, like the parables of prodigal son or hard-hearted creditor. Or it may suit the liturgical season. The homily should include also a *part* of what the participants should know about the theology of this sacrament; other parts should be foreseen coordinatedly over a cycle of two or three such liturgical occasions.

One point that should be emphasized is that sin means a renouncing of one's whole basic attitude of confidence in God, rather than merely infringing a concrete prescription, for which the pertinent formula has come to be that nauseating "how far can I go?" Also excluded is a mere shame for having fallen short of one's human nobility, which may involve pride or hypocrisy. "Our hearts may blame us, but God is greater than our hearts" (1 *Jn* 3, 20).

Again, confession is an imitation and a share of that setting foot on the road of reconciling man to God which Jesus took before us. Like other liturgies such as the Mass, penance has the function of "re-presenting"— not just evoking but really making present again — the moment in history when Jesus sought pardon for the human nature which he shared with us. The cross reveals the gravity of sin and the love and depths of God. The cross of Christ and the sacrament of penitence are a unique service of Christ for us.

8

Church as Sacrament

Thirdly, the confession is not individualistically toward God but through the Church. Really there are not many sacraments but one sacrament, the Church herself as the body of Christ. As Christ was tangibly present to communicate grace to us via his humanity "in the days of his flesh," so today he continues to be present and to communicate to us via the sacrament and the humanity of his Church. He is also present specially in the separate persons, actions, and objects that enter into the Church's sacramental actions. In this perspective the penitent will no longer feel that to accuse himself to another human is unworthy of the immediacy of his access to God.

Really there are two simultaneous dialogues. As pardon and advice are exchanged from man to man, so there is going on an exchange from God to man. It is quite different doubtless in that God's readiness to pardon over and over again, seventy times seven, can hardly even be conceived or be effected within the cadres of our psychology. God's dialogue is different also in that his pardon is already waiting before we get there to ask for it. But the human dialogue resembles the divine in that it is interpersonal (we did not say inter-individual) and involves a turning around in one's tracks which is also a turning to the other. Leaving inside the rite the individualism of each one's confession and absolution is not prejudicial to the ecclesial character of the whole gathering. Psychology itself warns against the inclination to replace this personal accusation with a more collective declaration of our "state of sinfulness."

The ecclesial dimension of confession should be brought out futher by relating it to the unity of the two commands of love of God and neighbor. Every fault of ours however private is an injury to the Church. To the Church that has been proximately wounded by our sin, we must proximately turn for pardon. The priest's absolving hand leads us back into the Church just as the catechumen was dramatically led inside the group in former celebrations.

The final point in our catechetical homily will be that the

more we get away from a too-magical notion of the sacraments, the more we will see how each is only a step or aspect in a harmonious spiritual totality. Sin is forgiven primarily by baptism, a plunging into Christ which continues and is renewed throughout our Christian life, especially at each reception of the Eucharist. Insofar as penance is our imperfect translation of *metanoia,* it is a conversion, a turning: but there cannot be a *second* about-face, only a second *affirmation* or re-present-making of our baptismal turning. And this kind of second step we all need, not merely those who have a lengthy period of grave sinfulness to turn away from.

It is better not to present this sacrament as a sponge wiping sins away, but rather as a *passage* or passover which makes grace superabound where sin had abounded. Sin is a fact of life. Where more is forgiven, there is more love (*Lk* 7, 47); not, of course, that we do evil so that good may be called out of it (*Rm* 3, 8; 6, 1). Rather, plunged by baptism into the death of Christ, we crucify our former man by death to sin with him.

Community penitential liturgies are rapidly becoming a fact of life. Those who have insight will make the most of this.

PART THREE: NEW APPROACH TO ORIGINAL SIN

Chapter Eleven

NEW THINKING ON ORIGINAL SIN

JAMES P. MACKEY and HERDER CORRESPONDENCE

Two of the most recent attempts to re-examine the doctrine of original sin, the first bearing more the character of speculative reconstruction, the second more that of scriptural exegesis, have not yet appeared in English translation. The first is Piet Schoonenberg's *Theologie der Sünde*, Einsiedeln 1966. (Two other works by this author have already been translated into English and in these the basic elements of the view he still holds in his latest book may be found. They are his *Man and Sin*, London 1965, and *God's World in the Making*, Pittsburg 1964.) The second work is H. Haag's *Biblische Schöpfungslehre und kirchliche Erbsündelehre*, Stuttgart, 1966. *And there are other books in English which re-examine the biblical texts that have normally been used to sustain the traditional doctrine of original sin: e.g., J. de Fraine, *The Bible and the Origin of Man*, Alba House, New York, 1962; A.-M. Dubarle, *The Biblical Doctrine of Original Sin*, Lon-

---

* Haag's work has recently been published in English under the title **Is Original Sin in Scripture** (Sheed & Ward, 1969).

don 1964; and H. Renckens, *Israel's Concept of the Beginning*, New York 1964.

These works illustrate in a very concrete manner the tension inherent in the Church's teaching mission precisely because there are *two* streams, scripture and tradition, that lead back to the original revelation-source. The possibility of such tension is easily seen when it is said, on the one hand, that scripture, like any written text needs a tradition of interpretation and, on the other hand, that every dogmatic formulation of the post-apostolic Church must be judged in the light of the original apostolic teaching as that can be found in the scriptures. So, the exegetes among the authors just mentioned show a marked tendency to take a very negative attitude to that doctrine of original sin which has become traditional, to point out what elements in it cannot be based on the biblical text. With very few exceptions they do not try to reconstruct a doctrine of original sin precisely on the basis of the biblical data. An extreme form of this attitude is found in J. Gross' two-volume *Entstehungsgeschichte des Erbsündendogmas, Entwicklungsgeschichte des Erbsündendogmas,* Munich 1960-1963; he denies that there is any notion of original sin in scripture and regards the notion as an invention of St. Augustine. A dogmatic theologian like Schoonenberg, on the other hand, does take full account of the latest findings of scriptural exegesis, but goes on to attempt a full speculative elaboration of these findings with the help of the best philosophical insights of our age.

The traditional doctrine of original sin can be gleaned from the Tridentine definition and from the normal elaborations of it in the standard manuals of Catholic theology. Trent (Denz. 787-792) defined that Adam by his sin lost the sanctity and justice in which he had been constituted, and that he lost this not only for himself but for us also. It maintained that Adam incurred the penalties of death and suffering for his sin, and it seems to imply at least that these penalties pass to all his progeny. It insisted that concupiscence, a certain tendency to sinfulness in us which remains even after baptism, is a result of the fall. It declared, finally, that original sin, as it existed in the progeny of

Adam, although it was transmitted by physical propagation, and did not come about by our own sinful and personal imitation of Adam's disobedience, is sin in the true and proper sense of that word.

The traditional theological elaboration of this defined dogma normally takes the following form (see, for instance, B. V. Miller, "The Fall of Man and Original Sin" in *The Teaching of the Catholic Church*, G. D. Smith, ed., London 1956). It first of all paints a picture of Adam in the idyllic state of innocence before the fall; Adam stood in holiness and justice before God, did not experience suffering, did not have to die and did not know that inherent tendency to evil-doing which is said to be characteristic of all later men. It points out that original sin in Adam's progeny is a state of sin which does not result from personal acts of their own, but rather from the personal act of Adam, that it consists essentially in the lack of sanctity and justice (usually interpreted as the lack of what is known as sanctifying grace) and involves also the presence of concupiscence and the prospect of death and suffering.

In an important analysis of the historical precedents to the Tridentine definition A. Vanneste has pointed out that speculation about Adam as an individual and particularly speculation about the state of this individual before his fall did not begin to play the large part we find it playing at the time of Trent and in later theology until fairly late in Christian history, until the time of Aquinas in fact (see his "Le Décret du Concile de Trente sur le péché originel," *Nouvelle Revue Théologique*, 87 [1965] 688-726 and 88 [1966] 581-602). It is the considered opinion of Vanneste that this emphasis on Adam and on his state before the fall is to be explained at least partly by the fact that it is easier to accept the inheritance of a state of deprivation than it is to accept the inheritance of sin. Of course, when later theologians had finished saying that the fallen state meant essentially the lack of certain things which God meant all men to have but yet did not owe them, they still faced the task of showing how this lack could be truly sinful, as Trent said it was, even in men who had done nothing personal to incur it and could have done nothing to avoid it. Faced with this task most of them said that the lack of sanctity and justice in unredeemed man was sin in a real but analogous sense of the word, since it did involve a real alienation from God even if it did not involve any individual responsibility for this. Unfortunately, however, the Tridentine insistence on the true and proper sinfulness of the fallen state led most theologians to postulate some voluntary involvement of the whole race in the fall. Since this could not be a *personal* voluntareity on the part of the individual sons of Adam, they introduced into the theology of original sin the idea of the human race as a corporate personality bearing corporate responsibility for an act performed through its head, Adam. The concept of corporate responsibility is as characteristic of the traditional theology of original sin in recent times, as it is questionable.

Difficulties within Theology

The difficulties surrounding this presentation of the doctrine of original sin are so many and at times so intractable that they certainly demand the radical rethinking of the doctrine that is going on in contemporary theology. Some of the difficulties arise within the Catholic Church itself: from vagueness about some aspects of the doctrine or from tension between some elements in the doctrine of original sin and certain other doctrines of the faith.

There is, for instance, a great vagueness about the Tridentine declaration that original sin is transmitted, not by imitation, but by propagation. How can sin, which belongs essentially to the ethico-religious sphere, be transmitted in the biological process of generation? Within the terms of the traditional theory this question is not so difficult to answer as it might seem. One need only regard generation as the pure condition for the placing of the new human being in this graceless world, and not itself a process by which sin is transmitted. Undoubtedly the Council Fathers at Trent held, most of them, the Augustinian view that "libidinous" generation corrupted the flesh and in this way infected the soul with guilt (see Karl Rahner, "Theological Reflections on Monogenism" in his *Theological Investigations,* I, London 1961, p. 246), but it is by no means necessary to say that this view was defined by Trent. Of course, if the further concept of corporate responsibility is introduced to explain how the race after Adam is guilty of its graceless state, the objections to this concept must be faced—objections which are raised far more strongly outside the Catholic Church than inside it.

Perhaps more serious for the formulation of the doctrine that has by now become traditional is the difficulty of harmonizing the alleged effects of Adam's fall with the Christian teaching of the universality of God's salvific will. One could say, of course, on the old formulation, that even in the graceless ages between Adam and Christ, in the graceless places that have not yet heard of Christ, God, in view of Christ's works, found and finds ways of saving those who do the best they can.

Stimulus from Science and Philosophy

Significantly enough, the most serious difficulties for the usual doctrine of original sin, the most insistent stimulus for re-thinking, come from the realm of secular science and thought. This is significant as illustrating the fact that development of dogma occurs precisely through our attempts to embody our Christian insights in the ever-developing thought-patterns of our times. The Christian revelation was first formulated in the concepts and categories of Judaism at the time of Christ, and it has been necessary for man's retention and understanding of it ever since that he translate it into the concepts and categories of each succeeding age. The challenge from secular science and philosophy, of course, is never an unambiguous one for theology. It certainly can make theology see that the price it has to pay for saving the consistency of a past synthesis is too high in terms of realism. It could also tempt theology to reject some of the true insights of the past just because they were expressed in an idiom that is no longer current.

The first and most obvious challenge from modern science to the traditional doctrine of original sin takes issue with the latter's insistence on monogenism. Rahner's statement, "We assume that from the point of view of the natural sciences polygenism even as a scientific hypothesis possesses no greater probability than monogenism" (p. 286), is no longer an accurate assessment of the climate of responsible scientific opinion, if it was that even at the time he wrote it. The zoologist P. M. C. Davies, of Nottingham University, wrote in *The Tablet*, 30 June 1966: "To state that the entire human race has descended from a single pair of individuals is to make a biological statement that contradicts the considered opinion of most biologists" (p. 875). He is aware that genetic arguments have been brought forward to show that the monogenistic origin of the human race is possible and feasible (see John J. O'Rourke, "Some Considerations about Polygenism," *Theological Studies*, 26 [1965] 407-416); yet he said in his address to the Nicholas Callan Society at Maynooth, 23 June 1966: "Although it is true to say that the origin of the human race in this way (i.e., monogenistically) is not biologically impossible — certainly biology cannot yet disprove it — from all that we know of genetics and evolution this manner of origin seems — to say the least of it — unlikely. Certainly the elaborate genetical arguments which have been constructed to account for the origin of man in a biblical way, seem to me contrived and rather improbable."

It would be a mistake, however, to think that the brunt of the modern scientific challenge to the traditional doctrine of original sin bears on this very specific point about monogenism. The challenge is at once more diffuse and more radical. And science does not concern itself with the evolution solely of man's *body* (see, for instance, *Evolution after Darwin*, Sol Tax, ed., Vol. II, *The Evolution of Man: Mind, Culture and Society*, Chicago 1960). The modern evolutionary evidence affects one's outlook on the evolution of the whole man, physically, mentally, culturally and, therefore, religiously.

On the negative side, the picture of a state of primeval perfection in which man did not have to die and did not experience any physical suffering, in which, moreover, man's moral faculties were so fully developed and his fall so correspondingly complete that the whole of subsequent history, and even the work of Christ, must be seen mainly as an attempt to recover his original status, is not at all easy to harmonize with the picture which modern science paints — the picture of an extremely gradual evolution from extreme primitiveness to that mastery of mind over matter and over its own aggressiveness which we call civilization. On the more positive side, the scientific world-view is quite capable of facing the traditional theology of original sin with a rival explanation of the apparently permanent proclivity to evil in human society. This, it can say, is due to the fact that man's perception of true moral values is as painfully slow as his mastery over an often hostile universe. So the emphasis is laid on the possibility of human progress rather than on the acceptance of divine redemption, and the guilt complex connected with the doctrine of original sin is thought to be retarding rather than helpful to this possibility (see *The Humanist Frame,* J. Huxley, ed., London 1961).

Recently also an insistent attack has been mounted, mainly by philosophers interested in moral theory, on the concept of corporate responsibility in the Christian theology of original sin. This attack is well documented in the works of H. D. Lewis, professor of philosophy of religion in King's College, London (*Morals and the New Theology,* London 1947, and *Morals and Revelation,* London 1951). It is simply an offense to the moral reason of man, in Lewis' view, to suggest that moral responsibility and, therefore, moral guilt can be other than strictly individual. There can be no such thing as corporate responsibility in the sense that a group should be thought to share responsibility for an act which the majority of its members did not perform and which they could have done nothing to prevent.

Of course not all non-Christian thinkers of our time raise objections to every facet of the Christian doctrine of original sin. One might hesitate to appeal to Jung's psychology of the collective unconscious, for instance, especially in the context of the largely behaviorist-orientated psychology of the English-speaking world. One might not even be altogether happy to claim as independent witness the fact that concepts of all-pervasive and unavoidable guilt loom large in the existentialist philosophies of men like Heidegger and Jaspers, and co-exist in these with the typically existentialist emphasis on individual freedom, since existentialism itself has its roots in the work of a religious thinker, Kierkegaard, who had a vested interest in the Christian concept of original sin. Nevertheless, there is value in the fact that these thinkers feel that they need to retain the concept in order precisely to explain the existential condition of man, even though they no longer subscribe to Christian belief. There is particular value in Albert Camus' belief that it is man's longing for a lost or rejected heaven that drives him to excesses and to inhumanity towards his fellowman. For an account of the original guilt idea in non-Christian thinkers see L. Scheffczyk, "Die Erbschuld zwischen Naturalismus und Existentialismus" (*Münchener Theologische Zeitschrift,* 15 Jhg., pp. 17ff).

Papal Teaching

The popes have, on more than one occasion, expressed their support for full freedom of truly scientific research. They have often expressed their thanks for the help which theologians and other experts have given them in the fulfillment of their office as keepers and interpreters of the whole body of the Christian truth, their great reverence, even, for the work of such men (*Acta Apostolicae Sedis,* 58 [1966] p. 1169). Yet they are always very conscious of the fact that their own particular task is to guard the whole deposit of the Christian faith. It is only to be expected then that in times of suggested change, when the scientific and philosophical challenges from the secular sphere carry, at one and the same time, prospects for advance and seeds of dissolution, and when no adequate reformulation of traditional teaching is yet agreed, the pope should warn about the dangers of diluting the Christian truth and should show personal preference still for traditional formulas.

So Pius XII in his encyclical *Humani Generis* (1950), having granted his subjects freedom to debate the biological theory concerning the evolution of the human body, refused them similar freedom to debate in the same way the "conjectural opinion" of polygenism, "since it is in no way apparent how such an opinion can be reconciled with what the revealed sources of truth and the acts of the Church's teaching authority lay down on the subject of original sin, which is the result of a sin really committed by one individual, Adam, and which is passed on to all men by generation, and so is in each one of us and belongs to each of us" (Denz. 2328). Despite the second half of that quotation theologians have consistently maintained that the Pope did not here utter a doctrinal condemnation of polygenism, that he simply stated its apparent incompatibility with the doctrine of original sin and, consequently, made a disciplinary decision about debating it. Prohibition of public debate does not imply prohibition of research.

Research, in fact, continued and in recent years some attempts were made to reformulate the teaching of original sin in such a way that it could be harmonized with polygenism (see Z. Alszeghy and M. Flick, "Il peccato originale in prospettiva evoluzionistica." *Gregorianum*, No. 2, Vol. 47, pp. 201-225). Then, on 11 July 1966, Paul VI addressed these words to a group of scientists and theologians in Rome taking part in a symposium on original sin: "It is evident that the explanations of original sin given by some modern authors will seem to you irreconcilable with true Catholic doctrine. Starting from the undemonstrated premise of polygenism, they deny, more or less clearly, that that sin from which so many cesspools of evil have come to mankind was first of all the disobedience of Adam, 'first man,' figure of the future Man, committed at the beginning of history. Consequently, these explanations do not even agree with the teaching of scripture, of sacred tradition and of the Church's teaching authority, according to which the sin of the first man is transmitted to all his descendants not through imitation but through propagation, 'is in each one as his own,' and is 'the death of the soul,' that is, privation, and not simple lack, of holiness and justice even in newborn babies" (*AAS*, 58 [1966] p. 654). Perhaps the most sanguine view of this statement was taken by A.-M. Dubarle writing in *Le Monde*, 6 August 1966. Since the paragraph in the Pope's address immediately following the one quoted above condemned, in addition, any theories of original sin deriving from evolution theory in general which run counter to traditional and defined doctrine, Dubarle maintained that the Pope was implicitly relaxing the discipline of *Humani Generis*.

The Pope did not say what recent reconstructions of the theology of original sin he had in mind, if any, when he gave this address. There were two people at least in his audience who had published attempts to reconcile original-sin theory with polygenism, Flick and Alszeghy. A circular letter from Cardinal Ottaviani to bishops and heads of religious orders was even less specific and, therefore, less helpful from this point of view. The letter, on 24 July 1966, bade the bishops to take note, and to notify him, of "risky and deviating interpretations" of, among other things, the Tridentine definition on original sin. No indication was given as to what interpretations precisely were straying, much less as to how precisely they were straying.

Most recent writers, with a very few exceptions (for instance, M. M. Labourdette, *Le péché originel et les origines de l'homme,* Paris 1953, pp. 33ff), maintain that Trent did not pronounce definitively on monogenism or on the historicity of Adam as an individual. Even Rahner who, at least when he wrote the work referred to above, believed that monogenism was definable, does not believe that it was in fact defined by Trent. Like others he makes a distinction between that which is directly asserted in a solemn definition and that which is only concurrently asserted (p. 245) and he maintains that only the former is defined. In effect, what is being said is that Trent's teaching on original sin was given still in the oldest biblical forms. In other words, theologians are arriving at the view that a distinction which is now applied regularly to the Bible must also be applied to conciliar statements. The distinction applied to biblical texts is the distinction between what the sacred authors intentionally taught and what they thought but did not teach. In practice, since both we and they regard the Bible as a handbook of salvation, the distinction lies between the teaching on the true redemptive relationship between God and man and any literary form or natural conceptual framework in which this is expressed. We may even have to assert in some cases that *we* see where this distinction lies even when the sacred authors or council fathers did not. It is doubtful if modern theology has yet seen the full implications of this for the real extent and structure of change in the Church, and of the historical conditioning of truth.

The New Exegesis

From the point of view of the scripture scholars the doctrinal formulation of the teaching on original sin has leaned too heavily on official pronouncements, most of which date from a time when biblical exegesis was not what it is today. For too long exegesis was simply pressed into service in order to establish this doctrinal edifice. Their feeling is that a deeper understanding of the doctrine of original sin must be sought in the light of new exegesis, not the other way round.

Perhaps the most basic principle for a better understanding of the two classic biblical texts on original sin — chapters two and three of the Book of Genesis and chapter five of *the Epistle to the Romans* — is the principle put forward by Renckens that the texts attempt to explain present and apparently permanent realities rather than the historical, or pre-historical, origin of things. "Again and again, we have to force ourselves to return to the most elementary principle of all exegesis: The first condition of any reliable judgment about the paradise narrative, or any other biblical text, is that our own point of view should as far as possible be the same as that of the sacred author. And his concern here is first of all to convey something about the disastrous present, which is at first sight so difficult to reconcile with the content of his faith in God. In the process of doing this, he is obliged to go back and consider the historical event of man's first sin, which has cut across the line of God's original saving purpose. . . . The biblical evidence concerning the state of affairs which existed before this first sin does not allow us to make any kind of historical reconstruction of it, since its central point of reference is a judgment of value about *present* reality. All the narrative is saying, in the last resort, is that if things had gone as Yahweh had intended, man and the world in which he lives would have looked quite different. That they are as they in fact are, is not to be blamed upon Yahweh, but on sin, that of the past as well as that of the present. And the believer must therefore see in suffering and death more than a mere necessity of nature" (op. cit., pp. 291-2).

Romans 5:12-20 is a kind of meditation on the kerygma of *Rm* 3:24, "Both Jew and pagan sinned and forfeited God's glory, and both are justified through the free gift of his grace by being redeemed in Christ Jesus." A multiple comparison of the old man and the new man is put before us, with the motifs of antithesis and supersedence overlapping. Two Adams are contrasted, as heads and embodiments of two humanities (see K. Condon, "The Biblical Doctrine of Original Sin," *Irish Theological Quarterly,* 34 [1967] 20-36).

It is the opinion of P. Lengsfeld that the Christ-Adam parallel in *Rm* 5 contains no teaching at all about an historical Adam as an individual man (*Adam und Christus,* Essen 1965, p. 115). Perhaps the point is explained best by C. H. Dodd. Commenting on the fact that, for St. Paul, sin is not an inherent taint but a real spiritual force for wickedness in the world, which Paul sometimes seems to personify, Dodd continues: "How sin came into human nature is a question which Paul does not answer very satisfactorily. He sometimes traces it to an historic transgression of a human ancestor in the remote past. This was the common account given in contemporary Judaism. But in other passages he suggests a different origin. In the background of his world stand the 'world rulers' or 'elemental spirits.' They have some special relation to the material world, and it does not appear that in relation to it they are necessarily evil. But if man becomes subject to them, then he is fallen to a state of unnatural slavery" (*The Meaning of Paul for Today,* London, 1958, p. 62). St. Paul does not commit himself, therefore, to any particular explanation of the rule of sin in the world. Indeed, as D. J. O'Connor pointed out at a study session of the Irish Theological Association on original sin, on 2 November 1966, Paul is quite capable of using the single-ancestor model even in a context where he himself explicitly recognizes that not all those about whom he speaks are natural sons of the ancestor. In chapter 4 of the same *Epistle to the Romans* he describes Abraham as the father of all those who live by faith even though he realizes that some, the uncircumcized, are not descended from his people. It is the model of faith that interests him, not the genealogy.

It might seem then that the main exercise of biblical exegesis with regard to the usual doctrine of original sin is a debunking one. Most of De Fraine's book is devoted to showing that monogenism is not the teaching of any text of scripture, in the Old or New Testament. And if one asks the question: Is there in the Bible any teaching about the inheritance of sin or the transmission of sin? the answers are hesitant. According to Haag, there is certainly no question in the Bible of a passive inheritance of sin (p. 64), and Schoonenberg points out that Paul has nothing to say about the existence of original sin in the unbaptized child (*Theologie der Sünde,* p. 153).

Haag is also of the opinion that the Genesis narrative can establish nothing about man's freedom from suffering before the fall (p. 51) and the fact that even in Genesis 2:7, that is, before the narrative of the fall begins, man is seen to be formed of the dust of the earth, essentially corruptible stuff, should cast some doubt on any view that the sacred author thought that man, before the fall, was destined to escape biological death (p. 52). Evidently, in the fall narrative itself, some more ancient mythological material is used, for instance, the old Babylonian *Epic of Gilgamesh,* and this deals with man's puzzlement at, and at-

tempt to rid himself of, his condemnation to biological death.
Nevertheless, exegetes do normally point out that when the Bible
deals with death as the wages of sin it is not thinking only, perhaps not even principally, of biological death. It is thinking,
rather, of the falling away, the destruction, of human nature at
all levels once man is alienated from his true destiny in God. So
in *Rm* 5:21 death is contrasted with eternal life with God in
heaven, not simply with continued life in this world. Death, according to the "new theology," is not simply a radical change at
the biological level; it is an experience for man. The man who is
united with God in love dies a very different death from the
man whose ideals are all within this present world (see Karl
Rahner, "On the Theology of Death," *Modern Catholic Thinkers,*
A. R. Caponigri, ed., London 1960, or Ladislaus Boros, *The Mystery of Death,* New York 1965).

The Present Debate

Small wonder that the speculative theologian should feel un-
comfortable with original sin at the moment. Between the devil
of exegetical unhelpfulness and the deep blue sea of apparent
papal intransigence, he is also aware that the same sea is infested
by scientific sharks already sharpening their teeth for him.

The decisive argument for original sin, as Vanneste has
pointed out (pp. 598-600), is neither the biblical texts just mentioned nor the practice of infant baptism. In fact, he says, one
can regret the exaggerated interest, even in recent times, in the
baptism of infants. Of course the definition of original sin must
be able to show how infants are saved from it by baptism, but we
do not define original sin by first concentrating on the case of
infants. The decisive argument for original sin is the implication
of the basic truth of the faith, namely, that Christ came to save
all men from sin. If Christ died to save us from sin (1 *Cor* 15:3)
then we are all sinners; if Christ was reconciling the world to God
(2 *Cor.* 5:19), then there is a "sin of the world," that is, some
kind of solidarity in sin. Possibly a more positive contribution

may yet be expected from the exegetes on the biblical view of our real solidarity in sin. Meanwhile, dogmatic theologians have been trying to formulate some explanations of it.

Some, like Rahner and Scheffczyk, have expressed the view that such solidarity in sin must be grounded in a very special unity of the race, the unity, in fact, of single ancestry. Schoonenberg accepts that this is an ideal form of unity, but it might not be the *fact* (*God's World in the Making*, p. 74).

P. Smulders (*Theologie und Evolution,* Essen 1963) attempts to integrate the doctrine of original sin fully into an evolutionary framework. His view is that mankind from the beginning was called to the fulness of the Body of Christ, a status to be achieved in very gradual steps by cooperation between God and man over the long ages. But mankind was unfaithful to this call, not simply by a single major sin at the very beginning, but by a "snowball" effect of sins from the beginning (p. 234) so that the sinfulness of mankind increased with growth in civilization. This sinfulness meant that mankind was refusing its God-given destiny, was closing in on itself, and was continually creating a spiritual atmosphere or situation which newcomers to the race would both inherit and transmit.

The attempted reconstruction of Flick and Alszeghy is even more indebted to the evolutionary view of human existence (see "Original Sin and Evolution," *The Tablet,* 17 Sept. 1966, pp. 1039-1041). They specifically envisage a polygenistic origin for the human race. They propose that the first true men were neither fully installed in the "sanctifying-grace" relationship with God — they were simply being prepared for this by preliminary graces — nor were they yet fully moral agents. These writers then seek the best of both worlds by envisaging the case that one individual at the beginning did finally arrive at full moral status, in fact did not commit himself to God's plan, but rather rejected it and in doing this involved the rest of the morally evolving race in his fall. The price they have to pay for wanting the best of both worlds is the reintroduction of the very questionable concept of corporate responsibility. Yet without this concept it is not possible to say how the lapse of one individual could cause the fallen status of others with whom neither he nor any of his contemporaries nor any of their progeny might have come in contact. It certainly seems that the acceptance of polygenism will mean the accepance of a multiple origin of human sinfulness.

Vanneste shows that this is not necessarily in opposition to Trent's insistence on the unicity of original sin (p. 723) — *origine unum* (Denz. 790) — because that phrase was simply meant to combat the opinion of some Protestant theologians who identified original sin too closely with concupiscence and so tended to dilute it into the many actual sins to which concupiscence can give rise. It would seem, therefore, that we may have to say that the exact details of the remote origin of sin escape us, but we can certainly see sin as a force in history that precedes us, indeed precedes any period of history, any civilization that we know.

There seems little prospect of proving that the lack of grace and of the preternatural gifts in the long ages between hominization and the coming of Christ was more than a mere lack, that it constituted in fact a sinful state. To make this case, as the traditional formulation of doctrine tried to make it, involves either saying that men in those ages lacked something they "ought" to have had — but how can a man ought to have something which he can do nothing to provide himself with? — or in using, again, the concept of corporate responsibility. In order to say that sin reigned from Adam to Christ, it is necessary to admit that grace was also available in the normal structures of human existence from Adam to Christ, for sin means the rejection of God and not simply the absence of God from man's world. The concept of the sacred tradition (or traditions) of the race as that which carried in its own tenacious manner the awareness of God's approaches to man, as that which was helped on and developed by the hidden saints and prophets with whom God provided these lost ages, until it received its definitive confirmation and fulfillment in the coming of Christ — this concept is necessary for the true understanding of the reign of sin in the long history of man. Every sin is, at least implicitly, a readiness to substitute some other ideal for that of personal union with God. Since there are sinners in the human race there are traditions of these substitute ideals challenging the sacred ideal for the allegiance of men's minds even before men take definitive decisions of their own (see the chapter on "Fall" in J. P. Mackey's *Life and Grace,* Dublin and Melbourne 1966).

Schoonenberg, in both *Man and Sin* and *Theologie der Sünde,* has been at pains to show that as men are ministers of grace to each other, preaching God's word and witnessing to him in their lives, so they may also be ministers of "graceless situations" to each other. This is never merely a matter of bad example. Rather is it, especially with parents and children, a question of instilling substitute ideals, thus shaping the mental attitude, the spiritual direction of others. It is a question of the formation of mind, character, personality, just as much as biological generation forms the body. The race's solidarity in sin, therefore, is a matter neither of a simple summation of actual sins nor of some passive reception of a curious type of guilt. It is a question of a spiritual atmosphere, created by the traditions of men, forming men's moral and religious attitudes in a way that jeopardizes their possibility of responding to God's call, which is also carried to them in the sacred tradition. It is the "flesh" of St. Paul, the "world," used in a pejorative sense, of St. John, that which stands hostile to the grace of God in human history, and grows as the grace of God grows until the great confrontation in the death and resurrection of Christ. Because of it, death is no longer simply a transition point but rather a radical break with this world, for this world, because of human traditions, stands under the reign of sin. Yet, because he was faithful to his Father on earth, Christ was raised from the dead, and we are now baptized in the likeness of his death and resurrection (*Rm* 6:3ff).

These modern attempts to reconstruct the theology of original sin are subtle and many-sided. They try to knit the best of biblical exegesis with the best of human discovery. They do not do away with the mystery of sin as the foolishness, the ultimately absurd in this world, standing against man's best interests and God's will. They have already influenced the presentation of the doctrine of original sin in the Dutch catechism for adults (see Herder Correspondence, Jan. 1967, pp. 6-7), and it is to be hoped that they will soon have an influence on a better formulation of the doctrine for children as well.

They do not deny the historicity of man's fall, though they are agnostic about the time, nature and number of its first occurrence. In fact, as Schoonenberg insists, they give back to sin its historical dimension. Certainly they give back to Christology its central and due place in theology, in the Christian understanding of life. Too often in theological textbooks and even in modern catechetical programs, it is the destructive work of Adam which is described in detail first; only then is Christ introduced, called upon to restore what one man lost (see the Irish *Syllabus of Religious Instruction for Post-Primary Schools and Colleges,* p. 7). More recent theology prefers the pauline perspective (*Rm* 5) for which the center of interest is Christ's person and work.

His coming is seen more positively as the culmination of all God's historical approaches to mankind. Looking out from this center — and only from this vantage point — the theologian can see that men are and always have been bound together in hostility to God or indifference to him, to their own destruction. At this point the theology of sin is truly Christian.

Chapter Twelve

EVOLUTION AND ORIGINAL SIN

PIERRE SMULDERS, S.J.

The evolutionist viewpoint and the doctrine of original sin may seem to be directly opposed to each other. The evolutionist, who sees every origin as imperfect and defective, is confronted with the picture of a first man endowed with magnificent privileges and dominating paradise. Recent advances in exegesis have accentuated the uneasiness many feel in this matter.

Theology risks disfiguring reality when it treats the dogmas of faith as separate units. Our teaching on sin, particularly original sin, finds its proper context only in subordination to the total message of salvation. Original sin is *felix culpa*. It makes sense only in a mankind destined to become the body of the Incarnate Word of God. Salvation in Christ dominates human history and limits the power of sin.

Unfortunately attention has centered on the extreme cases of original sin committed by Adam and contracted by new-born infants. This focus misses the central thrust of the doctrine that all men are sinners. We must remember that the story of the Fall grew out of Israel's consciousness of her sinfulness and of man's solidarity in sin. Original sin loses its existential meaning when separated from the experience of sin among adults. For Scripture is chiefly interested in sin among adults rather than infants, and the Council of Trent retained this emphasis.

But after Trent the perspective changed. The accent shifted from the experience of adult life to the condition of infants, from solidarity in sin to exclusive concern with what original sin meant for each person, from a dynamic power that oriented men to personal sins to a static reality identical for adults and infants.

Larger Context Eases Tension

If we again place the doctrine of original sin in the larger context of consciousness of personal and collective sin, we can rediscover its full meaning. We will see original sin as a power of sin that grows along with mankind itself, because each sinner gives it a new force and impulse. Thus the opposition will diminish between the dogma and the modern historical and evolutionist view.

According to the Bible the Father created the world and mankind for Christ. "He is a likeness of the unseen God, born before any creature, for it was through him that everything was created in heaven and on earth . . . He existed before all things and he sustains and embraces them all" (*Col* 1, 15-17). In God's design everything is oriented to the Incarnation. From its first beginnings mankind is destined to grow up to the fullness of the body of Christ.

Sin Rejects Divine Plan

Against this destiny man sinned from the beginning. The first man had to make his choice like every man that was to come after him. Would he give himself to God in faith, or would he prefer his own human power? Everywhere we find the same central sin, in paradise, in the Tower of Babel, in the idolatry of the golden calf, in the wicked politics of the later kings, in the unbelief of the Jews who demanded a messiah according to their own ideas. In love with his own greatness and power, man wishes to suffice for himself. He wishes to develop himself without recognizing that he himself is a gift of God and that God is the goal of his liberty. In its depths, every sin is a rejection of God and implicitly a refusal to build oneself up in the body of Christ.

How are sin and concupiscence connected? Concupiscence, according to Trent, is from sin and leads to sin. It is not, in the first instance, an inclination to evil things but to the pursuit of good things in an evil manner. When man refuses the gift of God, he inevitably seeks something infinite outside God. His inclination becomes disordered, immoderate, and unbalanced. He demands of creatures what only the Creator can give him.

This is the concupiscence described by Scripture and the Church. It seeks absolute values in things, in pleasure, in wealth, in honor, in power over the world, as opposed to an ordered quest of finite values which seeks them only as they are related to God. Concupiscence consists in the tendency to make of earthly goods something absolute. Augustine calls it the love of self carried to the contempt of God.

Therefore concupiscence is not mainly or exclusively discord between sense desire and will. Perhaps it is seen most clearly in this discord, but its root is in the will. True concupiscence shows itself in vanity, ambition, pride, in the self-love that penetrates even the best intentions. St. Paul speaks for all men when he says: "I do not do what I want to do, I do things that I hate" (*Rm* 7, 15). Man is disjointed and divided against himself.

The goods of this earth are the gifts which God has given man the task of subjecting and using. But man has made these goods serve his own self-love. He makes absolute values out of pleasure, wealth, honor, power. Men know the fragility of these idols, but continue to venerate them and seek salvation in them. The goods of this world cease to be a springboard to God and become a wall that shuts out the horizon of heaven.

Brings Social Divisions

Society likewise becomes disjointed. Man rejects God's call to a life of love and builds a divided society. The Tower of Babel is the biblical symbol of national idolatry which results in hatred and war. Spreading wars and cruel tyrannies arise when man spurns love of God and of the neighbor which provides the only solid foundation for lasting peace and a just social order.

In this framework, original sin appears as the weight of evil that burdens every man by his birth and his solidarity with mankind, prior to all his sins, but ratified and freely accepted by each personal sin. Theology ordinarily describes original sin on the analogy of "habit," an inclination of the will resulting from personal choices. But original sin can also be depicted as the situation in which man finds himself because he enters a world where sin reigns. Man's environment — especially its institutions, value systems, and peculiar web of inter-personal relations — can influence the formation of personality. Man develops by his contacts with other men. If certain values are absent from his environment, man can hardly develop them in himself. He unconsciously adopts from others the attitudes that in large part determine his own conscious conduct. For example, the idea that money and luxury are the main goals of education, study, and work so surrounds children brought up in our western culture that few escape the powerful force of this atmosphere.

Not Purely Static Reality

This environment of sinful mankind which children enter just by being born largely makes up the concrete social form of original sin. Personal sins augment the weight of evil and sin that burdens other men and posterity. Hence we can see that original sin is not a purely static reality, but something that grows with the growth of mankind itself, it is a parasite that penetrates a seed and then spreads throughout the tree to the extremities of its roots and branches.

But the real essence of original sin is more hidden and profound; it is found in concupiscence and especially in deviation from our God-appointed destiny. The Godless world is so powerful only because it finds in each human heart an echo and an accomplice. "When anyone is tempted, it is by his own desire that he is enticed and allured" (*Jn* 1, 14). Paul calls this evil tendency the "flesh." The flesh is not the body as distinct from the soul. It is the whole man, but without the Spirit; it is man given over to the powers of sin and death. "The desires of the flesh are against the Spirit" (*Gal* 5, 17). Thus the center of gravity of sin is within man, in the revolt of the passions, and especially in the deep egoism which lodges in the will.

Here lies the deepest root of original sin. Created and destined for love, man always aspires, at least unconsciously, for love as the final flowering of his being; but in his depths he has cultivated a profound egoism. He lacks the uprightness that ought to direct him beyond himself toward God. Man is spiritually dead, for union with God is his real life. God calls man to membership in the body of Christ and to union with the Father. But man obstinately refuses to pass beyond self into this infinite love. He folds in upon himself and turns away from God.

How original sin can exist in man prior to all personal choice is a mystery, but perhaps no more a mystery than man's call to form the body of God's incarnate Son. In the covenant of paradise, mankind could have constructed this body by developing itself in the course of history: each generation could have handed down a positive orientation to this destiny. History is a process in which what follows depends upon what precedes. Therefore if mankind was to achieve this destiny by its history, parents could have given their children an existential orientation for its accomplishment. The parents' "yes" to God's call would have directed the children forward.

"No" passed on to posterity

Inversely, the "no" of generation after generation com-

municates a deviation to posterity. Not only is each man born
into a world marked by sin, but the very existence received from
his parents lacks the proper orientation to the divine destiny.

However, we must not see human history as a unilateral progress of sin, for it is primarily a history of grace and redemption.
Even the paradise story ends with a promise of redemption.
God continues building up the body of his Son, and man continues to share in this work.

The confrontation of the dogma of original sin with evolutionist thought underlines the dissonance between the modest
origins of mankind which evolution postulates and the universal
range which dogma attributes to Adam's act. Revelation teaches
that the ancestors of the human race caused original sin. Likewise the Council of Trent had defined that Adam's sin lost for us
the holiness and justice which he had received from God and
that Adam transmitted to the whole human race sin itself which
is the death of the soul. "One man's disobedience made the mass
of mankind sinners" (*Rm* 5,19). Genesis also teaches this truth.
The inspired writer intends to assign the cause of the misery and
wickedness of mankind and to explain our present condition.
Adam is not only an image or a type, but the *real cause* of the
estrangement between God and mankind which the constant
infidelity of the Chosen People and the perversity of the pagans
had made so clear. For Israel the history of mankind is not a
cycle but a road, and the universality of sin can be accounted
for only by a sin committed at the start of the road. We have
here a narrative of very mysterious and obscure facts; yet they
are facts.

This causality of Adam's act does not exclude the causality
of other sins. The sin in paradise is only "sin's beginning" (*Sir*
25, 23), the breach by which sin entered the world to assert
thereafter its domination. Genesis relates a succession of falls
which affect more or less the destiny of posterity.

A similar situation occurs in each person's life. Personal sins
are not committed outside of original sin but are its fulfillment.
By his personal sins every adult confirms and makes his own
the fall of Adam. We cannot raise a watertight division between

original sin and personal sin. Revelation describes original sin less as a state than as an orientation to ever new sins.

For St. Paul personal sins are a consequence of Adam's sin which alienates his whole posterity from God and puts it under the domination of sin and death. Adam's children condemn themselves to the full terror of this domination by personally confirming their alienation from God.

These considerations dispel various difficulties raised against the usual presentation of original sin. Adam's sin does not have to be a superhuman act. It may have been a primitive sin of a primitive man, although of a man sufficiently evolved to make a moral act, to accept or reject grace. But Adam's sin went on snowballing. His descendants confirmed their inherited sin on the level of their own higher culture, with their more mature conscience. Original sin develops with the development of mankind.

Adam's Sin Repeatedly Ours

There is a certain hypocrisy in the complaint that the sin of a remote ancestor makes us guilty before God. As if we are not continually making Adam's revolt our own! We are ever fashioning idols of money, pleasure, and power. Our personal sins proclaim and confirm incessantly the dominion of sin introduced by Adam.

When the Council of Trent teaches the transmission of original sin "by propagation, not by imitation," it indicates that man incurs original sin by entrance within fallen mankind. Procreation can include not only the strictly biological aspects, but also all the factors by which mankind makes someone its member, including education, environment, and example.

Formerly the paradise story was regarded as an eye-witness report transmitted from Adam to Moses. This view is outdated. The narrative is history insofar as the sacred author teaches what was the beginning of the history in which we live. The writer informs us that at the origin of mankind a drama unfolded like that which took place at the beginning of the history of the Chosen People, a divine covenant of grace and salvation to which man was unfaithful from the beginning. Therefore we should not look for exact information about geography, biology, or psychology in the story. Genesis teaches that man's alienation from God, his concupiscence, hostility, and death do not correspond to God's original plan. These evils result from an ancient sin that is constantly being renewed. Thus there was a time without such misery, but the Bible does not indicate how long this time lasted.

This view sets aside certain difficulties raised by the evolutionist view of the world. The theologian must carefully scrutinize the standard view which endowed the first man with perfect knowledge, harmony between sense life and moral life, and immortality. The privileges which the Greek mind attributed to the first man for the sole reason that he is the source of all that comes to fruition throughout history are not imposed by revelation and so may be freely questioned.

Open to Improvement

In teaching that concupiscence and death result from sin, Scripture and the Church indirectly teach that Adam was preserved from concupiscence and death. But there seems to be no obligation to hold that Adam possessed these privileges with full perfection rather than as dispositions open to improvement. By fidelity to God, could not the first man have progressively freed himself from the law of concupiscence and death?

Scripture and the Church teach no more than a preservation from concupiscence and death such as they reign in our experience. The Bible restricts itself to death *such as we know it*: the anguished end of our life and projects. The Bible asserts that this death results conjointly from a punishment and from our earthly origin. Scripture and the Church teach that Adam was preserved from the brutal death, alone deserving of the name, which is a punishment for sin. They seem to make no pronouncement about death as our natural end. Apparently we are not obliged to picture man in paradise as utterly preserved from the law of decay which awaits every organism living on earth.

The same considerations can be applied to freedom from concupiscence. Man in paradise did not know the concupiscence experienced by fallen man. Concupiscence is more a division within the will than a discord between sensual and moral tendencies. Perhaps Adam's freedom from concupiscence was compatible with struggle and tensions which he could gradually bring to perfect moral integration.

Again, a sober view of the privileges of paradise will possibly disarm much of the opposition aroused by the ordinary presentation. There remains the central privilege of paradise which is the supernatural call to build up mankind in the body of Christ and the aptitude for this task which sanctifying grace and the infused virtues confer. The first man received the Holy Spirit who enabled him to love the Father above all else and his fellow man as himself. Against this privilege the evolutionist cannot object. If he acknowledges a spiritual soul, he will recognize the possibility through grace of personal encounter with God. The conferral of grace opened to body and instinct a new opportunity of consecration to the service of the Spirit of escaping the slavery of instinct and matter. Yet this need include no sudden and total break with the inherited corporality and psychism of animality.

Chapter Thirteen

ORIGINAL SIN AND MAN'S SITUATION

Modern men even modern Catholics, find it difficult to admit that sin is a fact. Imperfection, weakness, inability, tragedy, yes — but sin? Yet we know from Scripture and from Christ's crucifixion that we are truly sinners. Our imperfect lives include the evil of true sin, the refusal of faith and love.

It may be admitted that much usually taken to be the result of sin is in fact simply part of a world that is incomplete and developing. Some would say that original sin is no more than a primitive way of expressing man's necessary metaphysical insufficiency. But the contention here is that there exists a community of sin, just as men share together in Christ's redemption. This "original" sin affects man's origin and whole existence precisely because it is common to the individual and all his fellows.

John expresses man's community in sin by the phrase, "the sin of the world." This expression is rooted in the OT experience of Israel where community was as primary as the individual. Not only kings, but patriarchs and heads of families determined the fate of their communities by their individual behavior. This is put most forcefully in Yahweh's word about the fathers' guilt haunting four generations and their goodness extending to the thousandth generation (cf. *Ex* 20, 5). And the pagans were also considered guilty before God. The NT term, "world," seldom means creation as pleasing to God. In the Johannine writings, it refers to the world hardened in sin, rejecting and hating Jesus, closed to his revelation and bound up in evil most of the time.

Individual Responsible, Too

This collective consideration of the people of God and of mankind as a whole does not exclude the individual's own responsibility. That "God repays each man according to his works" is clearly applied to individuals in the prophets and wisdom literature. At the time of the exile, both Jeremiah and Ezekiel oppose the complaint of the people that God is punishing them for what their forefathers had done. To the objection that "the fathers have eaten sour grapes," Jeremiah replies. "Everyone dies through his own guilt" (*Jr* 31, 29). Ezekiel adds that father and son are equal, that only he who sins will die — then he adds examples of personal responsibility.

The more primitive notion of community passed as the individual was thrown on his own resources, particularly during the exile. In Scripture, individual responsibility is one aspect of man's relationship to God and runs parallel to his solidarity with others. The sin of the community, the sin of the world, is more than the sum of personal sins viewed individually, yet it is not constituted by the transmission of guilt from one person to another. What then is the connecting link that joins the sins of the fathers to those of their children?

"Situation" Described

We have to speak of the influence which one man's decision has on that of another in such a way that the freedom of the second man is preserved. The notion of situation can be helpful here. My free act puts the other in a situation which presents him with good or evil, provides support or withdraws it, and communicates values and norms.

So the situation determines another's freedom insofar as he cannot but respond to the good or evil that confronts him — or else not respond at all. Whatever his decision. It is a matter of his own free choosing. I do not influence his actual reacting but rather the determinate context in which he freely takes a stand. The context or situation so links our free decisions that history itself might be described as the interplay of human decision and situation.

The dictionary defines situation as "a totality of circumstances in which one sees himself placed at a definite moment." At first glance, it seems the circumstances merely affect a person from the outside. But our inquiry concerns the *inner* determination of the situated person, his subjection to the situation, his being-handed-over to it. This feature is the constitutive element of the sin of a community, the sin of the world.

The situated character of human existence is no contradiction of man's freedom. It is a matter of the determinate conditions that meet man's freedom within its own sphere of action, of that limit upon the objects man encounters and hence the limited number of insights and opportunities they can provide. Men possess a *situated* freedom; every human choice is conditioned by past decisions and restricts future possibilities. Such would be a formal sketch of the way one person's freedom situates another's.

But what is the concrete meaning of saying that a person is situated by the sin of others? One way to explore this problem is afforded by our experience of bad example. Why does it leave me at such a disadvantage? First of all, such behavior does not provide the appeal of real values. Then it stands as an invitation to evil. By his action, the other person equivalently says, "This is the way it goes; I feel fine doing it; it makes sense in my life; is this not the way for you, too?" Any moral behavior influences us both as an objective statement and personal affirmation of values.

Example Situates

Moreover, deprivation of good example can be just as catastrophic as the lived example of evil. Not only in our early formative years, but through the whole of life we depend on others and measure our behavior against theirs. Social pressure added to the force of example can make a given choice in a situation as difficult as that of a martyr. Such pressure spreads bad example, but is more dangerous because it excludes the good example everyone needs, especially young people. If true values and norms are not provided for the young or are lived hypocritically, young people can hardly come to live in a moral way.

The situations so far described are those which condition our conscious living — we meet them and give them part of their meaning and form. But there is another type of situation in which values and norms can be obscured. This sort of situation precedes the individual's existence, encompasses it, and influences his life prior to and independently of any conscious decision on his part.

The simplest example of this latter case would be that of a child born into a family living by theft or prostitution, where the values of honesty and chastity are simply absent. Here the child's need to be morally educated cannot be filled. In such a family the child is absolutely unable to be honest. For a person can only esteem and pursue a value which he has somehow come to recognize as such. If values are not presented in this way, a person cannot choose to realize it for himself. This impossibility is absolute, unlike the situation where one is subject to bad example and social pressure.

Grace Also Missing

Sin not only damages interpersonal relations: it is also the refusal of grace — the relationship between God and man. So one individual's sin places another in a situation where not only values and norms are missing, but where grace is absent as well. Since the whole of humanity is an educative community, man stands as mediator to his fellows in his graced union with God. Even classical theology has to assume this in the case of Adam's sin, unless his influence in salvation history is explained merely extrinsically, by a divine will-act.

Catholic thought has viewed the offices, charisms, and intercession of the Church as participating in Christ's mediation. This participation also occurs in the case of Israel and the rest of mankind — on its way to Christ's Church. This is why St. Paul can call Abraham our father in faith.

Whether the relation between mediation and grace is understood as causal or simply conditional makes no difference. Every contact by which a person communicates his interior life to another witnesses at the same time to his relationship to God in grace. Because of the Incarnation there will generally be no such thing as grace unless one's fellow men have played their role. Thus grace is bound up with man's role as mediator. In like manner, sin — the rejection of grace — has a grace-robbing effect on one's fellows, placing them in a situation deprived of grace. Solidarity in sin creates a situation of blindness to value and the privation of grace.

This solidarity can take on dramatic implications. There are "historical sins" in which a whole community is involved — liberalism, colonialism, anti-Semitism, racial discrimination, lust for war. These are the modern versions of such ancient crimes as war, exploitation, economic and sexual salvery. To this the Bible adds specifically religious sins — idolatry, magical attitudes, killing of prophets, rejection of Christ.

The sin of the world and the salvation of the world develop together. The sin of the world is the negative side of salvation history. Man's refusal destroys not only his personal grace-life, but also breaks off the interpersonal mediation of grace and thus creates for others a truly "grace-less" situation.

Sources Indicated

The classical doctrine on original sin is based on Genesis as interpreted by Paul in Romans 5 and later elaborated by Augustine. Our contention in this article is drawn from three sources in Scripture and tradition. The sinfulness of Israel and mankind as a whole is used instead of Genesis. John's notion of the sin of the world is used in place of Paul's view of one man's sin. Instead of Augustine's elaboration of original sin we are substituting a Greek or even Pelagian tendency, but extending the Pelagian doctrine on bad example until it is orthodox once more. Is such a view of original sin identical with the classical explanation? Does it merely complete or really modify the classical position essentially?

Since we understand original sin as man's historical situation, there is no need to deny a historical fall. Adam should be multiplied, not done away with! But can the human condition of original sin (*peccatum originale originatum*) truly be equated with situatedness because of the sins of others?

At least there seem to be verbal objections. The Eastern Church speaks of original sin as original death. The Latin West maintains with *Rm* 5, 12 and Augustine that in Adam all sinned. Councils such as Carthage and Trent speak of a *sin* transferred to all men from Adam — not of a penalty. Augustine claims that hell is the destiny of children dying in original sin. (As regards children, historical development of the theological views — from hell to a state of natural perfection minus the beatific vision — indicates that original sin differs from personal sin in its consequences.)

This distinction between the two is supported by both magisterial statements and theological speculation. Scholastic theology sees original sin as a passive habit man receives, *in* our will but not *from* it, rather *from* Adam's sinful choice. Except for the language, this is precisely what is meant by man's situatedness. The condition of original sin lies *in* our will, affects our freedom, not because of the subject's own decision or attitude, but insofar as his freedom is situated by the sins of others.

If we compare the meaning of the sinful human situation with the notion of original sin, the sin of one man entails the breaking off of the general mediation of grace for others. This

can be a situatedness that precedes and comprises all the free
decisions of an individual. Such a situation in regard to grace
would then be characterized as the absence of grace — and what
is this but original sin? But the classical explanation of original
sin also included the loss of the preternatural gifts. This may be
included as a part of man's situation, but is better treated with
Adam and paradise.

Older Explanation Differs

What about the fall itself (*peccatum originale originans*) in
both theories? Here they do not correspond. The traditional explanation has pointed to a single sin of the first parent; ours con-
tends that the fall is the whole history of sinful deeds. Two
questions are in order: Does this proposal simply complete the
classical explanation by adding the sins of others? Or does it
so modify past theory that the first fall is robbed of its unique
significance?

The sins of men, especially of those who determine the life-
situation of a given person, seem to have some importance along
with the sin of Adam. Yet no Catholic has clearly affirmed this.
The statements of Scripture about the sins of the fathers are so
strong that Augustine himself allowed that they have influence.
This notion lasted through medieval times and was discussed at
Trent without being condemned.

Sins of Others Added

The idea that the fall includes the sins of others besides Adam
is clearly plausible because of the fact that mankind as a whole
is an educative community and mediates grace as well. The historical community conditions a person's existential situation even
before he is born. And if the classical explanation of original sin
is carried further, the notion that the fall is the whole history of

sinful deeds seems a *necessary* consequence. Traditionally, generation has been seen as the link between Adam and his posterity of later centuries.

But what is meant by generation? Its influence can be direct as when a person inherits physical defects. But it can also have indirect effects, as in the case of a child born in New York because its parents had just moved there. Even in classical theology original sin can only be understood by analogy with a person's inheriting a given historical situation. For sin and the lack of grace are personal matters not subject to transmission like a person's biological make-up. Because of God's salvific will there has never been a graceless vacuum since Adam. How, then, could the loss of grace from Adam's sin come to men unless others refused God's offer and broke off the mediation of grace?

Did Adam have a special influence, then? Chronologically there had to be a first sinner, of course, but his importance seems to be less than that of his later descendants. And this explanation does not require that the first sinner was the first man.

This brings up the whole problem of monogenism — a problem not solved or even raised in Scripture or in Church teaching before the twentieth century. The notion that the whole human race has descended from one couple seems a presupposition based on an outdated picture of the world. According to Jedin and Smulders, canon three of Trent's treatment of original sin intended to emphasize that the unity of original sin lies only in its origin without further characterizing this origin. The point was to affirm that each man has *his own* original sin.

The sole direct statement regarding monogenism was that of *Humani generis*. The encyclical merely states that it is not clear how polygenism and original sin can be reconciled. It leaves open the possibility that monogenism may not be an essential part of the doctrine of original sin. Perhaps a more important consideration looks to the reasons why the teaching on original sin gives such importance to one first sinner who is parent of all mankind. There seem to be two reasons operative: the loss of the preternatural gifts and the universality of original sin. So the question is whether the loss of the preternatural gifts and the universality of sin can be explained apart from monogenism or not.

Biological or Not?

The nature of the preternatural gifts is quite important, for if they are part of man's biological make-up they are transmitted directly through generation and one parent couple is a necessity. K. Rahner has tried to explain these gifts in terms of anthropology. Immortality and integrity do not entail a different structure of human nature. Rather in the state of original justice the relation between person and nature in each man would be characterized by total conscious possession and free self-determination. Since original sin our nature and spontaneous tendencies are not completely at the disposal of our freedom. Before sin, death and suffering could be accepted without their hindering or obscuring personal decisions.

A question can clarify a point in Rahner's explanation. Where is the basis for the difference in the relation between nature and person before and after the fall? If it is within man's essential structure, there would seem to have been a higher form of humanity at the wrong end of man's evolution. Hence the basis must be found in grace. Grace is always a personalizing and unifying factor for a person in regard to God, his fellows, and himself. Grace enables man to find God in everything without being forced to leave self and the world. So the preternatural gifts would be present in the same measure as grace. There would be no difference between the effects of the first sin and any later sin.

Monogenism Not Essential

Is the universality of original sin essentially bound up with monogenism? If original sin is located within a history of sin, it would seem possible that Christ's redemption could so take hold of a milieu that its history would be characterized by faith, hope, and love and that the men born in it would begin life with grace and without original sin. Yet the Church teaches a universality for original sin such that children born of Christian parents can be freed by baptism alone. But could not the influence of all mankind as an educative community explain the universality of original sin?

In my book. *Man and Sin,* I sought an explanation in that historical decision by which Christ himself was rejected. R. Guardini took this to be the second fall and so I was led to call it the completion of the fall. This led to the hypothesis that at the crucifixion grace was irrevocably rejected in its source.

But if one considers original sin to be not only the situation of the infant upon birth, but rather to situate man's whole existence, then original sin is in fact universal. Because sin has entered into the world, every man will meet it in some form or other. This corresponds to the preaching of many of the Church fathers, who saw baptism for infants as protection against future temptations. Admittedly, there are many points that are still unclear.

Yet even with further clarification original sin will remain a mystery. It stands as the dark side and counterpart of the mystery of God's redemption. From his first breath each man is situated both by the fall of "Adam" and by the redemption of Christ. Baptism is needed because of original sin, but this same baptism is the sacramental affirmation that man lives from birth in a redeemed situation as well. Original sin signifies that each man belongs to a sinful humanity. So baptism, though it must be completed by Christian education and the other sacraments, means that the baptized person has been received into the saving community of Christ's Church.

Chapter Fourteen

A CATECHESIS ON ORIGINAL SIN

MARCEL VAN CASTER, S.J.

A catechesis on orignal sin can be developed in two directions.
The first starts from the data of revelation and applies them to
the actual human situation. The second, having previously
analysed the actual situation, inteprets it in the light of
revelation.

We will successively follow these two paths which very
clearly delineate a *twofold catechetical approach.* Then in relation to each, we will pursue *a critical inquiry* that is both doctrinal and methodological. Finally, we will state *a few concrete
requirements* pertaining to a true catechesis on original sin.

I. THE DATA OF DIVINE REVELATION
APPLIED TO THE ACTUAL HUMAN SITUATION

The first pages of the Bible, which deal with Adam's sin and
the struggle man waged against evil, are the fruits of a reflection
the writer elaborated under divine inspiration, whilst bearing
in mind Israel's long experience of sin which reigns in the world.

Similarly, a catechesis on original sin (in the twofold sense of "Adam's sin" and the "sin-in-which-all-men-are-born") would benefit by taking into account *the totality* of God's plan, as it was fulfilled in Jesus Christ and is continued within the Church.

1. *The Gift of Divine Life in a Concrete Situation*

God's plan consists in communicating *divine life* to man in his concrete existence, that is to say in a *way that corresponds to all the essential dimensions of human existence.* The latter is a spiritual and corporeal existence, one that is personal and communal, progressive on earth and definitive in life hereafter. We should note carefully that the "corporeal" situation is the foundation of "mediations" operated by the body and therefore the foundation of the influences interacting between persons, for they belong to the human "community."

God's concrete intention is that every man should receive his natural spiritual life (his soul) through the corporeal mediation of his parents who insert him into a fostering and educative community (the family, society). This community must help him to progress towards the full development of his personal and social being.

In the same way, God desires man to receive supernatural life, or at least the right dispositions for welcoming it, *through the mediation* of a fostering and educative *community.* The latter, acting supernaturally through sensible signs, could be termed a "quasi-sacrament." The whole of this community, and all the means of grace available to it, are ultimately "personalized" in the One who is the center of all: Jesus Christ.

2. *Man's Original Attitude and its Consequences*

What was the spiritual reaction of "humanity in its origins" regarding this plan of God? What were the internal consequences of the attitude adopted, bearing in mind the influence which is fatally exercised through the *mediation* of the community?

The *first human beings* (Adam and Eve), who formed the origins of the human community, committed sin. The biblical account does not provide us with the historical circumstances; it presents the fault of our first parents as one in which they both collaborated. Thus, they made the human community bear a sinful influence, whereas it was destined to be a mediation of divine life.

Their children are born in a community that has turned away from God; at birth, they find themselves deprived of the supernatural life God intended to communicate to them. They are born with *original sin*, that is to say in a state contrary to God's intention.

3. *The Seeds of Redemption*

But within this sinful community, *God* has progressively introduced elements of redemption, centered in Jesus Christ.

1. *From the very beginning,* God works in the heart of sinful man. He continues to call him; he helps him to accept suffering and death as hardships which bring about repentance; however, he has not revealed to us at what precise moment he grants forgiveness and reconciliation to repentant sinners who do not know Christ. In spite of his divine attentions, sin develops throughout the human race.

We can allow that as man acquires greater aptitudes of every kind, humanity places them in fact in the service of good and evil.

2. The main historical preparation for salvation is provided by the special graces given to the *people of Israel*. God has chosen this people so that it might bring forth Jesus and welcome him as the Savior. One might say that from this chosen community he has created a "sacrament-of-preparation."

But sin develops as well amongst the chosen people.

3. *Jesus Christ,* sent by the Father, realizes the plan of "com-

munion" between God and man. He is the perfect "mediator" of
this plan. In him, humanity is perfectly re-orientated towards
God; in him, that is to say through the relations which all the
members have with their Head.

These relations, which are at first but mutual bonds formed
by a common participation in human nature, become an active
personal union through participation in the faith and life of the
Church "community," the body of Christ.

Jesus gives life to the community whose head he is, by communicating his Spirit to it. He has established his Church, moreover, as a *"community-Sacrament"* of the salvation he brings.
In particular, he has endowed her with an initial "sacrament"
(in the strict sense): *baptism,* which is precisely the *efficacious
symbolic action* whereby every man can effectively form part of
the community of salvation.

4. *The Actual Religious Situation*

The actual religious situation of humanity is therefore chiefly
characterized by the active presence of the Church considered
as a "sacrament of salvation." In different ways, all men find
themselves in a state of tension between two influences: that of
the Church and that of the "world."

In the derogatory sense, the "world" is the environment ruled
by sin, the *absolute* anthropocentric mentality. The Church is
the environment in which supernatural life is given sacramentally, and together with this life, the strength progressively to wage
a victorious struggle against sin.

Insofar as she is a community of supernatural life, the Church
is not *"of" the sinful world;* she stems *from* God; she is not *of*
those who possess an absolute anthropocentric mentality.

But the Church is *"in" the sinful world.* Her faithful share
their daily life with men whose mentality is deeply opposed to
the Gospel.

To the extent that Christians are unfaithful to the spirit they receive from Christ within the Church, the world still remains active "in" the members of the Church.

But fortunately, the presence of the Church in the world need not be considered as a threat; she is more particularly destined to fulfill her action of *converting the world,* and to achieve this in two ways:

— as a *reaction* against the influence of the "world," understood in the derogatory sense;

— as a Christian *transformation* of the world, understood here in the positive sense of "the whole of creation" providing the human environment.

Finally, in the world (according to its general meaning) there is an influence of grace which transcends the limits of the Church's sacramental presence. Just as before the coming of Christ on earth, even now God prepares the hearts of those who do not yet know him; and the action of Christ, sending forth his Spirit, can already unite "anonymous Christians" with the Church in an invisible way. Their implicit Christianity tends towards its explicit realization which it will achieve by participating sacramentally in the life of the Christian community.

5. *Interior Dispositions and Tendencies*

Approached in this way, the entire question still requires closer scrutiny with regard to man's *interior dispositions.* The latter are indissolubly united to the communal influences which operate through exterior mediations (the manifestations of the environment). Man's reaction to these influences does in fact depend on the particular state of his interior tendencies.

In every spiritual creature, there is a *tendency to unite with God* and a corresponding *tendency to self-withdrawal.* The first is perfected and strengthened through supernatural grace; the second is aggravated by original sin.

— Throughout the history of humanity, the good tendency persists for it stems from the deepest ontological orientation. In varying degrees, it is assisted by the graces which prepare men for salvation.

— But throughout history a state of disorder likewise endures and is introduced in every human person because the mediations of the general human environment are vitiated by sin.

Salvation, which comes to us through Christ, only cancels out the privation of supernatural life, but it does not instantly heal our wounded nature and does not correct or totally redress our inclination to sin. It merely gives us sufficient inner strength to combat and conquer the latter progressively.

Because of the dynamic *connection between inner tendencies and environmental influences,* the tension every man feels existing between the interior poles of his being undergoes constant modifications. These are determined by the ratio of forces developing between the action of the Church and the action of the "world."

Finally, this entire question should not primarily be understood in terms of *activity.* According as we commit *our freedom* in conformity with our orientation towards God or else in the direction of sin (in harmony with the Church or in league with the "world"), we collaborate either in the growth of Christian salvation or in those things that hinder its progress.

II. THE ACTUAL HUMAN SITUATION
ENLIGHTENED BY DIVINE REVELATION

A catechesis on original sin can be developed in the contrary direction which we are outlining below. This will enable us to draw some conclusions applicable to both procedures.

Man desires happiness but, in his search for it, he comes up against obstacles. The evils he encounters are situated at various levels: some directly concern projects and human values to be realized on earth, others concern religious values and hopes that extend even beyond time.

These evils arise from two different causes: on the one hand, there is man's inability to work upon the "data" of existence, as

in the case of famine or sickness; on the other, he uses his freedom wrongly: he harms himself, for instance through intemper-
ance, and he also harms others, as illustrated by the fact of war.

The continuous development of the sciences and technology—
especially in the world of today — enables us to combat the first
cause with increasing skill; but what about man's use of his own
freedom?

1. *The Use of Freedom*

We commit our freedom in response to inner promptings and
external influences. Both can work in the direction of good or
evil.

As our present study is concerned with the *sources of the
wrong use of will,* and with original sin especially, the negative
aspect will claim our attention more particularly; we should
never forget, however, that the sources of good are also constantly active, and according to different modes.

1. The *inner source* of freedom's misuse resides in our *unruly
passions.* These should not be considered as merely accompany-
ing others which could be termed well-controlled passions; for
the expression is used to designate inner inclinations when they
threaten to develop at the cost of the order which must reign
in the totality of human life, and especially in our relations to
God.

The unruliness of passions stems from the fact that man does
not attribute a "relative" significance to human possessions, as
indeed he should according to the very nature of things. This
situation arises when the desire for material goods prevents the
flowering of personal values as a whole; it equally arises when
individual gain is sought at the cost of the relationships which
must exist between people. Hence the existence of cupidity, pride,
injustice, and above all of the refusal to see the world and mankind in relation to God.

2. The *external source* of freedom's misuse is to be found in
the *social environment* insofar as its members who obey their

unruly passions are responsible for the prevalence of a *mentality that is inconsistent with the legitimate order of values.*

The man who commits his freedom by complying to his unruly passions and by conforming to the vitiated elements in the mentality of the environment, whilst yet remaining aware that his actions are contrary to God's will, falls into a state of sin.

We should distinguish several meanings in the use of the terms "sin" and "sinner." The most current meaning is the one that applies to a *determined act* called actual sin; but the most important refers to a permanent attitude known as a *state of sin.* We shall see that here likewise, we will have to make a subsequent distinction between the state resulting from our personal commitments and the one in which we find ourselves before we even gain the use of our freedom, namely by the fact of participating in the general situation of humanity.

2. The Universality of Good and Evil as Two Interior Poles of Tension

All men are fundamentally orientated towards God through a natural summons; and revelation teaches us that they are orientated towards him to an even greater degree through a supernatural summons. This *ontological summons towards good* is a permanent one. Without even being aware of it, men perform actions which, to a greater or lesser degree, are perfectly consistent with their search for God or with their desire for a more complete union with him.

But it is equally true of all men that this search and desire are hindered by sin.

Two terms are used to designate the *universality of evil,* and these respectively correspond to two aspects:

a) To express the fact that the universality of evil goes back to humanity's origins and that it establishes a state of sin as a situation in which every man participates through his kinship with humanity, we speak of *"original sin."* This term indicates that as a result of the sin committed at the birth of humanity, we are born deprived of the supernatural life God wished to communicate to us through the mediation of the natural human community. This privation includes an absence of the strength which would suffice to conquer the interior and exterior sources of evil.

b) To express the totality of the sinful acts committed by mankind, as well as the general manifestation of the unruly passions which remain unconquered, and to designate more particularly the attitude of opposition to God which is displayed in the form of power and unrestrained pleasure, we speak of *"the sin of the world."* This sin therefore mainly resides in the "human environment's" claim to be self-sufficient, to set itself up as an absolute, and to repudiate its relationship with God.

These two aspects of evil's universality must be considered simultaneously if we are to grasp the *concrete need for salvation* which is specific to humanity as a whole.

We should not envisage mankind in its totality as being purely devoted to evil; for the profound orientation towards God is engraved in all men, and God himself has given them graces throughout the history of humanity. But it remains true that before coming in contact with Christ the Savior, man experiences an existential situation in which the internal consequences of his first parents' sin, and the ascendancy of the scandal evolved through the "sin of the world," prevent him from orientating his whole life towards God according to the plan of communion God had conceived for him. It is through Christ that this existential situation of man changes.

3. The Transformation of Man's Situation Through and in Jesus Christ

1. Jesus is God's envoy, the supreme envoy, who comes to proclaim that God wishes to share his life with men, and that to achieve this aim, assisted by his strength, they must conquer sin. Through his preaching, he opposes the scandal that reigns in the world.

But the implications of his message are even more far-reach-ing. For this message expresses an experience that Jesus himself is *living*. He has received supernatural life from the Father, both in his soul and in his human body; and he responds to the Father's love in a perfect manner. *The religious situation of humanity first changed "in" Jesus Christ.* In him there was no sin but instead, a perfect love of God.

2. It follows that the evil which sets itself against God will equally set itself against Jesus Christ. In his human life, this opposition will cause him to experience the full impact of violent resistance. Jesus *"bears" the sins of the world.*

But through his fidelity, he brings humanity obedience where there was but disobedience; and through the divine strength he communicates (notably the strength to forgive and to resist evil), *he "takes away" the sins of the world.* At least he does so "in principle," for we have to put his strength into practice; but he already does so in fact "with the birth of a new dynamism," for an illness is "conquered" when its true remedy is available. Insofar as he is the visible and efficacious sign of the radiance of divine grace, Jesus Christ is the supreme "sacrament."

3. This strength, which destroys sin and communicates the new life, is one that Jesus possesses as the head of a renewed human community, and as a *principle of universality.* That is why he also delivers us from original sin. This aspect of salvation is illuminated when we express it in terms of "beginning," "head," "participation." One might say that Adam is the very beginning, the first head, etc.; and that Jesus Christ is the new beginning, etc. But it would be more correct and more profound to say that Adam is the preparatory beginning, destined to make possible the true and definite beginning which radiates from the fully established center. This center, which is Jesus Christ, therefore constitutes the complete and definite beginning.

4. Salvation, or divine life communicated to man, is then first realized in Jesus Christ and, stemming from him, it radiates within us insofar as *we participate* in his life. This means that humanity's existential situation first changes *in Jesus Christ* who is its definite Head; and *through him,* this situation equally

changes within us, thanks to the power of his radiance as "God's sacrament for all men."

Let us now examine the further consequences of this truth.

4. *Our Progressive Participation in the Divinizing Transformation*

1. The transformation, *already operated* from the very beginning of Christianity, includes the following elements:

— Jesus himself, as the Head of humanity, lives in a situation that has been totally transformed by his resurrection.

— He acts within the community whose Head he is: 1) *in all men* by the grace of his summons, and in relation to the "signs" these men encounter on their journey; 2) *in the members of his Church,* by sending them his Spirit who communicates supernatural life.

— He has established his Church which, as a living and visible community, is a "human-divine environment of grace" and, as an institution, has received "sacraments" in which God communicates grace.

The first of these sacraments brings man, who belonged to the environment of the "world," into the environment of the Church. In the Church community, man receives the grace of which he had been deprived because the world was incapable of being its mediation.

Regarding the possibility of the non-baptized being "anonymous Christians," consult our previous remarks in section I, no. 4.

2. Our participation in the transformation operated by Jesus Christ covers a range of varying stages and degrees.

— As men, we belong to those who are called to be "the community living in Jesus Christ."

Through baptism, we are delivered from the state of original sin which pertains to the "world," for we receive supernatural life through the mediation of the "Christian environment." But this participation, which is already a living one, is destined to develop progressively, both internally and externally. God makes his love grow within us and renders us increasingly capable of a generous response.

— Our unruly passions are not cancelled through baptism, but the strength needed to combat them is placed at our disposal.

Similarly, the sin of the world continues to be a cause of our temptation, but it has lost its hold over us; we are able to resist it with increasing firmness.

— Salvation (the progressive transformation of our entire being), communicated to us through the sacraments, begins by affecting us at the religious level and in the depths of our being. We have to make its effects shine forth progressively in our moral conduct. The morality of our actions will then ward off the evils resulting from the wrong use of our will.

— Finally, this Christian influence must equally unfold in all social environments in order to transform their mentality and reform their structures, thus enabling them to become more adapted to the life led by a Christian.

This social radiance of Christianity should go together with an earnest attempt to illuminate the signs of Christian salvation, and in a way that all men — Christians and others — might be more effectively prompted to respond to God's interior action. These signs are provided by two types of "witness" which we are required to give: 1) the witness that proclaims the life, death and resurrection of Jesus Christ, interpreted according to their authentic meaning; 2) the witness of incarnated faith and charity, interpreted likewise as manifestations of a profound Christian vitality.

3. Thus man's existential situation, already actively and fundamentally transformed by Jesus Christ, undergoes constant transformation according to the co-operation given by mankind. The opposition to God's summons, whether offered by baptized Christians or others, develops the sin of the world. A faithful response to grace, given either by acknowledged or by anonymous Christians, causes humanity to progress towards the fullness of participation in the life of Jesus Christ, a fullness that it

will enjoy as a perfect and definite transformation of its former self in communion with God.

III. CRITICAL REFLECTIONS:

DOCTRINAL AND METHODOLOGICAL

We begin by proposing a positive critical investigation that is not meant to be taught explicitly; it is suggested with the aim of enabling teachers to realize that the schemas offered in the two previous sections are *consistent* with the data provided by Holy Scripture and by the magisterium.

We will then examine certain *questions posed by scientific criticism,* and which largely remain "open" questions from the stand-point of revelation.

A final series of critical observations refers to the defects inherent in certain presentations of original sin.

1. Doctrinal Precisions

1. *The Nature of Original Sin and its Mode of Transmission*

Let us begin by specifying the points of doctrine which express the "sinful situation" of every man who comes into the world.

1. On the religious and moral plane, every man is born (a simplified term to replace "who comes into the world") in a state of privation and disorientation, irrespective of his physical and psychic state of health.

He is deprived of supernatural life; he experiences an inclination to evil in a way that is not merely natural: an inclination that leads him to seek the enjoyment of earthly goods *as an absolute,* to consider himself, either individually or socially, as an end and an ultimate norm, and to refuse all transcendence which would have to be received as a supernatural gift.

2. *Original* sin consists essentially in a privation of grace

resulting from Adam's sin, and in man's disorientation in relation
to God. How does original sin relate to concupiscence, understood as a disorderly tendency man experiences with regard to
himself and to earthly goods?

— On the one hand, original sin results in heightened concupiscence. This being so, concupiscence does not cause the
privation of grace, but, on the contrary, the privation of grace
entails the actual situation of concupiscence. After baptism,
concupiscence remains, but the grace whereby man is enabled
to resist his unruly passions is placed at his disposal.

— On the other, God habitually adopts a mode of action corresponding to man's mode of existence; in particular, he begins
by making certain preparations for the reception of grace, and
man is called to contribute to them personally and/or socially.
This grace, which takes away original sin, is given by Christ the
Savior within a "social environment" which provides its members
with a normal preparation and constant support. When man
gains the use of his freedom, he must also undergo "personal"
conversion, which means that in principle he must turn away
from the habit of complying with his unruly tendencies in order
to welcome grace.[1]

3. *The terminology currently adopted,* particularly since the
Council of Trent, should be interpreted bearing in mind that
several expressions are only used analogically in relation to
their everyday meaning.

The situation we have just described is known as *"sin."* We
should first note the analogical meaning of "actual sin" (an act
committed by the person in question), "habitual sin" (the state
subsequent to this act) — and "original sin" which is of another
kind; we could call it "situational," but this term might be equally misleading.

---

1. This two-fold relation entails important consequences with regard
to all aspects of pastoral work. In this connection, the observations made
by Fr. Bro, in **L'enseignement religieux et les disciplines profanes,** Ligel,
1964, pp. 99-100, and by Fr. de Premare, in **Repenser la mission,** D.D.B.,
1965, p. 216, can be usefully compared with those of Fr. Frisque, **ibid.,**
pp. 312-313.

We are dealing with sin nonetheless, for: 1) it is a situation contrary to God's will; and 2) one in which I am not orientated towards God in the way he desires.

Finally, this situation is said to be transmitted *"through generation."* This in no way implies that the act *of generation* is sinful, nor that *biological* descent is determinative in the matter. The terminology which in certain languages speaks of sin "referring to our origins" (in particular: original sin) is expressed in other languages in terms of heredity: "Erbsünde." The latter terminology is more closely related to the biblical expressions which contrast the inheritance we receive from Adam with the one in which we participate through our kinship with Christ. It is therefore obvious that the "personalist" kinship is the important one. — The expression "through generation" signifies that every man enters into this sinful situation by reason of the fact that he belongs to the human kind. In other words, original sin is transmitted *through our kinship with the human community, in the state of sin in which it finds itself before coming into contact with Christ.* Consequently, this sin will be taken away (which means that the situation will be transformed) through our kinship with the ecclesiastical community which is a new "generation" as it were, for it is the mediator of the grace flowing from Jesus Christ, its Head.

4. This "mode" (termed generation or kinship) equally throws light on the *special nature of original sin.* The human person is not merely an independent being co-existing with others; he is a being-existing-with-others; he is a being-existing-in-relationship-with-other-men.

My kinship with the human community is a constituent of my person; it is something that "belongs to me essentially." But the human community has turned away from God through the sin of our first parents, the sins committed throughout history, and the "mentality" prevailing in the world at large as long as it does not welcome Christ. Therefore, insofar as my relation to this world is a constituent of my personalist existence, I participate ontologically in the fact of having turned away from God. But when I assume another kind of relationship (notably through my kinship with the community which dwells in the Spirit of Christ the Savior), my situation is transformed, and I too am transformed in the essential elements of my personal being.

The terminology which emphasizes the constitutive significance of belonging to a particular milieu of human beings is therefore very enlightening. Nonetheless, we should avoid oversimplifying our analogies. There are essential *dissimilarities* between the respective "heads" of the two communities, and between the two separate modes of belonging. Our solidarity with Adam is ontological according to a mode that is both biological and sociological; our participation in the life of Jesus Christ is ontological according to a sacramental mode (or one referring to a direct inner gift) and according to a mode expressing the environment's personalist influence; in particular, the mode expressing the prophetic function of the Church and enabling us to know Christ the Savior to whom we must freely adhere.

5. This explains, moreover, why the two forms of belonging can to a certain extent co-exist in Christians. In other words, the consequences of original sin — and therefore certain affinities with the sinful world — endure whilst being resisted by the strength which flows from grace; this strength derives from our kinship with the community whose Head is Christ. The second form of belonging can triumph but progressively over the first, and our Christian transformation will only be complete after death.

We should equally distinguish between our biological kinship with the human race, in a given state of physical health and cultural development, on the one hand, and our kinship with the world, considered as an area of religious influence, on the other. This distinction also applies to the questions that arise concerning the situation of our very origins.

2. The Mediation of the Community

As for *the way in which we should conceive the mediation of the community,* revelation gives us but few indications. Theological reflection on this subject develops from certain data mainly provided by the ecclesiastic dimension of the sacraments; and previous to that, they were derived from the general principle according to which God acts towards man in relation to the latter's dispositions. We will attempt to outline the question as follows:

1. God intends to bring man into supernatural communion with him. He "calls" him. If man adopts a welcoming attitude, God gives him supernatural life; but if man adopts the contrary attitude, he is deprived of supernatural life.

2. The first human beings should have transmitted natural life in a situation of such a kind that their children would have possessed "social dispositions" favorable to supernatural life. By "social dispositions" we mean the "communal relationships" which belong to the constituent elements of man's personal being (family, profession, friendships, country, culture, etc.).

3. But as a result of their sin, our first parents did the contrary, which was to transmit life in such a way that their children now participate in a human community unfavorably disposed towards supernatural life.

4. Christ began his work of salvation by summoning men to conversion. It was necessary for them to acquire dispositions enabling them to welcome the Kingdom of God. When his "hour" of salvific radiance had come, he established sacramental signs within his Church. These are his gestures extended by those to whom he gives sacramental power.

5. We should note carefully that the sacraments (conferred according to their normally expressive mode) are gestures which have a double function:

— firstly, they summon man to adopt a living attitude of welcome; man prepares himself by being converted from his unfavorable dispositions and by revitalizing his faith;

— then, they express the fact that God bestows his grace and that man receives it.

6. The Church is the communal environment wherein these sacramental actions take place.

Therefore, the mediation of the community also has this *double function*: 1) that of being an active environment which fosters the right dispositions for welcoming grace; 2) and, in accordance with divine institution, that of accomplishing sacramental gestures as expressive forms of the action whereby God bestows supernatural life.

It is clear that these facts have important consequences regarding the organization of pastoral work in general and the inclusion of a catechesis, comprising various stages, within the total context of pastoral activity. As we cannot develop these consequences within the limits of the present article, we are merely unfolding the significance of the communal mediation, conceived in this way, in relation to original sin and man's deliverance from it.

3. *The Mediation of the Community and "Original" Sin*

As each man enters this world, he participates in a communal situation that is distorted: his social dispositions are unfavorable to supernatural life; that is why he is deprived of the latter.

The reason for this privation of grace is not a purely external decision on God's part, nor merely the natural inability of parents to transmit grace to their children. The ontological reason lies in a reality existing within every man and forming an obstacle to grace. More particularly, it is his refusal to accept the supernatural.

This refusal is expressed according to various modes. It is a voluntary refusal, both from the personal and from the communal point of view, in the case of those who, socially speaking, live in accordance with a closed anthropocentrism. It is rarely an explicit and definite refusal; often, it is found to be an *implicit and provisional refusal which takes the form of voluntarily neglecting to care about God, or to show any interest in him, in order to devote oneself entirely (in a psychologically exclusive way and for the time being) to the pursuit of worldly human values.*

Before man gains the use of his personal freedom, this same refusal exists through his *participation in the mentality of refusal* which reigns in the community as long as the latter is not converted, saved and endowed with grace by Christ. This situation, which is sinful through participation before becoming sinful through personal choice, goes back to our origins; its cause lies in the sin of our first parents; it is called: original sin.

Man is summoned to conversion through the testimony of the Church. She provides an environment in which supernatural life develops in relation to favorable social dispositions. The one who is ready to welcome grace enters within the ecclesiastical community; he shares favorable social dispositions and, through sacramental action, he receives supernatural life. He is thus delivered from original sin.

However, the consequences of belonging to the original environment, and in particular the influence of "the sin of the world," are still felt in every human person and in the Church insofar as she is formed of men "journeying towards" their eschatological fulfillment. The situation of Christians, therefore, is one of men who are delivered from original sin and furnished with supernatural strength so that they may progressively conquer the influences which are opposed to their life in union with God. We find ourselves in this existential situation of the Christian because we share the "existential situation" of Jesus Christ, our Head; we participate in it according to our mode, that of converted sinners. Supernatural life is communicated to us through the sending of the Spirit whose radiance stems from the Head and fills all the members of the ecclesiastical community.

2. Questions relating to our "Origins"

The difference between the literary form adopted in the first chapters of Genesis and the literary form of modern scientific writings obliges us to make a fundamental distinction between the religious content of these chapters and the colorful presentation of this content.

1. It is fairly safe to presume that the biological and cultural situation of our first parents was a very imperfect one and that mankind has undergone an increasing *evolution* regarding technical progress and its awareness of human potentialities.[2]

2. The question of the *number* of beings corresponding to what we are taught by faith on the subject of our "first parents" is connected with that of the meaning we should attribute to "human universality in its source."

What Was the Object of Original Sin?

Did the sin committed by "Adam and Eve" consist of *one* act? Of *several* acts leading to a decisive choice? On what object precisely did this choice bear?

Revelation does not give us a detailed answer to these questions. It is permissible to conceive this sin as the rejection of a reality surpassing man's power; either as the rejection of a norm of action superior to the one man *chooses for himself*, or as a refusal to accept a higher life and a higher happiness which would not be the outcome of powers man possesses as a human being, but the fruit of a superior gratuitous gift bestowed by God and enabling man to find his happiness in communion with divine life. The basis of sin would therefore be the atheistic orientation which furthers human self-sufficiency either individually or socially.

Man's relations to God are incarnated in the attitude he adopts towards the material world, and above all in his relationships with his fellow-creatures. As humanity acquires greater technical power and develops social relationships, good and evil *extend their scope*.

The attitude whereby man, although aware that he is called to live with God in a relationship of dependence and love, nevertheless seeks self-development (hominization) *solely* through social collaboration and interhuman communion, this same attitude of human self-sufficiency marks out sin as the opposite of

---

2. On this subject, consult **Dieu nous parle**, II, p. 380.

consent to God's supernatural love which must be the motive force of a perfect communion between men.

A picturesque and brief description of this attitude is given in the biblical account of the tower of Babel. This chapter of Genesis sets the sin of man's origins within a broader framework in which one simultaneously realizes that, on the one hand, the evil now extending is a consequence of the evil which began, and that, on the other hand, evil once initiated extends its scope in man's social life. And this occurs more through the collective responsibility of self-sufficient groups than through the cumulative effect of individual sins.

However, we have to discover even more complex *implications* between the person and the community. On the one hand, the most prominent sins are those committed by the individual against the people considered to be the "bride" of God. On the other, the development of the sense of the human person will subsequently introduce distinctions in the concept of responsibility. Finally, in the modern world, individuals become once again aware that they share a common responsibility for good or evil, either through their achievements or through their omissions regarding other individuals or other groups. At present, then, we are fully alive to the role played by freedom in common responsibility, but every day, we also gain a clearer understanding of the role played by "social mediations" in the exercising of this freedom through consent or refusal. One of the characteristics of modern times is precisely the way in which these implications are extended to the dimensions of humanity as a whole.

All this can be found at the beginning of humanity as well as in its subsequent development, and it is expressed either implicitly or explicitly. If it is possible "to be a Christian implicitly," there is also the possibility of "implicitly rejecting supernatural life and the Christian message."

3. Faulty presentations of original sin

Just as Redemption, which belongs to the supernatural order, original sin, founded on the interdependence of men within God's supernatural plan, is a mysterious reality which cannot possibly be presented in an exhaustive and perfect manner. The same applies to the Christian mystery as a whole, which is the object of catechesis. Nonetheless, it is possible and also very necessary to avoid defects conceived in such a way as to exclude an essential element.

These major defects in presentation follow two opposite directions corresponding (in a general way) to a disregard for either the *immanence or the transcendence* of the mystery. To state this more precisely: in the first case, because transcendence has been conceived too extrinsically, the presentation of immanence lacks a sense of reality; in the second case, the opposite occurs. In recent centuries, catechesis has been more inclined to evince the first defect; in present times, our conception of original sin is chiefly characterized by the second defect. We shall now consider a few examples.

1. *A Presentation Over-stressing "Extrinsicality"*

In the present context, "extrinsic" signifies "imputed from without," as a "juridical" condemnation which is heaped upon us, whereas in fact we have committed no misconduct and have no means of explaining why we are in a "culpable situation" except in terms of the judge's arbitrary decision.

A schema which insufficiently avoids the *extrinsic emphasis* runs along these lines. We hope that this type of schema will be increasingly abandoned in practice:

Adam received sanctifying grace, exemption from concupiscence, and exemption from suffering. (He is placed in a world so very different from our own that it seems external to our reality.) Through his sin, Adam lost grace and the two previous exemptions. We are born in the same triple privation. (Is the cause of our inner privation an external one? How can a privation of grace, resulting from another person's sin, be a personal sin for each individual? Is this sin imputed to us through a fiction of the juridical imagination? According to which justice?) Redemption is operated by Christ who acts instead of us (are his actions external to ours, and are ours useless?); his merits are *applied* to us in baptism (what does this "application" mean? how does it realize an immanent justice?). However, grace alone is restored to us on earth (why not the two exemptions? Could Christ's power to restore be lesser that Adam's ability to lose?).

The element lacking in this type of presentation is the interior ontological dimension of the human community, not only at the biological level but especially at the level of interpersonal influences exercised through the mediation of the body and of external signs. With regard to a more authentic way of conceiving redemption we recommend the reader to consult our monograph on this subject.[3]

2. A Presentation Liable to "Immanentism"

In the present context, "immanentism" would consist in depriving the sources of sin or its consequences of practically all "supernatural" dimensions; everything is explained in terms of psychology, the environmental influence; one intends to "demythologize," to "naturalize." "Mystery" is entirely ruled out.

The general mentality of our time insists on the communal dimension of good and evil in man. By integrating this dimension into our way of conceiving original sin, we can avoid the danger of a too extrinsic approach; but inevitably, some are tempted to react by succumbing to the opposite defect, that of *immanentism;* they forget that the immanence of a mystery is the immanence of a transcendence which must be acknowledged as such.

Original sin is then presented unilaterally, in terms of an

---

3. Cf. **The Redemption,** Paulist Press, N.J.

awareness of a permanent social reality which is present throughout the history of humanity and the life of each human being. The account of our origins would be *no more than* a mythical expression of humanity's wretched condition which is permanent and therefore actual. Each man would be Adam, not only with regard to the summons towards good and evil which he apprehends, but also with regard to his correct or wrong use of freedom. Further, each man would be one who passively undergoes the good or bad influence of every other Adam. And thus the whole of humanity would constantly exist in an active and passive state of sin. Real sin, however, would not be present in the individual except insofar as he freely obeys a natural inner inclination towards evil (which conditions freedom of choice) or a bad social influence (an analogous social condition). Some writers no longer even mention the supernatural order explicitly. In fact, one or two go so far as to say that everything we read in the biblical account of man's origins is but a transposition of details which refer to his final ends. At the beginning, there would only have been God's intention to lead man towards the full flowering of his being.

To counter these theories, which have been elaborated too unilaterally, and according to the *horizontal dimension* of reality, we should respect the totality of revelation's data and their authentic interpretation.

It is important, therefore, to remember the *vertical dimension*: the difference between the first human beings, before the fall, and ourselves. Here we might note a few indications on these various points.

Before the fall, humanity existed in a state of innocence and, in the supernatural order, it had received at least the gift of a divine summons and of the strength enabling it to respond to this summons. This state of innocence can no longer be rediscovered as such in every human being.

We are born into a sinful situation before we even gain the use of our freedom.

Evil, moral evil, or sin, should not be solely conceived as a disorder which prevails amongst men (according to the horizontal dimension) even if we add that this disorder is contrary to God's will. Above all, man is a being capable of entering into a relationship with God himself, and belongs fundamentally to that particular plane, for it is a refusal made to a summons of God which has been recognized as such. Man does not wish to acknowledge the true nature of this summons because he will not admit his obligation to answer it. However, he cannot avoid answering, for refusing to respond when the summons is sufficiently clear is the equivalent of answering with a refusal.

SELECTED BIBLIOGRAPHY

Anciaux, P., **The Sacrament of Penance,** New York: Sheed & Ward, 1962.

Aquinas, St. Thomas, Summa Theologica, Ia IIae, q. 23-40; IIIa, q. 84-90.

Barton, J. M., **Penance and Absolution,** New York: Hawthorn Books, 1961.

Bausch, W. J., **It Is the Lord: Sin and Confession Revisited,** Notre Dame, Ind.: Fides Publishers, 1970.

Betz, O., **Making Sense of Confession,** Chicago: Franciscan Herald Press, 1968.

Boros, L., **The Mystery of Death,** New York: Herder & Herder, Inc., 1965.

Bücher, A., **Studies in Sin and Atonement in the Rabbinic Literature of the First Century,** London: Oxford University Press, 1928.

Carra de Vaux Saint-Cyr, M.-B. et al, **The Sacrament of Penance,** Glen Rock, N.J.: Paulist Press, 1966.

Chery, H. C., **Frequent Confession,** London: Blackfriars, 1954.

Community of St. Severin, **Confession,** Chicago: Fides Publishers, 1959.

Coudreau, F., **Catechesis and Sin,** New York: The Macmillan Company, 1962.

De Fraine, J., **The Bible and the Origin of Man,** New York: Alba House, 1967.

Delhaye, P., ed., **Pastoral Treatment of Sin,** New York: Desclee, 1968.

De Lubac, H., **Catholicism,** London: Burns & Oates, 1950.

De Rosa, P., **Christ and Original Sin,** Milwaukee: Bruce Publishing Co., 1967.

Dirksen, A. H., **The New Testament Concept of the Metanoia,** Washington, D.C.: Catholic University Press, 1932.

Dubarle, A. M., **The Biblical Doctrine of Original Sin,** New York: Herder & Herder, Inc., 1964.

Galtier, P., **Sin and Penance,** St. Louis: B. Herder, 1932.

Gelin, A., **Sin in the Bible,** New York: Desclee, 1965.

Godin, A., **The Pastor as Counselor,** Dublin: M. H. Gill and Son, 1966.

Goldbrunner, J., **Realization,** New York: Herder & Herder, Inc., 1966.

Haag, H., **Is Original Sin in Scripture,** New York: Sheed & Ward, 1969.

Hagmaier, G. and R. Gleason, **Counselling the Catholic,** New York: Sheed & Ward, 1959.

Häring, B., **The Law of Christ** 1, Westminster, Md.: Newman Press, 1961.

——————, **Shalom: Peace; the Sacrament of Reconciliation,** New York: Farrar, Straus, 1968.

Heggen, F. J., **Confession and the Service of Penance,** Notre Dame, Indiana: University of Notre Dame Press, 1968.

Henry, A., ed. **Christ in His Sacraments,** Theology Library, Vol. IV. Chicago: Fides Publishers, 1958. pp. 205-274.

Hulsbosch, A., **God in Creation and Evolution,** New York: Sheed & Ward, 1965.

Kierkegaard, S., **The Sickness unto Death,** Garden City, N.Y.: Doubleday, 1954.

Krumm, J., **The Art of Being a Sinner,** New York: Seabury Press, 1967.

Lehmeier, L., **The Ecclesial Dimension of the Sacrament of Penance from a Catechetical Point of View,** Cebu City, Phillippines: University of San Carlos, 1967.

Ligier, L., **Pêché d'Adam et pêché du monde,** 2 vols., Paris: 1955; 1961.

Lumiere et Vie, Special issue, "La Pêché," Vol. I, No. 5, August, 1952.

Mackey, J. P., **Life and Grace,** Dublin: M. H. Gill and Son, 1966.

May, W. F., **A Catalogue of Sins: Contemporary Examination of Christian Conscience,** New York: Holt, Rinehart and Winston, 1967.

Monden, L., **Sin, Liberty and Law,** New York: Sheed & Ward, 1965.

Mortimer, R. C., **The Origins of Private Penance in the Western Church,** Oxford: Clarendon Press, 1939.

Nesmy, C. J., **Conscience and Confession,** Chicago: Franciscan Herald Press, 1965.

O'Callaghan, D., ed., **Sin and Repentance,** New York: Alba House, 1967.

Oraison, M., **Love, Sin and Suffering,** New York: The Macmillan Co., 1964.

——————, **Morality for Our Time,** Garden City, N.Y.: Doubleday & Co., 1968.

——————, **Sin,** New York: The Macmillan Co., 1962.

Palachovsky, V. and C. Vogel, **Sin in the Orthodox Church and Protestant Churches,** New York: Desclee, 1966.

Palmer, P., **Sacraments and Forgiveness,** Westminster, Md.: Newman Press, 1959.

Paul VI, Pope, **Poenitemini** (Constitution on Penance). Appears in English translation in **The Jurist**, Vol. 26, April, 1966, pp. 246-64.

Poschmann, B., **Penance and the Anointing of the Sick**, New York: Herder & Herder, Inc., 1964.

Pottebaum, G., **Go in Peace: Four Celebrations in Preparation for Penance**, New York: Herder & Herder, 1969.

Rahner, K., **Theological Investigations**, Vol. II, Baltimore: Helicon Press, Inc., 1963.

Regnier, J., **What is Sin?** Cork: Mercier Press, 1961.

Renckens, H., **Israel's Concept of the Beginning**, New York: Herder & Herder, Inc., 1964.

Richter, S., **Metanoia: Christian Penance and Confession**, New York: Sheed & Ward, 1966.

Ricoeur, P., **The Symbolism of Evil**, New York: Harper and Row, 1967.

Riga, P., **Sin and Penance**, Milwaukee; Bruce Publishing Co., 1962.

Rondet, H., **The Theology of Sin**, Notre Dame, Indiana: Fides Publishers, Inc., 1960.

Schnackenburg, R., **The Moral Theology of the New Testament**, London: Burns & Oates, 1964.

Schoonenberg, P., **Man and Sin**, Notre Dame, Indiana: University of Notre Dame Press, 1965.

—————, **God's World in the Making**, Pittsburgh: Duquesne Univ. Press, 1964.

Sheerin, J., **The Sacrament of Freedom**, Milwaukee: Bruce Publishing Co., 1961.

Snoeck, A., **Confession and Psychotherapy**, Westminster, Md.,: Newman Press, 1964.

Thurian, M., **Confession**, London: SCM Press, 1958.

Trooster, S., **Evolution and the Doctrine of Original Sin**, Glen Rock, N.J.: Newman Press, 1968.

Uleyn, A., **Is It I Lord? Pastoral Psychology and the Recognition of Guilt**, New York: Holt, Rinehart and Winston, 1969.

Van Zeller, H., **Approach to Penance**, New York: Sheed & Ward, 1957.

Von Speyr, A., **Confession: The Encounter with Christ in Penance**, New York: Herder & Herder, Inc.: 1964.

CONTRIBUTORS

Paul Anciaux, O.S.B. is professor of Pastoral Theology at the Grand Seminaire in Malines, Belgium. He is also director of continuing education for priests in the Malines-Brussels archdiocese. He has written numerous articles on moral and sacramental theology. His book *The Sacrament of Penance* appeared in English in 1962.

Louis Monden, S.J. is a member of the Theology Faculty of Heverlee-Louvain, Belgium. He is also professor of Modern Religious Problems at St. Ignatius College, Antwerp and professor of Religion and Psychology at John XXIII Seminary, Louvain. He is associate editor of *Streven* and a regular contributor to such journals as *Choisir* and *Lexicon für Theologie und Kirche*.

Marie-Bruno Carra De Vaux Saint-Cyr, O.P. is professor of Doctrinal History at the Monastery of Arbresle in France.

James F. Filella, S.J. is Vice Principal for Arts and professor of Psychology at St. Xavier's College in Bombay, India. He has written a number of articles on psychological and educational subjects in such journals as *Thought, Catholic Psychological Record* and *Journal of Educational and Vocational Guidance*.

Jerome Murphy-O'Connor, O.P. is professor of New Testament and Intertestamental Literature at the Ecole Biblique in Jerusalem. He has published a number of articles on New Testament topics in leading theological journals. His books include *Paul on Preaching* (1964) and *Paul and Qumran: Studies in N.T. Exegesis* (1967).

Gabriel -M. Nissim, O.P. is supervisor of the Institute of Pastoral Catechesis in Paris. He has taught and written extensively on the subject of liturgical and catechetical renewal. He plans a future work on the initiation of children into the eucharistic celebration.

Robert O'Connell, S.J. is Associate Professor of Philosophy at Fordham University in New York. He has written extensively on St. Augustine's theology of man and on the works of Teilhard de Chardin. Among his published books are *St. Augustine's Early Theology of Man* (1968) and *St. Augustine's Confessions* (1969).

Kevin O'Shea, C.Ss.R., a professor of Pastoral and Moral Theology at St. Mary's Monastery in Ballarat, Australia, is currently on research leave. He has contributed articles dealing with moral, pastoral and spiritual theology in such journals as *Theological Studies, The Irish Theological Quarterly* and *The Thomist.*

Piet Schoonenberg, S.J. is professor of Dogmatic Theology at the Catholic University of Nijmegen in the Netherlands. He has written extensively on a wide range of theological subjects. His two recent books translated into English are *God's World in the Making* and *Man and Sin.*

Pierre Smulders, S.J. is professor of Dogmatic Theology and Patrology at the University of Maastricht in the Netherlands. He has written extensively on the Council of Trent, the doctrine of the Trinity and Sacramental Theology.

Paul Tremblay is the diocesan director of religious education, Chicoutimi, P.Q., Canada.

Bruce Vawter, C.M. is professor of Scripture at St. Thomas Seminary, Denver and at De Paul University in Chicago. He is a frequent lecturer and writer on biblical topics. His books include *Conscience of Israel, Path Through Genesis* and *The Four Gospels.*

Marcel Van Caster, S.J. is on the staff of Lumen Vitae, the international center for studies in Religious Education in Brussels. He is an experienced lecturer and writer on a wide area of theological topics. Among his published books are *Redemption, Themes of Catechesis* and *God's World Today.*

James P. Mackey is professor of Dogmatic Theology at St. John's College, Waterford, Ireland. He is a frequent contributor of articles to theological and philosophical journals and is the author of *The Modern Theology of Tradition, Life and Grace* and *Tradition and Change in the Church.*

Michael J. Taylor, S.J. is Associate Professor of Theology at Seattle University. He has taught theology on the college level — especially the Sacraments — for the past eleven years and has published, apart from this volume, four other titles: *The Protestant Liturgical Renewal* (1963), *Liturgy and Christian Unity* (1965), *Liturgical Renewal in the Christian Churches* (1967) and *The Sacred and the Secular* (1968).